THE
9/11
PROPHECY

THE
9/11
PROPHECY

STARTLING EVIDENCE
THE ENDTIMES HAVE BEGUN

JAMES F.
FITZGERALD

WND Books

THE 9/11 PROPHECY

WND Books, Inc.
Washington, D.C.

Book designed by Mark Karis

WND Books are available at special discounts for bulk purchases. WND Books, Inc., also publishes books in electronic formats. For more information call (541) 474-1776 or visit www.wndbooks.com.

First Edition

Hardcover ISBN: 9781938067082
eBook ISBN: 9781938067099

Library of Congress information available

Printed in the United States of America
10 9 8 7 6 5 4 3 2 1

CONTENTS

INTRODUCTION

I N THE PAST TWENTY MONTHS, as of the time of this writing, two different books have been published showing in remarkable ways that 9/11 was God's judgment on America for its sin. One is *The Harbinger,* by Rabbi Jonathan Cahn. The other is my book, *The 9/11 Prophecy.*

When I first heard about Cahn's application of the Isaiah 9:10 prophecy to the events following 9/11, I could easily believe it was true. As the reader will soon see, I knew for a fact 9/11 was a divine judgment, because the Lord had sent my team and me to New York City with His deliberate warning in 2000, months before it ever happened (Amos 3:6–7).

Furthermore, the idea of the sycamore tree and the location of St. Paul's Chapel both figured prominently in my own testimony. For one thing, I was accompanied on our mission of warning in 2000 by my wife, whose original Dutch ancestors had legal possession of both the World Trade Center property *and* the Chapel property at the time of New York City's founding in the 1600s. What were the odds of this "coincidence"? And there was much more, as I tell. That's why when I heard of Cahn's message, I was quickly convinced of its authenticity.

Nonetheless, the amount of controversy *The Harbinger* stirred up gave me pause. I had also purposely avoided reading the actual book until my own was submitted for publication. Once my book was submitted, however, I began looking into critical reviews of *The Harbinger*. The most thorough treatment I discovered was a one-hour-and-thirty-three-minute critique by Chris Rosebrough that came highly recommended because it "dismantled" Cahn's claim that the pattern of Isaiah 9:10 was repeated following 9/11. Its major point was that if Cahn claimed the same pattern was repeated with the 9/11 attack, then there had to be "a prior warning," just as Isaiah gave northern Israel prior knowledge that the Assyrians would attack them and what would happen. The critique said that because that didn't happen with 9/11 and there was no prior warning, Cahn's idea of a pattern did not hold up. If there were a real pattern, God would have provided prior warning.

I was blown away by this online argument at Pirate Christian Radio! What the critique called for is exactly what my book claims did happen. God did provide prior warning. In His mercy He sent a specific deliberate warning to New York City fourteen months before 9/11, through His own Word, and did so in full public view at Madison Square Garden (even though He didn't really need to because we already have the Scriptures in our possession which we are taught are sufficient for correction and instruction and that the OT was also written for our instruction). I was so excited by the point of this critique that I could hardly sleep that night.

Second, Rosebrough noted that the preceding verses to Isaiah 9:10 foretell the coming of the Messiah, which he gave as another reason for dismissing Cahn's pattern. But again, that is also exactly what my book claims. I seek to prove from Scripture, history, and providence that 9/11 began the biblical events of the endtimes that usher in the Second

Coming. For this very reason, what Scripture could be more appropriate for God to use as a providential sign after 9/11 than Isaiah 9:10 as a pattern to recognize? In fact, paying only slight attention to *The Harbinger* as I finished my book, I had wondered why, out of all the many other verses in the Bible and out of all the many other countries in the world and throughout history, the Lord would use that one particular verse as a pattern for the post-9/11 events in America. Why this particular verse now, and why for America? But once I looked carefully and saw its context, I was amazed. Here, in context with the 9:10 passage, was the promise of the coming of Messiah as a way to give the Jewish believers hope in the midst of judgment. And that was the very message of my book. The attack on 9/11 was not some arbitrary judgment, but in fact God's instrument to begin the endtime events that lead to the second coming of the Lord.

I could hardly believe it. Rosebrough's thorough critique turned out to be instructive to me—"as iron sharpens iron"—and actually helped make my case for *The 9/11 Prophecy*. Because its primary objections were met, it would also help confirm the validity of *The Harbinger*'s application of the Isaiah 9:10 pattern to the events of 9/11 and our future. Having said that, I don't believe God now gives anyone's words the infallible nature of the Scriptures. What Christian in his right mind does? All of us are prone to mistakes and errors. So why would anyone expect that any of God's messengers today must be 100 percent infallible before we listen to anything they say? Who is infallible? Yet, why then don't preachers merely read the Bible verbatim on Sundays and say nothing else? Why do they preach? Do they believe God works through them? Yet who of them claims to be infallible and perfect in every point? But if not, then why do some hold up such a standard for a writer and teacher like Cahn before they listen? Must he be exactly perfect at every single point before we see and believe that God has called and is using him with his teaching about Isaiah 9:10?

In terms of proving 9/11 to be a definite divine judgment on America, Cahn and I have come at it in two different ways. In his book, he shows how the pattern of Isaiah 9:10 has providently reappeared in convincing detail after 9/11 as a harbinger of further judgment if we don't repent. In my book, I show how the Lord led us to New York City with His warning before it happened. I also show the attack's amazing connection to the book of Revelation and its role in the endtimes. Because I show how 9/11 was in fact the opening salvo of the endtime judgments, I believe we will not see this nation return, but fall, to pave the way for the appearing of Antichrist. My earnest hope, however, is that God will use the witness of these two books to help stir an awakening in this nation that we love so much (see 2 Cor. 13:1; Deut. 19:15).

I also believe the Lord has given us these extraordinary signs because the time is extraordinary. The Islamist attack on 9/11 was the beginning of the endtimes. The Lord is calling His Church to awake and see His hand at work and get busy in the time we have.

PROLOGUE

Now the word of the LORD came to Jonah the son of Amittai, saying, "Arise, go to Nineveh, that great city, and cry out against it; for their wickedness has come up before Me."

—Jonah 1:1–2 NKJV

EFORE THE LORD SENT New York City warning in the summer of 2000, He led a watchman to see through Scripture and providence that *this great city would soon suffer a surprise attack in a single hour.*[1] Tall buildings would be destroyed, with fire and smoke visible from sea. Many would die. It was not a vague vision or mere premonition.

Through His Word and providence, the Lord also led the watchman to believe *this attack on the world's preeminent city would be a prophetic sign.*[2] This judgment's unique nature would point to Mystery Babylon's sudden destruction in a single hour by Antichrist as foretold in Revelation.[3] Its severity would foreshadow this prophecy's sure and ultimate fulfillment before the return of Christ.[4]

To send His warning, the Lord even opened a door in New York City at a time of intense future speculation—*the Millennium Year*. And as He would have it, His warning was not hidden in a corner. On July 9, 2000, the names of His watchman and His warning were prominently posted at Madison Square Garden in the heart of the city.[5] Yet, hardly anyone paid attention to the prophetic words written in bright lights upon the marquee of the most famous arena in America. Three days this watchman was in the city to deliver God's warning through His Word. And he was not alone. A team of witnesses was with him; they know this is true.

And I know it is true because I am that watchman the Lord sent on a deliberate mission to forewarn New York City with His holy Word more than a year before 9/11. Unlike Jonah of old, however, I was convinced God's judgment would happen this time. For New York, unlike Nineveh, would never even hear the Lord's warning through His Word, much less heed it.[6]

When this very judgment struck at the hands of Islamic terrorists on September 11, 2001, *the shocking magnitude of such a surprise attack at the dawn of the Third Millennium was a further sign*.[7] Because of what I knew, I soon could see its purpose in the events that followed. This audacious attack had set in motion two of the most critical endtime prophecies in the Bible: *the beginning of sorrows* and the judgments of *the book of Revelation*.[8] The prophetic events they foretold would commence the final generation of forty years or less in human history that Jesus taught would come at the end of the age.[9] And here they were before our eyes!

I was astonished by these things. Not only had God's judgment been a surprise attack and a prophetic sign as I had believed, but it had proved to be a powerful catalyst. The spectacular strike on America by just nineteen jihadists in the first year of the New Millennium had turned the course of history in a single hour. God's judgment on 9/11 had begun the endtimes.[10]

To guide and encourage me to write the testimony of this book, the Lord confirmed the reality of our warning and the truth of these insights in three amazing ways—each a matter of public record before the attack—that I might write boldly about *the things I have seen, the things which are, and the things which will take place*.[11] In many ways I dread what I see through His Word and providence, but that won't make these things go away—they belong to the great unfolding plan of our good and holy God and the coming of His kingdom and the return of Christ.[12] Even now the seals of Revelation 6:1 and Daniel 12:4 are being opened. Who can but prophesy?[13] The first rider has ridden.[14] The second waits in the wings.[15] Can you not see them?

Now I cry like a Jonah of the final generation[16]: "When America falls from power, just as Scripture prophesies, an Islamic Beast will arise to conquer the world!"[17] In the dark years ahead, half the planet's population will perish by global war, famine, and pestilence, as is written.[18] Many will die by persecution.[19] And in Allah's name, Antichrist will destroy Mystery Babylon.[20] But this Beast and his False Prophet will be cast down at the gates of Jerusalem by Jesus Christ, just as He promised in His Word.[21]

"Yes, these events are under way even now.[22] The decades of the final generation began with God's judgment on 9/11.[23] Scripture, history, and providence all declare that this is true!"[24]

To tell its story, this book weaves three main threads: the undeniable testimony of the Lord's intentional warning to New York City through our premiere of *The Book of Revelation* before 9/11, the evidence of my lifelong calling to be this watchman on the wall, and how 9/11 initiated the endtime judgments of the final generation. Filled with fresh insight, it also sheds new light on Paul's veiled prophecy of the two great events that must precede the ascendancy of Antichrist, "the lawless one," before the Lord's Second Coming.[25] In the process, America's major hidden role in prophetic Scripture is uncovered for all to see.[26]

There is much to tell that is amazing. I was sent to knowingly deliver God's warning to New York City before 9/11. By His mercy and grace, this knowledge, along with years of study, training, and preparation, has given me a unique expertise in understanding New Testament prophecies begun by the attack.[27] Now this book seeks to help others see where we are in history from a biblical light, why things happening must happen, and how they fulfill essential endtimes prophecies—prophecies that demonstrate the utter trustworthiness of the Lord's Word and His absolute power ruling over history.[28] Finally, when all is fulfilled as is written, and the Gospel has penetrated every language, tribe, nation, and people on Earth, the Lord Jesus will return to save His own for eternity. Indeed, He told us this good news in advance that we might possess an unshakable faith and hope, even in the face of what is coming upon the world *in this very generation.*[29]

PART 1

DIVINE REVELATION

When disaster comes to a city, has not the LORD caused it? Surely the Sovereign LORD does nothing without revealing his plan to his servants the prophets.

—Amos 3:6–7 NIV

I WAS CAREFULLY REVIEWING OUR master tape of *The Book of Revelation* in June 2000 when the Holy Spirit suddenly opened my eyes through His Word to see the certainty of a future divine judgment upon New York City.

THE BOOK OF REVELATION

Prior to our production of *The Book of Revelation,* the Bible's most famous prophetic book had never been produced in its entirety. It had taken us almost a year. To support the text on-screen, we had created five hundred scenes of relevant imagery in our computers—some with as many as a hundred layers of video, each layer having multiple special effects.

The Book of Revelation was the fifth production in our quest to produce the whole New Testament as a dynamic videobook. By then I had been working on the *WatchWORD Bible* project nearly nine years. I had envisioned it as an innovative way to increase biblical literacy in a media age: viewers would watch, read, and hear the Bible all at once. I was convinced nothing could be more important than helping more people read, believe, and obey God's Word. It was the written revelation of His work in human history to bring salvation to all who put their faith in Jesus Christ, who died for sin and rose again in victory. Its divinely inspired story, teaching, and principles had changed the lives of untold millions and the course of nations, including our own. Yet people no longer read as much, and the majority remained ignorant of its truths. How, then, could they be transformed in their hearts and minds? By producing God's Word on video, we hoped to increase Bible reading as a catalyst for a spiritual awakening. Beyond this impassioned vision I had no idea of what God was preparing us for. In fact, because of the constant difficulties and setbacks we had faced, I often questioned whether the project had been truly His will, or just a grave mistake.

But when our duplicator saw scenes of *The Book of Revelation*, he urged me to submit our production to film festivals. I applied to two in the spring of 2000. In mid-June we were thrilled to learn it was accepted by the 2000 New York International Independent Film and Video Festival. It would be introduced at the festival's grand opening at Madison Square Garden on July 7, 2000, a few days past the Fourth of July.

After years of laboring in obscurity, we finally had a chance to make our work known to an important audience. *The Book of Revelation* would premiere two days after the grand opening on a Saturday night in the media capital of the world. This thought gave me real hope that we might finally attract the attention and help we so desperately needed. Though attending the festival would be a financial strain we could barely manage, I saw it as a necessary investment.

As a final precaution, I decided to review our entire 110-minute production one more time for any possible problems. It was the week before we left. I sat by myself in the edit room in our home, carefully reviewing chapter after chapter, until I reached chapter 18. Then, partway through, one verse suddenly jumped out at me: "*This was the greatest city ever.*"

As soon as I heard these words about *the greatest city ever*, two unexpected thoughts collided in my mind. The translation of this prophecy about the destruction of great Babylon had struck me so forcibly because the city we were going to in a week certainly considered itself "the greatest city" in the world—and maybe ever. And this thought had jarred a memory.

I recalled a book from the 1980s by New York pastor David Wilkerson, about America's sudden destruction by judgment, including fire, rioting, and the utter collapse of order in New York City.[1] Many folks at the TV ministry where I then worked saw the moral decline of our nation as ample provocation for such judgment and were convinced of the imminent truth of this vision. I had never read Wilkerson's book, *Set the Trumpet to Thy Mouth*. The idea of New York City's complete collapse out of the blue made little sense to me in my understanding of how God worked and the season we were in. First, there would be progressive warnings and preliminary judgments. But recalling all these things, I thought Revelation would surely never predict the destruction of a particular city in a future United States of America.

Nonetheless, the thought of Wilkerson's book made me wonder about New York City. Wanting to assuage my curiosity and be certain, I went upstairs to review the fall of Babylon in Revelation 17–18. At a glance, chapter 17 held nothing I could see with any obvious relevance to New York City. But what I found in chapter 18 stunned me. Three separate groups spoke there about Antichrist's destruction of the great city of Babylon.

Scanning quickly for any possible connections with New York, I came to the first group in verses 9–10, where all the kings of the earth "slept with her and shared in her luxury," calling her "that great and powerful city" (CEV).

About to pass over the archaic language of *all the kings* as not relevant to a modern city in a twenty-first-century democratic republic, I suddenly remembered the United Nations. Genuinely surprised, I saw at least the possibility for an application of this verse to the global assembly of nations headquartered in New York. By hosting the UN, with its formal gathering of world leaders, New York did in fact play queen to *all the kings* and did so quite unlike any other city on Earth. In God's providence such an important circumstance was surely not incidental.

With new attentiveness I continued further. Verses 11–15 stated that every merchant on Earth *had become rich because of her*.

Again I was struck by what I read. As everyone knew, more than any other city on the face of the earth, New York was synonymous with world commerce and finance. It had the preeminent stock exchange. The whole world looked to Wall Street as the recognized economic epicenter of the planet. The crash of 1929 had begun there and circled the globe. There were other great cities of commerce, but New York was surely in a class by itself.

Going on to verses 17–19, I read that every captain, passenger, and sailor who traded by the sea had cried at the sight of the smoke of her ruin, "*This was the greatest city ever.*" This was the verse that had first caught my attention.

With total amazement now I considered that New York was situated quite unlike any other city of its rank in the world. Not one other—not Rome; Washington, DC; London; Paris; Berlin; Moscow; Peking; or Tokyo—was located directly on an ocean or a sea. In this respect, New York City was entirely unique. As I well knew, she sat as a great port at the mouth of a broad river right on the Atlantic Ocean, with perhaps the finest natural harbor on Earth.

That all three attributes describing mystery Babylon in chapter 18 should fit New York City in a way *without parallel* in the modern world astonished me.

I hurried to my commentaries. They presented familiar concepts. Babylon symbolized the ancient Roman capital on seven hills as "the world-centre of organized godlessness."[2] Babylon represented all cities as man-made centers that were by nature under the power of evil and in rebellion against God. Babylon stood for the world's entire socioeconomic system in defiant opposition to the Creator. But nothing in my commentaries pointed to a specific modern city like New York as a type of Babylon. Of course, I knew they could never confirm such an idea. Still, what an amazing *type* of Babylon she was! Though surely not *the* Babylon of chapter 18, New York seemed to fit Babylon's description better than any other city I could think of or even foresee in the future.

Founded in the early 1600s by Dutch traders, New York had required centuries to rise to its prominence. She was now a city without parallel. With her natural setting, heritage, power, prestige, and infrastructure, I thought her unique economic and cultural preeminence in the world would be difficult to overcome and replace in a hundred years without significant intervention.

JUDGMENT

For the first time I found myself wondering seriously if the prophecies about Babylon may actually have some particular current application to New York City.

"Fallen!" shouts the angel. "Babylon has fallen!" The Scriptures teach that before the end of the world, the great city of Babylon will be destroyed for her sins and wickedness, "because her judge is the powerful Lord God" (Rev. 18:2, 8 CEV).

If God has promised to destroy the great city of Babylon in the future, I reasoned, and New York has grown into such a unique and preeminent "type" of Babylon, how could she hope to escape a similar judgment? Yet how could this really be? New York City was a symbol to the world of what was best about the United States, its freedoms, and its success as a melting pot. To many she had been their doorway to the land of opportunity. She stood for the *American Dream*.

And what about the good we did in the world as Americans? What about our missions, our postwar programs, our aid to impoverished nations, our beneficial technologies, our many educational contributions? Surely, I thought, these things were mitigating factors in our defense.

But did these mean God would never and could never hold us to account for our great and growing national sins of immorality, greed, idolatry, and murder (Rev. 2:13–16)? New York City played a central role in promoting such sins when she could have done so much more good. The economic reins of America and the world were at her disposal. Through her powerful media she was privileged to be the world's chief herald, but for almost forty years city leaders had used their mighty influence to wage a relentless culture war. They had aggressively worked to undermine our spiritual heritage and alter national values. In the name of art, freedom, and profit, they had actively promoted the spread of decadence and immorality as new, enlightened virtues. They even financed their export to corrupt the rest of the world.

For almost thirty years, her liberal media had actively supported and protected the silent murder of forty million babies their powerful voices should have helped protect (Prov. 31:8). Our courts had promulgated *the right* to abortion. They had called it a matter of individual privacy and choice, but almighty God was bound by justice to hold the city to account for complicity in this national sin of legalized murder.

For ideological reasons she had often overlooked the destruction of millions of innocent lives in Russia, China, and Southeast Asia. Time and again, she had turned a blind eye to the brutal suffering of millions in Africa. Frequently the victims were Christians.

At their worst, her powerful financial markets and institutions were driven by greed and fear, rather than by reasoned and rational investment. Corporate leaders and investors practiced manipulations, speculations, and a distorted form of capitalism that was without love of God or neighbor. Few realized that the very capitalism they said they practiced had developed under a Christian view of God and the ordered world He created, with its inherent principles and design. Narrowly focused on the bottom line and often ignorant of America's history, even the most successful businesspeople and traders were frequently blind to any spiritual dimension to their work and why we in America were so uniquely blessed. Their ceaseless drive for riches merely cried for endless consumption and materialism. Yet even they had foolishly stood aside as a third of their future markets were destroyed by abortion, with terrible consequences for the long-term future of our nation, to say nothing of the lives themselves. Some leaders had been willing to betray our best interests internationally for their own self-interest.

New York City had committed such grievous sins in a nation with a long Christian heritage. She was in a privileged position. She should have known better. The Scriptures taught that *to whom much is given, from him much will be required* (Luke 12:48 KJV). Would God ignore such sins forever? I knew He could not. With an awful realization, I began to believe this massive modern metropolis, home to millions of people, must surely be marked for God's particular judgment at some future time. But when might that be? I wondered.

Was her judgment vaguely distant, or near?

2

DIVINE PROVIDENCE

. . . according to the plan of him who works out everything in conformity with the purpose of his will . . .

—Ephesians 1:11 NIV

ITH AMAZEMENT I REALIZED the Lord was planning to warn the city of His coming wrath through the providential release of *The Book of Revelation* at the Millennium.

FESTIVAL TIMING

Seeking to understand the possible timing of any future judgment if I could, my thoughts immediately turned to the timing of our production of *The Book of Revelation*. The first word-for-word production of this great New Testament book about the end of the world was to be released in the year 2000—at the Millennium. It was only the second marker of a thousand years since Christ. Certainly, it would be the last before His coming again. Could the first production of this prophetic book at such a unique point in history be happenstance?

The apostle John had recorded his message more than nineteen hundred years earlier, closing the New Testament canon. In visionary language *The Book of Revelation* foretold God's ultimate victory over the powers of evil at the Second Coming of Jesus Christ. While no one knew the precise time of His return, Jesus had promised that signs would tell when it was near. Throughout the ages countless Christians had believed theirs was the time when He would return. In truth, great wars, deadly plagues, terrible earthquakes, and important dates had been *types and signs of what was to come*. For this very reason, they were easily misunderstood and misapplied in zeal and fear. Thus, the well-intentioned speculations of many bygone believers had always been impractical and unbiblical. For example, technology had never before been sufficiently advanced for an Antichrist to literally control *all* the buying and selling in the whole world, as prophesied in Revelation 13:17.

To avoid such speculative errors, the majority of believers made the opposite mistake: they considered all watchful observation to be completely useless and dangerous. They were just as unbiblical in their own way. Jesus said, "When you see all these things, you know that it is near" (Matt. 24:33 NIV). The Lord Himself taught that we would recognize the time of the end. It would become obvious, and He would have us be ready and watchful.

That's why I did not think it presumption to recognize that, for the first time in history, a convergence of things did truly point to the coming of the end. Ours was the first generation to possess sufficient power through nuclear, biological, and chemical weapons to threaten human existence on Earth. Multiplying populations compacted in larger and larger cities made it even easier to destroy masses of people. Fast, easy travel enabled the spread of diseases in a shrinking world. Powerful digital technologies provided unprecedented ability to communicate, calculate, and control. At the same time, how much longer could fallen humans beings sustain such a mind-boggling knowledge explosion, with its exponential change and development, without self-destructing? Technology, travel, and trade were breaking down barriers between nations, fueling a growing drive for global governance. Yet, consolidation of all power in the hands of a few carried the threat of totalitarian control and untold corruption.

Most important to me was the fact that Jesus said, "And this gospel . . . will be preached in the whole world . . . *and then the end shall come*" (Matt. 24:14 NIV; emphasis added). But until our time, fulfilling the Gospel mandate was never truly within reach as it was now. Great advances in technology and travel had made it possible to accomplish this unfinished task in our lifetime.

No doubt, missionaries in previous centuries believed the world could be reached in their time, but their hopes were well-intentioned wishful thinking. It wasn't that they hadn't tried hard enough. It was never really possible in their time, and they lacked sufficient information about peoples and languages to know the true size of the task. By the start of the twenty-first century, that information was no longer lacking. In the three previous decades, great strides had been made in measuring and quantifying the remaining missionary task. As I knew, it was more complex than simply reaching the individual "nations." According to organizations like Wycliffe Bible Translators, out of thousands of unique language and dialect groups in the world, more than a third were still without Scripture in their language; and, of an estimated twenty-four thousand "people groups," over a third remain "unreached" with the Gospel, requiring intentional cross-cultural missionary efforts.[1]

Also, I thought earlier missionaries hadn't taken into account other necessary prophecies about the end. What about the great army of two hundred million prophesied to come "from the East" (Rev. 9:16, 16:12 NKJV) that was to happen at the very same time humankind had the ability for centralized control over the entire world (Rev. 13:7–8, 14–17)? None of these things were ever truly possible before, but they were now approaching feasibility. Critical prophecies were reaching potential fulfillment at the same time missionary strategists believed even the smallest "unreached" people groups could be reached in our time and the Great Commission fulfilled.

All these things were part of my reflections as I thought about the unique timing of the release of *The Book of Revelation*. God had ordained it to happen at such a time; and at this particular time, no message was more relevant to the world. Releasing the first production of this great prophetic book at the dawn of the final Millennium had to be significant.

FESTIVAL LOCATION

Suddenly another thought struck me about our premiere. Its providential location. *The Book of Revelation* could have had its premiere anywhere. But because of the film festival, not only would it be released at the Millennium, but providence had so ordered that it happen in New York—the very city in the entire world that was most *a type of Babylon*. Could such a double providence of time and place *both* be just coincidence?

Not only that, but through the 2000 New York International Independent Film and Video Festival, providence had so ordained that our production be released at Madison Square Garden in the very center of the city.

With that thought, Jonah's story from the Old Testament instantly echoed in my mind. When God sent him to warn Nineveh, he had walked a day's journey *to the center* of that great city to call the people to turn to God or be doomed. This particular fact from his story had always stuck with me. Was the Lord speaking to me through this detail and the providence of our being in the center of the city? Was He showing me that we were to warn New York of the danger of His judgment while there? Were we to warn it as Jonah had Nineveh? But how could that be? The people of Nineveh had listened to Jonah. As a result, God's judgment was averted. But I knew something like that could never be replicated today in a place like New York, a vast, complex, teeming, modern metropolis.

Whom could we tell anyway? The mayor? The media? The Church?

And if we were to stand on a corner, preaching on the streets, with a message like Jonah's, even if true, what could we hope to accomplish? It would be pointless. We would merely sound crazy to any handful of people who might hear us. But instantly, I was reminded of the unique task to which God had called us. After years of effort, we had already completed the first production of all four Gospels. Now we had produced *The Book of Revelation* in its entirety for the first time. And this production had something far more powerful to it than Jonah's street preaching. It was nothing less than the written revelation of Jesus Christ Himself about the future of the human race at the end of time. It held a message of prophetic significance for New York City in particular and the world at large.

But who is going to pay attention to our production? my mind argued. We were completely unknown. No one would even be aware we were in the city.

Again Jonah came to mind. Nineveh had responded to his preaching as a divine warning from God. The people had repented, and the city was spared (Jon. 3:10); but New York would never even notice us. It was a massive, complicated city packed with competing messages. Ours would be just one more piece of media vying for attention. It was an unknown production that would be utterly lost in all the noise. And what would make people give consideration to our message above the other competing messages anyway? That it came from the Bible meant, if anything, they would be *less* inclined to listen to it. They had heard it all before. Our message would simply be ignored.

With that thought, I suddenly realized the problem of people's inattention was not my concern. The words of Revelation were not my words; they were not some sponsor's words. They were the infallible, inspired words of the almighty God *who honors His Word above His own name* (Ps. 138:2).

Instantly the hard reality became plain. I could see that the God of heaven had chosen to send His holy prophetic Word at this unique time to this particular city in a whole new way for the first time in history. Yet who would bother to perceive His purpose or hand of providence in it? Would His Church? All were busy, dull, and spiritually asleep. God was safely in His box. He would not act. He could not speak. Everything would just continue on as it always had (2 Pet. 3:3–4). How offensive this whole perception suddenly seemed! Almighty God was of no concern. We had rendered Him and His Word mute and irrelevant to the everyday busyness of our materialistic, self-centered lives.

How clear it was to me. God had ordained that *The Book of Revelation* be released in New York City for a purpose far beyond my simple plan to gain notice and support for our work. The Lord would speak to this city in a still, small voice through our production of His Word (1 Kings 19:11–12). He would speak and warn her, doing so in the very media language she understood. There would be no need to shout on street corners. If God could speak to me through *The Book of Revelation* and its providential timing and location, He could speak to others through it too.

The fact that no one would be listening was no excuse.

With a terrible shaft of insight, I then realized the Lord's judgment *must already be determined upon New York*. His coming wrath had to be more than a distant possibility that could be escaped. It must be an unavoidable certainty! For who would hear or heed His timely warning through *The Book of Revelation* when it came to the city at the Millennium? And without repentance, how could His wrath be averted?

Furthermore, if releasing *The Book of Revelation* in July 2000 was to serve notice of this coming judgment, His judgment would have to come in some relative proximity to His warning. How else could it serve as any reasonable notice? God's judgment must come at a time not too distant from His warning at the Millennium or it would make no sense.

3

UNAVOIDABLE JUDGMENT

I have determined to do this city harm, and not good, declares the LORD.

—Jeremiah 21:10 NIV

CONVINCED OF THE LORD'S IMMINENT JUDGMENT upon New York, I set my mind to foresee, if possible, what it could be—and was overwhelmed by what I saw.

SEVERITY

As I had reasoned, how could the city hope to escape God's wrath? She would not respond to His warning though He sent it in a most pointed and providential way. She would never even hear what God said, much less act upon it as Nineveh had (Luke 11:32). This could mean only one thing: there must be a consequence. If the Lord would send a warning that could be disregarded without consequence, what would be His point in sending it? To ignore His clear providential warning without any consequence would be to make it meaningless.

Thinking these things through, I had concluded that not only was His judgment coming, but that when it did come, it must also be serious. If it were not serious, why would the Lord go to such lengths to send a providential warning to the city at the Millennium? His judgment must be sufficiently severe to warrant such a unique, prophetic warning (Rom. 11:22).

But how severe would it be? I questioned.

The Bible taught that Babylon would be completely destroyed at the end of time, but I knew from Scripture that we were not yet there. Too much still had to be fulfilled, including the reign of Antichrist. And I thought New York City certainly could not be the Babylon of the Bible. She was merely a *type*.

For these reasons I quickly concluded that God's punishment could not possibly mean New York City's total destruction, now or in the near future. It made absolutely no sense to me in my understanding of God's nature and working that this great city would just be utterly destroyed right out of the blue. God was merciful and rational in His dealings with us. And the true Babylon's destruction waited for the end, with great warnings and judgments to precede it.

Therefore, I was convinced that any judgment upon New York now, though necessarily severe, must be limited in extent. In this way, God's judgment would be merciful, and it would also serve as a prelude, a sign, and a warning for the future. The time for *Babylon's* utter fall had not yet come, but was approaching.

Still, what would this limited, yet severe, judgment be?

SURPRISE ATTACK

If God's warning was to be seen in the description of Babylon's fall in Revelation 18, I reasoned His judgment must surely reflect this passage in some way. Otherwise, how could this specific prophecy serve as a providential warning at this particular time to this particular city? There would have to be an obvious connection with chapter 18 when it came, for if the judgment bore no distinct relation to the fall of Babylon, who would recognize it to be what God had threatened? A relationship would have to exist between the warning and the event. Some accident or calamity could be dismissed as a random act of nature, and it would never be seen with any certainty as a divine judgment.

Continuing to study chapter 18, I was struck by the particular repetition of a detail that accentuated the sudden and unexpected nature of Babylon's destruction. The passage repeated three times that her judgment came *in a single hour.* Surely, I thought, if this passage served as God's warning to New York City, her judgment would come quickly and suddenly, when she least expected it.

What, then, could this sudden and unexpected judgment possibly be?

In picturing Babylon's destruction in a single hour, Revelation 18:18 described "the smoke of [Babylon's] burning" (NIV). To reflect this description, I thought there would need to be great fire and smoke in New York City, and it would have to occur in a very short time. For these reasons, it seemed to me a huge natural disaster or some major accident made no sense as the means of judgment. An accident of sufficient magnitude would probably take far more than *a single hour* to get out of control—and some strange natural disaster that hit New York, but nowhere else, in a single hour seemed altogether too strange and unnatural.

Only one idea made any sense: a surprise attack. This would be sudden, unexpected, and severe, and could bring great destruction *in a single hour* with *smoke from her burning* rising so high it could be seen from the sea (Rev. 18:17–18). In a surprise attack, buildings would fall and many people would die. But how strange and horrible these thoughts were to consider! In this process, I had concluded that almighty God in His wrath had determined to bring an attack in judgment upon New York City; yet how could I possibly think such a dreadful thing? But, in the process of reasoning in my mind through Scripture and providence, one thought had led to another in a series of steps, each of which I could not deny to be true (see Prov. 25:2).

Still, the idea of anyone launching a major attack on New York that could happen by surprise seemed nearly impossible to conceive. How could a "surprise attack" on New York City take place at this point in history? Surely, with all our technology, we would be able to see it coming. Furthermore, the world was largely at peace. Who would suddenly attack the United States now? We were the planet's superpower.

BUT WHO?

Though I could hardly imagine a surprise attack on the city taking place anytime soon, I also wanted to believe it would be as far off as possible. But reasoning it through, I thought putting an attack more than a decade away *at most* made no sense. Beyond a decade would make our warning utterly irrelevant.

With this understanding, I then questioned who would be able to launch a surprise attack on New York City within a decade, and who would want to? Surveying the world quickly in my mind, I could conceive of just two potential attackers at the time; only one was a nation.

China could possibly have both reason and ability to do so. Her top military leaders were already on record saying that an inevitable show-down must take place with the United States in the future. Yet, I knew they believed they would not be prepared to win such a confrontation for at least two more decades. But perhaps China might have a sufficient missile capacity within a decade to attack us by surprise. Certainly, they could not do it before then, and how could they attack our East Coast with missiles from such a distance? While I half-imagined planes overhead, like air force bombers, in my mind's eye, I knew sending conventional bombers to remain undetected from such a distance would be impossible for anyone to carry out.

The only other group I could imagine with the will and ability to mount a surprise attack on New York was Islamic terrorists. While they had no air force and could not shoot missiles at that time, they could perhaps smuggle a nuclear weapon into the city. It was possible that small nuclear devices may have been stolen from the former Soviet Union. In that case, Islamic radicals could attack *at any time*; however, the thought of even a limited nuclear explosion in New York seemed too dreadful to contemplate. Surely such an awful thing would not happen soon. To be honest, though, I could see no reason why such a danger could be put off as far as a potential attack by China. While not ten years, I wanted to believe a terrorist attack on New York City wouldn't occur before two or three years, at the least.

Either way, whether by China or Islamic terrorists, the threat of a surprise attack appeared to me to be years away. This perception helped me push the awful inevitability into the vague future in my mind. I could not face the thought of it happening sooner, yet I couldn't deny I now believed the Lord had led me to see that New York City would suffer a terrible surprise attack within a decade of our warning. It was only a matter of time.

In spite of how preposterous all this would sound to the others, I knew I couldn't keep it to myself. I believed the Lord was sending us to New York City to bring warning of an imminent judgment. Furthermore, this judgment would be an intentional sign to the whole world that the prophecies of the endtime judgments and the future fall of Babylon were serious.

4

THREE WITNESSES

Every matter must be established by the testimony of two or three witnesses.

—2 Corinthians 13:1 NIV

I TOLD OUR LITTLE TEAM everything I had come to believe about God's purpose for sending us to New York at the Millennium with *The Book of Revelation*.

PRODUCTION TEAM

The four of us had been totally immersed in the production of *The Book of Revelation* for nearly a year. As a result, we had all been deeply affected by its prophetic message. Each of us could see its very real application to the future.

Regardless, I anticipated a string of arguments in response to what I was about to share, dismissing it as craziness. For me to believe God was preparing to warn New York City about something as specific as a future surprise attack, and that He would do it through our premiere, was one thing. To tell that to others was another! No doubt, I strongly believed in the importance of the work God had called us to do. We had sought with single focus to bring His Word to the world in a new way to help stir revival. Few had believed in the project; fewer had been willing to help. Yet, I had never stopped believing in the importance of what the Lord had called us to do in producing the Bible on video. Nonetheless, our little team had labored for years under great difficulty, and we were still hidden away, seemingly insignificant and invisible.

How, then, could I tell them that God had just led me to believe New York City would be attacked in the future, and our production of *The Book of Revelation* would serve as His warning to the city? It would sound ridiculous. They would hardly give me a chance to explain, saying, "Why would God show us such a thing? Who are we to warn a city like New York? Why would God choose us? Who would attack New York City anyway? Impossible!"

But, how could I withhold from them what I believed the Lord had shown me, despite what they would think? If God had truly spoken to me through His Word and providence about what would happen, how could I keep it to myself? If He was planning to warn New York through *The Book of Revelation*, I must tell them what I knew. To do otherwise would be to lack the courage of my conviction and to be thinking only of myself. As it was, I was convinced the Lord had given me a certainty of His coming judgment, the time frame within which it would occur, and even the type of judgment it would be. If I really believed these things were true, I needed to tell my team, or else I would be hiding the truth to wait and see.

Thinking all this through in a moment, I could see no good reason to wait. I should tell them now. Once the immediacy was gone and the clarity faded, it would only become harder to do. So I went downstairs and gathered them together in the production room.

THE GREATEST CITY EVER

"This morning," I said, "as I was reviewing our master tape for the trip, a verse in chapter 18 jumped out at me: 'This was the greatest city ever.'"

I related how this verse had caused me to think of an old book and about the city where we were to release our production. "New York is the business and media capital of the world," I said. "She certainly considers herself to be 'the greatest city ever.'"

I next related my surprise at discovering that the three attributes describing Mystery Babylon in Revelation 18 were all uniquely applicable to New York City, and then my amazement at realizing that the first production of *The Book of Revelation*, foretelling Babylon's sudden destruction, would be released in the city most reflecting the description of Babylon in our day. Furthermore, it would be released at the dawn of the Third Millennium, a time of great speculation about the future and the coming of Christ. "Nor will we be off in a corner somewhere," I said. "*The Book of Revelation* is being released at Madison Square Garden, right in the heart of the city."

I shared how these things had reminded me of the story of Jonah. He had been sent into the heart of Nineveh to warn that great city to turn to God or be doomed. We were being sent into the heart of Manhattan with God's prophetic Word. Only, unlike Nineveh, I said, New York City would never repent at such a warning. Hardly anyone would notice us—even releasing the first full production of *The Book of Revelation* in Madison Square Garden at the Millennium. No one would pay attention.

Guardedly I said that if God would send His providential warning to New York City that no one would heed, there must be a consequence. To me this meant that a judgment of some kind must already be determined upon the city (2 Chron. 25:1). Furthermore, it would have to take place in the relatively near future for our warning to serve any purpose.

A SEVERE JUDGMENT

Then I explained why I believed God's judgment could not mean the utter destruction of the city at this time. "New York is only a type of Babylon," I said. "And this is not the end, when Babylon will be totally destroyed.

Too much prophecy has yet to be fulfilled.

"But," I continued, "for God's judgment to be a sign of the fall of Babylon, it has to be severe. If it is not severe, people will just dismiss it. That can't be possible. Why would God send a special warning to New York City about His judgment if it isn't going to be severe?"

I told them how in Revelation 18 it was pointedly repeated three times that Babylon's destruction came "in a single hour" (vv. 10, 17, 19 ESV). In that short time, the smoke from her ruin had risen high into the heavens and could be seen from far at sea. I said that an accident would spread too slowly for God's judgment to come with great fire and smoke *in a single hour*, and a strange natural disaster would seem too obvious and out of place.

"I can only conceive of one thing that would reflect Babylon's destruction in a single hour," I concluded. "A surprise attack. If that's true, I can think of only two groups in the world who could or would do such a thing. One is China. They are developing rockets, but I don't think they will be ready to do something like this for at least ten years. The other group is Muslim terrorists. They could attack at any time. But I don't see how they could accomplish something of this magnitude for at least two or three more years."

Nonetheless, if premiering *The Book of Revelation* in New York was to be God's warning to the city, I believed a major attack could be no farther than a decade away at most. Yet, even as I explained these things, I wished I didn't believe they were true. I wanted somehow to be wrong, but I could see no other answer.

"I'm not claiming this to be prophetic," I said. Such a thought was too awful to even say or think. It would be like wishing to condemn the city to a terrible destruction. And what if I was wrong? I had had no actual vision or dream from God whereby I had seen a clear picture of these things. It was because of what I had read in Scripture and seen as its relation and application to the providential circumstances of time and place (1 Chron. 12:32). That is what had led me to the conclusion. I told my team I couldn't see otherwise. The Holy Spirit had captured my attention through the verse in Revelation 18, and then opened my eyes to its application with the knowledge of God's working that I'd come to understand through Scripture, history, and my own experience of decades as a Christian.

To my surprise, no one argued or had issue with anything I said. My wife Betty, who ran the office and aided in production, looked intent; both Joyce and her son Scott, who were the heart of our little production staff, responded in agreement. In fact, Joyce took occasion to express her deep concern at the danger our nation was in because of our sins and wondered how much longer God could look away without bringing judgment.

Before returning to our tasks, I ended with the only other thing I could think to say: "When we're in New York, we need to pray for God's mercy, *that in wrath, the Lord would remember mercy.*"

After 9/11, when the final toll was known, I could see how truly God had led us to pray in the city and that He had been merciful, as we'd prayed (Hab. 3:1–2).

5

FILM FESTIVAL

The LORD sent prophets to the people to bring them back to him.

—2 Chronicles 24:19 NIV

N JULY 2000 we delivered the Lord's providential warning to New York City through *The Book of Revelation.*

THURSDAY, JULY 7, 2000

Crossing the New Jersey marshlands as we approached the city, I saw Manhattan's skyline poking up on the horizon. Her buildings rose upwards in a tight cluster, and I was filled with instant apprehension and dread. How utterly strange it felt to see those tall, slender shapes now standing so peacefully silhouetted against the blue sky—as we came with the knowledge that they would be attacked in the imminent future with unexpected destruction, fire, and death.

That such a horrible thing could possibly be true still seemed so unbelievable. How could New York City really be attacked? Her buildings stood ahead of us with an undeniable aura of permanence and stability; but neither could I deny the knowledge of what God had shown me, and His specific purpose in sending us.

Upon arriving, we first picked up our promotional materials for the grand opening that evening. I then lunched with the man who ran the New York office for our duplicator and later rejoined the others to set up our display in Madison Square Garden. Finally, we made it to our hotel and changed for the event.

Nervous and filled with mixed emotions, the four of us then returned to the Garden to participate in the grand opening of the 2000 New York International Independent Film and Video Festival. We had no idea what to expect. Eager to gain awareness for our work, we wondered how *The Book of Revelation* would be received; yet, our hearts were heavy at the same time and filled with anxiety about the threat of judgment that hung over the city.

Scott, with a master's degree in drama, had long planned to dress up like John the Baptist. He would carry a big sign and call out to the crowds to draw attention to our production. But after what I'd shared the week before, the Lord had spoken to him as well through the story of David numbering Israel in disobedience to God. When offered the choice of punishments for his sin, David had asked for God's judgment rather than man's, for the Lord would be merciful (2 Sam. 24:11–14).

Knowing now why the Lord had sent us, Scott put his whole heart into crying out genuine words of warning to the tightly packed crowds of people flowing by, drinking and dressed with casual immodesty. No longer acting a part, Scott walked through the crush, sweating and crying aloud, "Repent! The kingdom of heaven is near!" and "Turn back to God," praying the whole time in his heart for mercy. At first we heard positive comments about the promotional gimmick. Most paid no attention, but as the evening wore on, people began complaining. "Tell him to stop," they said. "It was pretty cool for a while, but enough is enough," others said. "We're sick of hearing him."

We were also joined for the event by our composer Brian Hanson and his wife Cheryl, and by our close friends the Dickinsons, who had helped fund the production at a critical stage. Overdressed, we looked out of place in the young crowd. The festival was different from anything I had anticipated. For the most part, the other entries were dark, oppressive, provocative films. The contrast with *The Book of Revelation* could not have been more pronounced. I found it impossible to say more than a few polite words to the other producers and saw little to sincerely compliment.

People shuffled by our display for five or six hours, generally ignoring us and oblivious to any sense of an impending judgment. Watching them pass in the careless, noisy atmosphere only heightened my sense of God's displeasure with the complacency and His judgment looming over the city. Finally, the grand opening came to an end. I was only too eager to pull down our display and leave. I was physically and emotionally drained, standing all those hours, praying constantly that God would remember mercy upon New York.

When we reached our room for the night, I told Betty I felt such great foreboding. All that we had seen and experienced had disturbed me deeply. Tired as I was, I just wanted to sleep. The next thing I remembered, however, was being slowly awakened as out of a dream by loud screams and things breaking. Disoriented at first, I thought there must be a fire, but waking Betty, I soon realized the sounds were coming from a violent fight in the next room. A man and a woman were yelling and throwing objects. Finally, the hotel sent someone to stop it.

Wakened from sleep by this episode on this particular night seemed like just one more evidence of the widespread sin of the city, crying out for judgment. What were the odds of a fight breaking out in the middle of the night in the room next to ours in a grand hotel? This was not the film festival, with its bawdy, young crowd. The pervasiveness of sin and disregard for God were being exposed at all levels. There was no fear of the Lord in the people here; they were living as if He didn't exist. Fully awake in the dark, I had a heightened sense of His holy anger for this place that was brimming over with immorality and violence. The ugliness of what we had seen in one night only served to confirm what God had revealed to me through His Word before we came. Surely the Lord had determined that His judgment would fall upon this city.

SATURDAY, JULY 9, 2000

On the day of our premiere, unusually pleasant weather greeted us for July in New York.

It was especially nice because we had arranged a walking tour first thing in the morning with the Hansons. They had never been to New York before, so we cheerfully set out together, hoping to get to the top of the Empire State Building to see the view.

As we walked along, I felt I needed to share with them what God had shown me about our purpose for coming to New York. Brian had spent months writing the underscore for the production, composing the music, scene by scene, for twenty-two different chapters as we sent him our finished videos. He told me at the end that he had become emotionally exhausted in the process, due to the unrelenting soberness of the message. Before long we stood at the foot of the Empire State Building. On such a spectacular day in the city, people all around us busily went about their activities. Trying not to sound like some crazy eccentric, I explained how New York seemed to be a mirror image of the description of Babylon, how Scripture described Babylon's destruction at the end of time, and how I was convinced releasing *The Book of Revelation* here at the Millennium was the Lord's warning of an imminent judgment in a single hour that would reflect Babylon's fall.

"I believe it must be a surprise attack," I said, as we stopped for warm pretzels. Venturing to say such extreme things out loud on a bright, fine sunny day in New York City made me feel so completely foolish. Our dear friends looked about the city and nodded graciously as we went.

That Saturday evening, approximately a hundred people attended the world premiere of *The Book of Revelation*. News releases had been sent to papers and radio stations to promote the event. Though we had never seen most of those who came, we did recognize family friends who drove down from Connecticut; our former pastor, and his family; and the Webbs, who drove up from Princeton. Though we had also invited leaders from the American Bible Society, denominational headquarters, national ministries, and key churches, only our good friend Dick Castor, from the ABS board, and his wife, Connie, came.

Once *The Book of Revelation* started, the small audience sat absolutely still through the entire 110-minute production. Only one person walked out. When it came to an end, everyone remained frozen in silence. Suddenly the whole audience stood up and burst into applause. The director of the film festival came forward to have pictures taken with us, I said a few words and thanked our team, and it was over that quickly.

Gathering outside, about twenty of us agreed to celebrate over dinner at an acclaimed Italian restaurant that Connie Castor recommended. Grabbing several cabs, we soon reassembled at one long table in the restaurant and had a fine time together.

At one point in the conversation, Scott observed offhandedly that Manhattan Island's unique and compact geography forced its buildings to be tall and packed densely together. He pointed out how this feature would make her more vulnerable in the event of attack. But in the circumstances I found it impossible to share about God's purpose for our mission to the city. We were celebrating together, and our guests were unprepared for the message heavy on my heart, and I didn't know how to say it in any way that would be appropriate.

So with dinner and dessert over, the group shared warm regards and said good-byes, and we went our separate ways. I had said nothing about Revelation 18 and the surprise attack.

Going home the next morning was a relief. How anticlimactic our three days in the city now seemed. I just wanted to get on with raising the money we needed to shoot footage in Europe and the Middle East in order to finish the rest of the New Testament. I felt I had failed miserably through my inability to communicate what burned inside me so intensely about the certainty of the Lord's coming judgment. I had told only our composer and his wife, and I had done that poorly. No one who attended our premiere had considered any connection between its providential location in New York City or its timing at the Millennium. Nonetheless, we had done what the Lord had called us to do in releasing *The Book of Revelation* as a warning to the city. Later, I would understand that was all we were meant to do. I could not see the Lord's larger purpose and plan that this judgment would be no isolated event. But the time for my testimony would come after 9/11, when I could also witness to its purpose.

As it happened, out touring the morning of our premiere, Scott and Joyce rode past Madison Square Garden in a bus and saw our production and my name on the marquee. They immediately hopped off, excited at the chance to capture a record shot of our participation in the festival.

6

FOURTEEN MONTHS

Then the Lord said to me, "You have seen well, for I am ready to perform My word."

—Jeremiah 1:12 NKJV

I N JUST FOURTEEN MONTHS our warning mission to New York City would prove to be true.

TRIP TO EUROPE AND THE MIDDLE EAST

Returning home, I turned my attention to raising money to shoot the footage we needed in Europe and the Middle East to complete the rest of the New Testament. Nothing further had developed from the film festival in New York or its sister festival in Santa Monica in terms of increased awareness or support for our project. We also released *The Book of Revelation* in the new DVD format, but it attracted no interest at all from distributors, either. As usual, we were again under great financial pressure, just when we needed to focus on completing the New Testament as quickly as possible.

However, home only two weeks, I slipped on a magazine one night in the dark and fell on the hard arm of our couch, breaking ribs. On the same day Betty's mother in California fell and broke her ribs too. It seemed such an odd occurrence. Always priding myself for quick reactions and exceptional balance, I had never broken a bone in my life, in spite of my athletics. Why had it happened now, I questioned, when so many preparations had to be made for shooting essential footage in the Middle East? Had I angered God with my thoughts about New York City? Had I been judgmental to think and say the things I did? Had I reaped in my own body what I had sown with my thoughts and words? And why Betty's mother at the same time? Had God's displeasure with me overflowed to our family too? I prayed for discernment, but received no answer until after 9/11. The Lord was at work in ways I wouldn't see or understand until after the attack.

But after two months of no success in fund-raising for our trip, I was about to give up in total discouragement when Scott and I suddenly had the chance to go with a last-minute gift of ten thousand dollars, the minimum it would take. God had answered our prayers after all, just as it looked utterly hopeless. How overjoyed and relieved I was! We would finally be able to shoot all the footage we required for Paul's missionary journeys and to finish the New Testament. Our trip would take nearly the whole month of October. We had wanted to go six years. But God's timing was perfect. What I didn't know then was that I would learn things on this trip that would later shape my understanding of critical endtimes prophecy related to the purpose of 9/11.

What an incredible journey it turned out to be! We made nearly impossible connections every day. Using my experience with Eurail passes from a budget trip to Europe in college, we traveled by train from Paris to Rome to begin shooting there. Then we crossed Italy to the Adriatic Sea to sail to Greece. Landing there, we rode by train to Corinth, by bus to Athens, by train to Thessalonica, and by bus to Philippi and Neapolis, shooting in every location. Next we crossed the heavily guarded border into Turkey for six days, then went on to Damascus, Syria, and finally ended up in Beirut, Lebanon. Time and again, we made connections at the moment our buses and trains were pulling out.

Traveling on such short notice, reservations were impossible except for our first night in Rome. After that, we never knew where we would stay before arriving, but in amazing ways the names of friends were given to us to contact in almost every country. They offered advice and made daily calls on our behalf to book rooms and make arrangements.

Not knowing what to expect after Europe, we were concerned most of all about Turkey. The Greeks spoke harshly of their historic enemy. Adding to our trepidation, just as we arrived, the US Embassy alerted Americans to stay off the street following the attack on the USS *Cole*. But riding a bus through breathtakingly beautiful mountain countryside overlooking the Mediterranean, Scott and I were wonderfully encouraged by the largest, longest rainbow either of us had ever seen, which we took as a sign the Lord was with us in this place.

On our first night in Turkey, we stayed at Çanakkale, across the Dardanelles from the famed Gallipoli battlefields of World War I. Though I didn't know it, I would learn my first important lesson there. Almost a half-million casualties were suffered at Gallipoli when British, Australian, and New Zealand forces failed to capture this peninsula from its Turkish defenders. I would later realize this battle's enormous providential significance for the endtimes. The Allied debacle nearly ruined the promising career of a young Winston Churchill, but the great Turkish victory established a courageous young Colonel Ataturk, who rose to head Turkey after the war. It was this leader and his secular government that abolished the caliphate in 1924, an event that left the Islamic world leaderless for the first time in thirteen hundred years, and in its vacuum, planted seeds for the birth of the Muslim Brotherhood in Egypt, which would also spawn al-Qaeda and bin Laden.

The next day our bus passed by a series of roadside billboards advertising the ruins of ancient Troy. Seeing them, I suddenly grasped that Homer's fabled Troy must be closely related to the nearby biblical city of Troas, where Paul had been directed by the Holy Spirit. The story about Paul's famous voyage from Troas to Macedonia after a dream was recounted in Acts 16:6–12. Immediately, I wondered if there might be some interrelationship of stories and places with a larger providential meaning. Surely, Alexander the Great would have sailed near to this very spot to embark on his grand vision to conquer Asia for Greek glory and culture.

Only two days earlier, we had been in Philippi, where Paul first preached the Gospel on the European continent. Philippi had been named for Alexander's father, Philip, former king of Macedonia. It had also been the site of one of history's most pivotal battles, determining the future outcome of the Roman Empire just eighty years before Paul's arrival.

Instantly, I had an insight. The magnitude of it amazed me. The apostle Paul's story in Acts appeared to be Alexander's story *in perfect reverse*. In 334 BC, Alexander sailed *from Macedonia to conquer Asia* in what would be the most brilliant military campaign in human history. Almost four centuries later, Paul was called in the opposite direction to come over *to Macedonia from Asia*. Immediately, he sailed for Alexander's homeland—launching a spiritual campaign that in time *would conquer Greece, the Roman Empire, and eventually, the whole continent of Europe for the Gospel*, with vast implications for world history and eternity. I had never heard the idea before. Yet, here it was to be found in Scripture. Paul's *East to West* echoed in reverse Alexander's earlier *West to East*. In fact, Philippi, where Paul preached first in Europe, was the place where Alexander had prepared for his historic conquest of Asia. Certainly, none of this was lost to the learned apostle. He had to understand the great strategic and prophetic implications of his mission to the West. The Lord had led him with purpose to Macedonia from Asia. It was no small detour. It held the promise of a victory for the Gospel over the mighty Roman Empire, and with it, Europe, a victory that would shape a future Western civilization.

How these thoughts stirred my imagination to see a fresh vision of God's sovereign power and greatness, the King of heaven, who ruled over the kingdoms of men and revealed Himself in Scripture (Ps. 92:5)! As I later learned, Alexander *had intentionally* landed at Troy and slept with a treasured copy of Homer under his pillow. More amazingly, just like Paul, he had been encouraged in his undertaking by a dream. According to first-century Jewish historian Flavius Josephus, Alexander had dreamt of one in the likeness of the high priest of Jerusalem encouraging him to come and conquer Asia, promising he would be victorious. When Alexander approached Jerusalem with his army, the high priest came out to welcome this pagan prince to show him the prophecies in Scripture where he was destined to conquer Persia (Dan. 8:5–7, 20–21; Num. 24:24). History would later demonstrate that his rapid conquest of those regions proved to be God's preparation for the Gospel of Christ to spread quickly under a universal language and a future *Pax Romana*. Together, these providential circumstances would level the mountains and fill in the valleys for the coming of Messiah in the fullness of time. These very things would also enable Paul to take the Gospel *to Europe* to lay the foundation for an even greater victory for the Christian faith and the kingdom of God on that strategic continent. No wonder the Lord had prevented Paul from evangelizing to the east as he had twice sought to do in Asia and Bithynia (Acts 16:6–8). Not merely some random new outreach to another city across the Aegean Sea, in God's great, wise plan, Paul's mission to the European continent took a beachhead with vast implications for the rest of history. All this was to be discovered in Scripture with its implied connection between the historic military career of Alexander and the apostolic ministry of Paul. After 9/11, I would see much more to these providential events and their direct connection to the endtimes.

On our third day, Turkey held its national census. The government required everyone to stay indoors, so Scott spent the day shooting pictures of clouds from our hotel balcony. I remained in bed, having caught a cold the previous day on our air-conditioned bus. Lying still because my injured ribs ached when I coughed, and I felt miserable, I had time to think and pray about many things, including our warning to New York. Sick, in pain, and worried about our financial condition when we returned, I was still concerned about the Lord's possible displeasure with me regarding my thoughts about New York and could hardly listen with care. In this anxious state, I was unable to fully contemplate the implications of the *Cole* attack by radical Muslims and perhaps see it as a connection to the Lord's imminent judgment on the city. As time would tell, the *Cole* incident did point to who would carry out the surprise attack on New York. It would not be the Chinese. The city would be attacked by a small group of Islamic jihadists preparing even then.

The next day, despite Embassy warnings, we set out again to cross Turkey in a rented car. We then shot hours of footage in Ephesus, Antioch in Pisidea, the Sultan range, Iconium, and Tarsus, capturing scenes of extensive ruins and the most beautiful rugged mountains. In Adana, we took a bus to Antioch near the border with Syria.

On the way to Antioch, I prayed urgently about whether we should stay there or continue on to Damascus. Because of the census delay in Turkey, we were a day behind schedule, and I had a new contact to meet in Damascus. However, our bus driver couldn't speak English, and I thought it would be impossible to reach Damascus that day. Arriving soon at the terminal in Antioch, I stepped off the bus into a teeming sea of bustling passengers and shouting Turkish taxi drivers.

Just then a man walked around the bus, came right up to us, and said in perfect English, "Would anyone like to go to Damascus?"

"Yes!" I said in amazement. "When would we go?"

"The bus leaves in fifteen minutes," he said. "Just follow me."

Minutes later we were aboard the bus and on our way to Damascus. God had answered my prayer in a most unexpected way. We arrived in time to meet our friend for dinner at a fine Syrian restaurant. In the morning he took us to shoot in the actual underground room where the Lord had spoken to Ananias about Paul, and later to the window in the city wall where Paul had escaped in a basket (Acts 9). That night we ate dinner with our friend's family. The following morning he arranged for an experienced Christian taxi driver to take us through armed Syrian military checkpoints to Beirut. There we had a prearranged meeting with the leaders of SAT-7, a satellite TV ministry with offices in Lebanon, to draft an agreement for producing the Arabic New Testament for satellite broadcast throughout the Middle East, North Africa, and Europe. Of the world's many languages, our next version would be *Arabic*. It was less than a year before 9/11.

After our meeting in Beirut, Scott and I flew home to Pittsburgh. Thankful to be safe and alive, we had all the footage we needed to complete the New Testament. We could devote ourselves to finishing the production as quickly as possible. In the meantime, a good friend in Missouri suggested that Congressman Roy Blunt could deliver DVD copies of *The Book of Revelation* to President George W. Bush and Attorney General

John Ashcroft. I sent him three copies on June 19, 2001. Two months later, a formal thank-you arrived from the White House. The attorney general's hand-signed note was dated seven days after 9/11.

FINISHING THE NEW TESTAMENT

Having first offered in prayer to produce the Bible on video in November 1991, I could hardly believe it when we finished the last scene of the New Testament on Tuesday, September 4, 2001, nearly a decade later. Only six months' work remained as our composers wrote the final music for the last videos. Once their music came back, Scott would create the final mixed soundtracks and output the finished productions to master tape. After so many years it seemed almost inconceivable that we had actually produced the whole New Testament. In that long process, only God's grace had enabled us to finish what He had called us to start, when time and again it looked impossible (see Judg. 7:2). Thousands of scenes had been created to support the thousands of verses of Scripture. Tens of thousands of text elements had been composited on video and matched to the narration that had been carefully paced in thousands of places. The soundtrack had 130 original compositions.

Every aspect of the production had been carefully considered to communicate God's Word as effectively as we could. In countless ways, Scripture had guided our decisions: the priority of the written Word over everything else—font sizes, color and styles, dividing of text, use of dissolves, choice of scenes, coloring and use of actors, the use of narration, music and sound effects, pacing and choreography of elements, and the use of effects. Scripture had offered priceless practical insights, like: *It is written . . . the word of the Lord endures forever . . . Write it plainly . . . Faith comes by hearing . . . line upon line, precept upon precept . . . I did not shrink back from declaring to you the whole counsel of God . . . Do not neglect the public reading of scripture . . . Remember the word of the Lord . . . I beg you to read this letter to all His followers . . . How can they believe if they have never heard? . . . Teach them to do all that I have told you . . . all things to all people . . . making melody in your hearts to the Lord . . . Peace to you . . . a seamless garment . . . The south wind blew softly,* and many, many more.

In its various stages more than thirty people had been involved in the production. Among them, Mark Grover and Janet Dibble had helped to get it started. Don Wadsworth had narrated the text. The bulk of the production work had then been done by a mere handful of people: Joyce, Scott, Brian, Grace, Betty, and me. In particular, Betty had worked ceaselessly without pay, day after day, year after year, sitting at her desk in a cheap plastic lawn chair that was all we could afford. With such limited resources and staff, the task would have been impossible to accomplish without her; she influenced every area with her careful dedication and intelligence. How grateful I was for her and all that she did. We had now completed the first professional production of the entire New Testament in history. When I had the vision, we had been married just over ten years. The last scene finished rendering the day of our twentieth wedding anniversary—September 5, 2001. To me it was a sign of God's hand on our marriage and work together. I would shortly see how remarkably true this was. It was now six days before 9/11.

Elated to have reached this milestone in our production, the staff took a week's break. I sent a happy e-mail to SAT-7 that we could soon focus our attention on producing the Arabic New Testament—of all possible languages to work on next. As it happened, Joyce and Scott had gone to the Jersey Shore with old friends on their vacation break. During a hurricane there two years before, Joyce had shot dramatic footage that we used in *The Book of Revelation*. Since their friends had not yet seen the production, she and Scott planned to play the DVD their last night together—*September 11, 2001*. On that day, however, like everyone else around the world, they were shocked to see the tragedy unfolding in New York City. But as soon as Scott saw what was happening, he said, "This is it! This is chapter 18." Unable to watch, he went out on the beach, where he cried, prayed, and read Scripture. Having planned to celebrate a joyous milestone that very night, they watched *The Book of Revelation* with grief and amazement.

7

SEPTEMBER 11

Woe! Woe, O great city, O Babylon, city of power! In one hour your doom has come!

—Revelation 18:10 NIV

THE ATTACK ON NEW YORK CITY was a remarkable reflection of the fall of Babylon in chapter 18 of Revelation, just as God had led us to believe it would be.

THE NIGHT BEFORE

On Monday night before the attack, I'd been deeply stirred by my appointed Bible reading. I had finished Jeremiah the day earlier and planned to begin Lamentations before bed. However, once I started, I couldn't stop. I read all five chapters straight through.

It had been some time since I'd read Jeremiah's short book. The prophet's portrayal of God's wrath upon Judah for its long rebellion always caused me to approach it with a mixture of anxiety and trepidation, fearing the consequences of personal disobedience. But that night his words gripped me with a fresh sense of relevance to America. For months I had read through Isaiah and Jeremiah, and was reminded throughout of the book of Revelation by their similar imagery and threatenings. Now, reading Lamentations, I feared God's judgment on our nation. For decades we had gradually accustomed ourselves to accept ever-greater degrees of sinfulness. Few preachers warned about the genuine danger of approaching judgment. Even then, their talk of judgment was rarely more than a vague possibility in some distant future; almost never was it said we had already built up a reservoir of wrath that now awaited us. Somehow we never quite reached a level to deserve God's punishment; our collective sins were never quite bad enough for that. But how much longer could the Lord overlook our gross and blatant sin against Him?

Once more, I rehearsed in my mind how our Christian heritage was rapidly being lost. We had been a beacon of light and hope for centuries: feeding the hungry, forgiving enemies, rebuilding nations, dispensing knowledge and technology, and above all, spreading the Gospel around the globe. Yet despite these many good things, we were systematically turning our back on God and our biblical heritage. Our Congress had long since muzzled pastors by banning political speech from the pulpit. Our courts had outlawed the Bible and prayer in public schools without precedent. Then they legalized abortion, leading to the deaths of millions of babies. Our entertainment industry pushed the limits with ever more violent and depraved productions. To satisfy greed, our companies, financial institutions, and business leaders manipulated markets, engaged in illegal activities, sought excessive compensation, charged usurious interest of those least able to pay, and practiced a distorted capitalism that ignored the God whose principles made it possible. By and large, the American public went along with it all.

As I thought about these things, Jeremiah's words stirred in my spirit with awful urgency. Surely we must be approaching the time of God's wrath. How much longer would He or could He wait before pouring out His fury upon our nation? Kneeling by my chair, I begged God to have mercy on us, pleading intensely for an hour until I had a sense of peace and finally went off to bed. I hadn't prayed in such a concerted way for our country in some time.

9/11

The next morning I was still upstairs when Betty called out that a plane had crashed into the World Trade Center.

"That's impossible," I said, glancing out the window at a perfectly clear blue sky without clouds.

"But that's what they're reporting on the radio," she yelled back.

Turning on the TV, I was shocked to see an image of two tall buildings towering above the New York City skyline, with a long trail of ominous, dark smoke billowing out and away from the side of one. Newscasters talked in the background about what might have happened. On such a clear, cloudless morning, the picture looked completely absurd. *How could a pilot have done that?* I wondered. I yelled back down to Betty that she was right. Moments later, as I stared at the TV screen in total disbelief, a huge plane suddenly flew into view out of nowhere, impossibly low and heading right toward the towers. It disappeared into the second building as a massive fireball exploded outward from the other side.

Instantly, it was horribly clear what had happened. We were witnessing orchestrated terrorism. The planes had flown into the buildings on purpose. I was furious. How could this have been allowed? To let anyone hijack and crash one plane was unacceptable, but two planes? We soon learned the planes had flown all the way from Boston and crashed within nine minutes of each other. Both of them had been able to fly far off course without detection until too late.

Questions raced through my mind. How could the terrorists have gotten away with something like this that had to be carefully planned and coordinated in advance? Why weren't they stopped? How were our intelligence services caught so entirely off guard? Why had the airlines allowed armed terrorists to board the planes and get away with it? While angry at the terrorists, I thought, what else would you expect of them? I was more upset with the airlines and our leaders for allowing such an act. There was no excuse. This was America. We had the money, people, and technology to prevent terrorism like this from happening here.

Betty and I put everything else aside to watch. We sat transfixed. In time a small army of New York City's firefighters marched up the street, carrying their equipment to fight the fires.

Only later did we learn that men and women had jumped to their deaths from a hundred stories up rather than bear the inferno at their backs. Small groups had held hands together for the courage to jump. For thirty long seconds they'd plummeted, and nothing was left upon impact.

Before long the news reported that a third passenger plane had crashed into the Pentagon. It seemed inconceivable. What was going on? How many other planes were preparing to do the same thing?

And then, the unthinkable happened. Without warning the massive South Tower gave way. Collapsing upon itself like an accordion, floor upon floor, it gained momentum rapidly as it came cascading down from the top. The blast of air created a huge windstorm of dust, debris, and paper that rolled out for blocks in dense, billowing waves, coating everything in its wake.

The firefighters we had seen in the streets only minutes before had been courageously ascending the tower's stairwells. That quickly, hundreds were gone. Tears welled in my eyes. What we had just witnessed was incomprehensible. The sorrow was unspeakable. Less than half an hour later, the North Tower followed, simply melting before our eyes. The buildings were no longer there. The grief was oppressive and overwhelming.

Later, it was reported that the city had banned asbestos in construction when the towers were just halfway up. The architect had told the city it was a mistake. He said if ever there were a major fire above where the asbestos stopped, the buildings would fall. Hearing that, I thought engineers must have known almost immediately how hot it would get in the buildings and what would happen. Yet those brave firefighters had been sent to put out the flames. Was no one responsible for such knowledge?

Fewer than ten minutes after the second tower fell, a fourth plane was reported down near Pittsburgh. Flight 93 had crashed in a field outside Somerset. It was flying toward Washington. No one survived. Sometime after this report, Brian Hanson called from Florida. "I just wanted to make sure you're all right. I heard that one of the planes crashed near Pittsburgh."

"We're fine," I told him. "The plane went down near Somerset, which is quite a way from us."

"I'm glad to hear you're OK," he said. "I was concerned."

"I'm just so angry that our government and the airlines let something like this happen," I said. "All those firefighters who died in the buildings. I've been yelling at the television. There was no excuse."

We commiserated briefly. Then Brian said, "It's hard to believe we were in New York just a year ago."

His words hit me like a thunderbolt: *the surprise attack on New York City!* I couldn't believe I hadn't realized what was taking place. We spoke further, then hung up. I hadn't even thought about the film festival and our mission to the city until Brian's words. But I had expected missiles, or bombers, or a nuclear device. I hadn't looked for passenger planes flying into buildings, and at the outset it had not been clear just how devastating this act of terrorism would turn out to be. Only after the towers lay in rubble did it become apparent. But then it was clear. Just as the Lord had led me to believe it would be, the attack had been *severe* and *in a way sufficient* to gain our attention and the attention of the world without destroying the city.

My anger subsided. In its place I felt bone-deep sorrow. I could see our leaders were blind to the approaching danger, and their blindness was itself part of God's judgment. Though that thought didn't absolve them of their responsibility in allowing such a disaster to take place on our soil, it helped me begin to accept it. God had used our pride and complacency to punish us. The intelligence services had been isolated, limited, and careless. The government had been careless. The airlines had been careless. At almost every level our leaders doubted that terrorists could hurt us like this.

Over time I learned how many things had prepared us for punishment. For one, the 2000 presidential election was contested in an unprecedented way. Critical security planning was delayed by months. The new team underestimated the dangers. Key people were let go. After the first Trade Center bombing in 1993, the previous administration had two full terms to deal with the terror threat, but failed to truly comprehend our adversary. Although, bin Laden and al-Qaeda had declared war on America in 1996 and again in 1998, Janet Reno's Justice Department decided to treat Islamic terrorism as a crime. The CIA wanted to assassinate bin Laden.

The FBI wanted to bring him to trial in America as a criminal. The FBI's view won. As if to underscore the mistake with a strange irony, the man who had overseen the FBI's efforts to capture bin Laden alive had died on 9/11 in the collapse of the Trade Center. John O'Neill had just retired from the FBI in August and was hired to oversee security for the Center. Escaping initial injury, he stayed at his post and died doing his job with courage, but bin Laden had *still* killed him. He was a casualty of our grave misunderstanding of the adversary we faced.

However, the greatest responsibility for failing to adequately understand the true nature of our enemy fell to the former president. Bill Clinton had appeared to excel in his management of domestic issues, but America's popular president had failed in his responsibilities to oversee our national security as commander in chief, even after the terrorists' first attempt in 1993. Yet, in electing him the country was given what it deserved for its leadership. This immoral, politically gifted man had been an instrument in preparing us for chastening and worse.

In spite of these things, we had had multiple opportunities to halt the terrorists. Various people at many levels along the way weren't paying attention and had ignored obvious warnings. New regulations were put in place to prohibit interagency intelligence sharing—to protect our leaders from investigations of possible corruption, and the CIA knowingly withheld information it possessed that terrorists had entered the country. The FBI ignored several agents who begged for closer investigations of suspicious pilots. The few who saw things were not permitted to share or investigate. It was all heartbreaking and seemed so unnecessary. Yet, it had to happen. God had determined to judge our country for its sin by means of a terrible surprise attack. He would also send a great sign with enormous prophetic significance for America and the world.

REVELATION 18

Within days, two well-known TV preachers were accused of calling the attack an act of divine judgment, but both were immediately forced to publicly clarify what they said. No one wanted to hear it in the aftermath of such pain and suffering. One of the preachers was Pat Robertson, who had only said he believed that the Lord had lifted His hand of covering from us. Ironically, Robertson was the one who had told Russ and Norma Bixler to build a Christian TV station in Pittsburgh, where I would have the idea to produce the Bible on video that took us to the film festival in 2000. But wrestling with my own second thoughts about the attack, I couldn't deny what God had shown me through the book of Revelation. The terrorists had targeted the very city we had warned, the city I had come to see most reflected Babylon in the modern world.

But even beyond my imagining, the circumstances of the attack had echoed the passage in Revelation 18 in a number of profound and amazing ways. Occurring as it did on a weekday in the media capital of the world, the attack was televised live, with unprecedented global visibility. The images of New York could be seen in real time by every king, merchant, and sailor on Earth—the three witness groups described by John in his vision of Babylon's fall.

"*Every king on earth . . . will weep, when they see the smoke from that fire. Her sufferings will frighten them and they will stand at a distance and say, 'Pity that great and powerful city! Pity Babylon! In a single hour her judgment has come'*" (Rev. 18.9–10 CEV). New York, the great and powerful city that was host to all the world's leaders at the UN, had just suffered a devastating surprise attack in like manner. Many global leaders had called to express sympathy and shock at our sudden and unexpected suffering. With horror and amazement they had watched our burning, smoking buildings fall to the ground "in a single hour."

Revelation 18:16–17 says that all the rich merchants of the world "shouted, 'Pity the great city of Babylon! . . . In a single hour her riches disappeared'" (CEV). Standing proud sentinel on our coast, the world's most famous business icon had just been utterly destroyed by nineteen terrorists in hijacked airplanes. In a single hour the World Trade Center had melted in ruins. Nothing was left of its once-powerful presence for global trade. Mighty Wall Street lay buried beneath ashes and debris.

Every captain, passenger and sailor watched from a distance: "When they saw the smoke from her fire, they shouted, 'This was the greatest city ever!' . . . They threw dust on their heads . . . In a single hour the city was destroyed" (Rev. 18:18–19 CEV). All day long the cameras had displayed New York's skyline from across the harbor, with thick, dark clouds of smoke trailing high above for everyone to see. This great city on the seacoast had

been horribly wounded in a single hour. When its two tallest towers collapsed, everything—and everyone—had been covered by their dust.

All three passages had repeated that Babylon's destruction would
come in *a single hour*. In part, this fact was what had led me to believe
God's judgment upon the city would come as a surprise attack. How
could Revelation 18 be a warning to New York City, I had reasoned, if
her coming judgment did not reflect the prophecy? Almost incredibly, the
first building to fall had collapsed just *56 minutes* after being hit.

Beyond these things Revelation 18 prophesied that Babylon's judgment would come in a single day, with unexpected destruction, death,
and mourning: "Therefore her plagues will come in one day—death and
mourning and famine. And she will be utterly burned with fire" (v. 8
NKJV). Going about its normal business that day, New York City had
been totally unprepared for what hit it. Thousands had died in the falling
towers. Fire, fed by building materials and jet fuel, had melted the girders
and consumed what little was left of the ruins.

Of particular note, God had threatened in Revelation 18:5–6 that
Babylon must suffer *double* because her sins were *piled high*. Therefore
she would be destroyed with a *double portion* of judgment. In the attack,
the two highest skyscrapers in the world's richest city had been targeted,
and both fell. These two lofty symbols of power and wealth were gone
in a day. How amazing was it that there were even *two* tall buildings to
fall, not just one? One tower had been insufficient to project the grand
impression its builders intended. Mirror images of each other, the two
tall towers had been built shoulder to shoulder to create a dominating
physical presence to symbolize America's great financial might and success. It was for this reason that the terrorists chose them for destruction.
Yet in God's awful providence hadn't they, rather, been prepared for this
day and hour—duplicate symbols of our power and prosperity, standing
ready to pay a debt of divine justice, a *double portion* for God's wrath?

They both fell and collapsed in a heap.

In our production of *Revelation*, we had represented Babylon's double
judgment with the image of a single golden cup full of mire and filth that
morphed into *two gold cups that were identical*, just as the two buildings
were identical. We had used a cup because it was said that Babylon had
made the nations drunk with her evil wine. After the attack we discov-

ered that Jeremiah had actually referred to Babylon as *a golden cup* in the Lord's hand (Jer. 51:7). Amazingly, we also learned that the two matching landmarks were famous for turning brilliant gold when reflecting the evening sunset. After its golden cup imagery, the next verse in Jeremiah said, "Babylon will suddenly fall and be broken."

And the similarities with Revelation 18 did not stop there. These two towers in New York were not just any anonymous buildings. They were called the *World* Trade Center. They had been built for the purpose of expanding our global trade and business. Their very name recalled the verse that warns, "Every merchant on earth will mourn" (Rev. 18:11).

Even their nickname, Twin Towers, was an irony. The proud term *Towers* harked back to that notorious original built in open defiance to God in ancient Babylon, which had gained for itself the infamous name Tower of Babel (Gen. 11:3–9). These two towers were even filled with workers from all over the earth who spoke a babble of languages.

How could all these specific reflections and similarities, piled one upon another, be just coincidences when God had shown me in advance that a surprise attack would reflect the events of Revelation 18 and the fall of Babylon? To observe them after the fact and see a relationship with this Scripture, as many in fact did, was one thing; but that's not how it happened with us. The Lord had revealed it to me before it happened. Hadn't He done this so we could testify with absolute certainty that 9/11 was not just a terrorist attack, but a judgment of God and a distinct prophetic sign (Ps. 46:8)? If people didn't know this, why would they ever change their ways? Scripture also said, "Because they do not regard the works of the LORD, nor the operations of His hands, He shall destroy them and not build them up" (Ps. 28:5 NKJV).

MOURNING AND MERCY

In the aftermath of 9/11, the whole country was overcome by a collective mourning. Our peace and way of life as Americans had been violated, perhaps permanently altered by the sheer cruelty and magnitude of the unexpected attack. The lives of so many ordinary citizens had been snuffed out with no warning and with unbelievable brutality. Desperate family and friends posted pictures and messages near Ground Zero, trying to find husbands, wives, relatives, lovers, and friends. Many had jumped to their deaths and were not to be found. Some had died in the fire, and others were killed in the collapse. For days afterwards, firefighters, police officers, and volunteers risked their own lives, digging through dangerous rubble, hoping to find any comrades alive. When exhausted, they rested in the shelter of the historic little Episcopal church that had somehow miraculously survived in the shadow of the towers. But all hope of finding survivors in the vast debris soon vanished. Few were found alive.

Still, there was mercy amid the destruction. Fifty thousand people worked in the two buildings. When they first fell, the news reports said as many as 20,000 people or more may have been killed. But even as I heard that number, I turned to Betty and said with a quick sense, "God is merciful. I don't believe it will be more than 3,000 people." This proved true, reminding me how the Lord had led us to pray in the city, "that in wrath, the Lord would remember mercy." In the following weeks, the number reported killed declined until it stopped at 2,973 dead. This also included those who died at the Pentagon and those killed in the crash of Flight 93 near Somerset, Pennsylvania. The heroic passengers on that doomed plane had fought bravely to prevent the jihadists from reaching Washington.

Clearly, God *had* been merciful in judgment. Thanks to the courage of the passengers who gave their lives near Shanksville, our nation's capital was spared further destruction—it would have a major role to play in prophecy, as I was yet to learn. And seeing the shocking extent of the devastation in New York, as terrible as it was, it was a miracle that more people had not died. In sacrificing themselves, the firefighters had helped evacuate the buildings and saved lives. A stark, jagged cross exposed in the barren waste seemed to underscore this truth, and its powerful symbolism offered a silent comfort amid the rubble that was left.

Yet, an uncontrollable fire continued burning deep in the ruins for weeks. It smoldered and burned unquenched, despite a steady rain that turned thick dust everywhere nearly to cement. This eerie scene evoked a wake-up symbolism all its own, like a picture pointing to the fall of Babylon, with smoke rising from her fire; or worse, of the pit of hell, where the fires never go out (Rev. 18:8; Gen. 19:28; Mark 9:49; Rev. 14:9–11). These strange circumstances only seemed to underscore the truth of what God had shown me before our warning mission to New York in 2000 and the attack's genuine prophetic significance.

8

DIVINE JUDGMENT

When all this comes true—and it surely will—then they will know that a prophet has been among them.

—Ezekiel 33:33 NIV

DESPITE THE VAST NATIONAL OUTPOURING of grief, patriotism, and faith after 9/11, the Lord kept speaking to me daily through His Word in ways that confirmed the attack *had* been a divine judgment on America. None of it had been my imagination. In fact, the attack had even greater implications than I believed it would when the Lord sent us with His warning before it struck.

THE BOOK OF EZEKIEL

Beginning the book of Ezekiel the next day, I was astonished by what I read. Having finished all of Lamentations the evening of September 10, I intended to begin Ezekiel on September 11, but hadn't done it because Betty and I kept watching the news until well past bedtime. But once I began the next day, the Lord spoke to me through this book day after day through the patterns of His dealing with Israel, confirming the truth of what He had shown me the year before. Yes, the Lord *had* sent us to New York with *The Book of Revelation* to warn of His coming judgment. Yes, this attack *was* what He had led me to see through His Word and providence. Yet, thousands had died horribly at the hands of terrorists. Many of our people had acted honorably. How could I ever say to those who had lost loved ones and suffered so much that God had sent this tragedy? The country had immediately adopted the phrase *God bless America*. It was posted everywhere. Even the most unlikely people repeated it.

Then, as I began reading Ezekiel, I was startled by the first chapter. The prophet presented a picture of heaven and its creatures nearly identical to what John had described in his vision in Revelation. It was the same vision we had presented in New York City. The next day I read God's instructions to Ezekiel: "You shall speak my words to this rebellious house" (Ezek. 2:7). Had we not been sent to *speak* to New York? Had we not taken *God's own words* to do it? And were we not a "rebellious house"?

The following day I read, "But the house of Israel is not willing to listen to you because they are not willing to listen to me" (Ezek. 3:7 NIV). Similarly, while we had gone to the city with God's Word, no one paid attention to it: not the government, the media, or the Church. But it wasn't our message. God had spoken through His own prophetic Word, and now no one would believe the attacks were a purposeful act of God. Yet, it wasn't senseless. None of the deaths of those who died that day were meaningless or random. God had judged us severely for our corporate sins—and that in justice; but the death of nearly three thousand people, believers and unbelievers who died together was also a sober mercy—to warn us of greater danger still if we didn't repent of our rebellion.

Next I read, "Son of man, I have made you a watchman for the house of Israel; therefore hear a word from My mouth, and give them a warning from Me" (Ezek. 3:17 NKJV). It was as if the Lord were speaking directly to me and encouraging me to believe: *Yes, I did show these things to you, as to a* watchman *on the wall who sees the approaching danger.* His Spirit had opened my ears to hear His Word. We had gone to deliver His warning to New York City in July 2000.

In my next reading, the Lord told Ezekiel, "Lie on your left side and put the sin of the house of Israel upon yourself" (Ezek. 4:4 NIV). The prophet had been ordered by God to lie on his side and use his own body as a sign to Israel of her coming judgment. He did so 390 days, a day for each year of Israel's sins. He was to lie on his other side 40 days for the sins of Judah. After reading this, I instantly recalled my strange fall after our premiere. Betty's mother and I had each fallen on the same day on opposite sides of the country, and both of us had broken ribs. I had prayed to know why this happened, but never received an answer. Had God done in our two bodies what was about to happen to the towers in New York? Had it been for a sign and a testimony, even as with Ezekiel? Was that why we both fell and struck our sides? I had never broken a bone before!

Next I read, "Thus says the LORD God: 'Indeed I, even I, am against you and will execute judgments in your midst in the sight of the nations'" (Ezek. 5:8). Again, didn't this Scripture express the reality of what had just happened in New York? Wasn't it the Lord who executed His judgments on us in our own country? Though we publicly sought His blessing, wasn't He also *against us* because of our sin and lack of repentance? Hadn't all this been broadcast to the whole world by the New York media, literally in the sight of the nations, just as Scripture said?

Days later, I read, "But I the LORD will speak what I will, and it shall be fulfilled without delay. For in your days, you rebellious house, I will fulfill whatever I say, declares the Sovereign LORD" (Ezek. 12:25). Hadn't He fulfilled His judgment without delay, even as the verse said? In July 2000, I had hoped the Lord's judgment might be as much as a decade away. At the least, I had thought a surprise attack on New York could be no closer than two or three years from our warning. I had wanted to see it be as far off as possible. It had been just fourteen months. Again this Scripture underscored to me the fact of God's judgment upon our *rebellious house.*

In the next chapter, I read, "I will break down the wall . . . and bring it down to the ground, so that its foundation will be uncovered; it will fall, and you shall be consumed in the midst of it. Then you shall know that I am the LORD" (Ezek. 13:14 NKJV). How terrible and amazing this verse was to consider. The tower walls had been pierced by passenger planes acting as missiles. Two buildings more than one hundred stories high had been brought *down to the ground*, one in a single hour. Down to the very lowest levels, their foundations had been exposed to the entire watching world. Thousands of lives had been consumed *in the midst of it*, by the inferno and the collapse of the walls. This Scripture described God's method of bringing wrath and judgment upon a disobedient nation. We had witnessed this very thing. Were we so unbelieving as to deny God's hand in it? Were we so blind as to miss His purpose and His work? Had He not done this thing so that we would *know* He was the Lord, the holy God of heaven—and to warn us of that greater judgment that was eternal (Ps. 9:16)?

After the attack, many had asked why God would permit such a terrible thing to happen. How could a *good* God allow it? The awful suffering made no sense to them. Spiritual leaders had responded that we live in a fallen world, and God was bound to permit evil people to exercise their free wills. Pastors could only offer words of comfort and hope for the future (Jer. 8:11). But how could this be true? Had the Almighty sat impotent on the sidelines, watching? Had He been powerless to act while evil terrorists exercised their free wills? I knew it couldn't be so. Luther had taught me too well in *The Bondage of the Will*.

Again the following passage in Ezekiel spoke to me: "When a land sins against Me by persistent unfaithfulness, I will stretch out my hand against it . . . I bring a sword on that land, and say, 'Sword, go through the land'" (14:13, 17 NKJV). This Scripture spoke so directly to our situation. It clearly taught that God was the author of judgment when a nation sinned persistently against Him. When a "sword" attacked such a land in the form of invaders, it was God's *own hand* that was stretched out to bring punishment through them. Hadn't this thing happened to us? Contrary to what others said, these verses confirmed to me that the Lord was no helpless bystander on 9/11. He hadn't stood weakly aside to avoid interfering while evil people exercised their "free will." God had *sent* this sword upon us Himself to chasten and punish us!

So eager to see our sins in relative terms, we were only too ready to dismiss their gravity. But I knew God does not; He is no relativist. The sovereign Lord of heaven is absolutely holy and just, and has the right, even necessity, to punish our nation for sin. Were we so ignorant of God and His ways? He had just punished us by sending a sword upon our land. The Lord had done so to judge a rebellious country and to wake us up to turn us from our evil! As His righteous *sword*, He had used *unrighteous men* with evil plans inspired by Satan, the evil one himself. These wicked terrorists were the means of our chastisement (Hab. 1:13).

In the Old Testament, God had brought similar judgment upon nations over and over (Gen. 15:15; Deut. 7:1–2; Isa. 10:5–6, 26:10; Jer. 51:20–23; Hab. 1:5–8). The Israelites attacked the Canaanites, the Assyrians attacked the Israelites, and the Babylonians attacked the Assyrians. In each attack, God had judged the nation for sin. Indeed, He could not judge temporal nations in eternity because they had no souls. Nations had to be judged during their existence or not be judged at all; and if not judged, then God would be unjust. But when national judgments fell, good and bad alike were swept up in them.

As I knew, the Civil War was the greatest example of national judgment in our own history. Lincoln had proclaimed the war God's just punishment for the sin of slavery. For this reason, he said, the war called for humble endurance, as it would not end until divine justice was served. It remains our bloodiest conflict. Some 620,000 soldiers died, and that from a far smaller population. Yet, in a fearful justice, this terrible toll equaled the estimated number of slaves stolen out of Africa over centuries and imported to America. As the Lord promised, "Vengeance is Mine, [and] I will repay" (Rom. 12:19 NKJV). Neither did His holy justice overlook the generations born on this continent in a cruel captivity. While more Americans died in the Civil War than in all our other wars combined, that number of dead did not account for the thousands of amputees, crippled soldiers, broken families, ruined fortunes, and *countless* generations that would never taste life at all because their potential progenitors died from disease or in battle.

Yet even in national judgments, the Lord made gracious distinctions (Matt. 25:31–33). In the Civil War, believers and unbelievers died together by the tens of thousands, but these dead would not continue together in eternity. For unbelievers, death served no redemptive purpose whatsoever, and was only punishment for sin and preparation for judgment (Heb. 9:27). But for believers, their sufferings were *ultimately redemptive*. God's Word promised that "all things work together for the good of those who love God[,] . . . who are called according to his purpose" (Rom. 8:28 HCSB) and that their sufferings were "not worthy to be compared with the glory" that would be revealed to them (Rom. 8:18–28 KJV). Even bloody death in raging battle would be for them the path to eternal glory. In all these things, the Lord was good and righteous, in His judgment and in His mercy. It was no different on 9/11.

LACK OF REPENTANCE

Briefly, it had appeared that a great spiritual change might take place in the country after the attack. Church attendance soared. Bible sales spiked. For a period, people spoke openly about God and invoked His blessing on our nation. But real, lasting change never materialized.

The Church had largely failed to speak the truth about 9/11. It didn't say that God had called us to account as a nation for acting in rebellion to His holy laws. It didn't say that unless we changed course, worse would befall us. Unprepared to recognize God's purpose in 9/11, our pulpits mostly offered words of comfort for the grieving and hope of peace for the future. It was the terrorists who were guilty. Their free will, perverted by ignorance and misunderstanding, had led them to act as they did. We were the innocent, aggrieved party. We weren't being called to accountability for our sin through this tragedy. Despite all the lessons of Scripture and history about God's dealing with nations, we believed *our* God would never punish us in such a way. *Our* God was much too loving to ever do such a thing. How could *our* God be involved in any way in a barbaric act of terrorism that had killed so many innocent people? We had a different picture of the true and living God. We could pray, "God bless America" without any prior demand for national repentance. Our God would never punish us. But such faith was merely a form of distorted civil religion, and not an expression of true biblical Christianity. Such faith wouldn't answer people's deepest questions, and it wouldn't save anyone. Only the truth could do that, as painful as it was to receive.

Nonetheless, our government had had every right and responsibility to retaliate and defend against further acts of aggression and terrorism (Rom. 13:3–4). It was obligated to do so and galvanized for action. After years of denial by our leaders, immediate action was a good thing, a mercy to us, and as I would later see in Scripture, *a major prophetic event itself.*

But America's momentary spiritual attention was largely squandered by a Church lacking in discernment and compromised by the culture. It squandered a rare opportunity to speak boldly about the nature of our holy God and our urgent need for spiritual reformation. While Scripture taught, "The fear of the LORD is the beginning of wisdom" (Ps. 111:10 NKJV), the Church provided little spiritual self-analysis in the face of divine displeasure and wrath. No wonder attendance quickly dropped back. The majority of people simply returned to their previous behaviors. After some initial concern most realized nothing more was expected of them. The endlessly tolerant God of their imagination would bless them as they were. Why change?

No doubt a sobering of heart brought some to wonder about the deeper purpose of their lives. What were they doing, and why; for what were they living? Family and friends became dearer when one realized they could be taken in a moment without warning. What was truly important came into clearer focus. People's priorities shifted from superficial, selfish pursuits to truer, lasting values. Their faith became real and deeper.

But, while some were changed, it was soon clear that the country as a whole didn't change in the way called for by divine chastisement. Amid the bloodshed of the Civil War, our nation ended slavery. Yet now, our worst sins continued unabated and were soon carried out with even greater audacity and abandon. Did no one recognize God's purpose in 9/11? Could no one see what the God of heaven was demanding by way of repentance and faith (Ps. 36:1, 12)?

New York as a city soon did the exact opposite of what she should have done. She didn't humble herself before almighty God or seek His forgiveness for her sins. But how could such an enormous, pluralistic, materialistic, famously secular city ever do such a thing, do what she needed to do en masse to make a difference before the true and living God? It had never been in her genes; how could this city change now? From its birth New York had never been quite like the other great colonial cities of Boston and Philadelphia, both founded for primarily religious reasons. The Dutch had established this new world city first and foremost as a commercial trading center, a course from which it had never veered. In time, its great port became the destination for generations of immigrants seeking the opportunity for a better life.

It was no real surprise, then, that the city's first official act after 9/11 was to hold an interfaith prayer service to demonstrate the political unity and solidarity of the various religious groups in her midst. While seemingly sensible and sincere, a politically correct prayer meeting to a pantheon of deities would have little influence on the holy God of the Bible, who had acted on 9/11. Like King Ahab assembling the prophets of Baal on Mt. Carmel, the city with its good intentions and pious ignorance merely cried for greater wrath—officially breaking the first commandment and sanctioning the worship of false gods for the sake of unity and solidarity. But Jesus had said He had come in part to bring division, calling people either to choose Him or reject Him (Matt. 10:34).

Evidencing no genuine repentance, the city took other missteps. In the name of tolerance, it allowed new freedoms for Muslims while at the same time restricting the exercise of Christian faith in public schools. Simultaneously, the very city that had birthed the gay rights movement continued down the same path, establishing a special high school for homosexual and lesbian students so they could maintain their lifestyles without fear of ridicule or condemnation (see Jude 7). To top it off, the city planned to build an even taller tower on the site of the fallen Trade Center as a monument to its indomitable spirit (cf., Isa. 9:9–10). In spite of the fact that many individuals did come to find a genuine faith, the city as a whole seemed to have learned little from 9/11. I couldn't help but think of Jesus's firm rebuke to the Pharisees: "The men of Nineveh will rise up in the judgment with this generation and condemn it, because they repented" (Matt. 12:41 NKJV).

The country itself was not much different. While most Americans lived relatively decent lives of complacency and self-interest, God remained a low priority. Few repented in the face of His wrath, seeing no connection with 9/11. Our great corporate sins continued unabated, and we seemed set on flying in the face of our Creator's ordinances. Though the commandments forbid the sin of murder, and Scripture is clear that life begins at conception (Ex. 20:13; Ps. 139:13–16), our national policy of *legal abortion* was maintained. Our country persisted in this grievous sin even after suffering severe chastisement. Millions more babies had perished. But who was concerned? Who feared God?

Along with others I had long prayed for a turnaround. By way of precedent, the pagan Roman Empire had widely practiced abortion and infanticide, but these had gradually died away because the Christians valued life. Standing on the teachings of Scripture, they had changed the culture of Rome. Reverence for human life became a virtue of Western civilization. Couldn't that happen again, I had hoped? Even science now confirmed that life begins in the womb.

But how could science ever prove that humans are made in God's image? How could it prove that an *eternal being* is created at conception, and once created, this eternal being cannot be undone, even by abortion? Physical life could be stopped, but the soul cannot just go away as if it never existed. The soul of the human being is eternal. Scripture revealed this to be true and that taking an innocent life breaks God's holy law. I had myself had a hand in this heartless sin even before the Court declared it "legal" (see chapter 9). But once our country decided as a matter of its laws to justify what God condemns in His law, the whole nation bore guilt. Without repentance, it was only a matter of time before His just judgment must fall on us in even greater measure as a consequence. Further, if God is bound by justice to hold our whole nation to account for the sin of legalized abortion, how can anyone claim the *private right* to choose death for a baby because it is in *her* body? This so-called private decision affected us all before God. The whole nation must be judged for the sin it condoned. Those thinking otherwise lived in a fool's paradise.

What, then, *must* a just and holy God do to a nation that has murdered over 55 million infants it was called to nurture and protect? What must He do *in justice* to punish the unjust, premeditated killing of one-third of all the babies conceived in America over more than forty years? How long will He stand idle before He acts again? When He does, He has many arrows in His quiver (Ps. 7:12–13, 21:12). Will it be by poor national leadership and the increasing social, moral, and economic disintegration of our country? Will it be through problems created by mass illegal immigration? Will it be by means of the enforced euthanasia of an aging generation that had previously killed its own unborn? Or will it come more quickly, by war and disaster? Or, all these together?

And what more must God do about national efforts to *legalize* and *legitimize* homosexuality and gay marriage, even after His judgment on 9/11? In actual fact, homosexual inclination is not a sin; it was the practice of homosexuality in thought or deed that became sin. In His wisdom, God ordained sex to take place only between a man and a woman who are married to each other. Ignorant, well-intentioned people would say they didn't approve of homosexual behavior, but believed others should be free to practice it if they hurt no one else. However, the individual sin of the homosexual became corporate when it was legalized and condoned by law. God never gave such a right and would hold us all to account as citizens (Jude 7). Weren't the Old Testament stories about the destruction of Sodom and Gomorrah *written for our instruction* (Gen. 19:4–5, 24–25; 1 Cor. 10:11)? These cities were destroyed for the sins of some that the entire community condoned. When God judged them, Lot's own wife was destroyed, though she wasn't guilty of the sin herself. But she was there and suffered the consequences.

Similarly, when a nation like ours *approves* sinful behavior that God expressly *disapproves*, the whole nation must suffer the penalty in due course. This was a hard truth, and no one wanted to hear it, not even the Church. But it was true and actually loving to say so for the sake of the individuals and the country (1 Cor. 6:9–11). Yet, far from being the enemy of homosexuals, true Christians were their best friends in the world, even after God's judgment. Christians cared about them, prayed for them, and even helped to preserve them. Hadn't Abraham prayed for Sodom's preservation? In answer to his petitions, the Lord promised to spare the city had there been more righteous living there, but the city was too far gone.

Instead of being humbled in repentance after 9/11, liberal elites continued to force the God of the Bible out of public life. In the name of diversity, the only God acceptable was a multicultural god in a society where every belief and creed was held to be equal. Truth didn't matter. The one true God, who made heaven and earth, the triune God of our Christian heritage, could not be the exclusive God. For fear of offense, the name of His Son must never be uttered, true or not.

When *The Passion of the Christ* was produced two years after the attack, a howl of controversy erupted from New York and Hollywood. The greatest story ever told had become something to be feared, rejected, and marginalized. But the film's very proximity to 9/11 was a providential message of grace and warning. If God willingly suffered the brutal execution of His own Son on the cross to pay for human sin, why would we think He would just look the other way and never chasten and punish us for sinful behavior (Ps. 9:16)? Didn't Scripture warn, "How shall we escape if we ignore such a great salvation?" (Heb. 2:3 NIV)? The attack had been a painful call for repentance. Yet, that message was exactly what we were rejecting as a nation. And in America's case, wouldn't we be held to a higher standard for all the Gospel light we had received?

Before the attack, I had maintained hope that our culture war was winnable, and we might still return to our roots in the biblical Christianity that had so shaped the country and its institutions. I had hoped to be an influence with our project to produce the Bible on video to help more people read God's Word. But after the attack and its aftermath, I could see it was much too late in time for such a change in the course of our nation. With new eyes for Scripture, history, and providence, I perceived God's hand shaping world affairs on a scale that was astonishing to behold. The United States and the world seemed set on an irreversible course of biblical design.

I had also paid scant attention to Islamic terrorism before 9/11. We had been gravely misled by our leaders, who were ignorant or dishonest about Islam, and we had been misinformed by our media. Even our missionaries, in their own way, had misrepresented Islam as but one more religion whose adherents needed the Gospel. I had long dreamed of outreach to Muslims, and had set out to produce an Arabic New Testament to share God's Word with those followers of Islam who had been isolated from the Gospel for centuries. What I didn't know or understand, however, and what missionaries had not explained, was that Islam itself was much more than another religion. As I soon learned, it also called for a government system with a mission to bring the entire world under its totalitarian rule by force through jihad. In this political aspiration Islam was utterly unique among world religions. Domination under a single military religious leader had been its goal since the death of its founder in 632, almost exactly six hundred years after the crucifixion of Christ.

Furthermore, most Christians seemed blissfully ignorant of the prophetic implication of these things and what was happening before their eyes. In the face of the rapidly growing threat of militant Islamic revival, much of the American Church lived in denial, dreamed of escape, or paid almost no attention at all.

Nonetheless, as events unfolded and my learning grew, I could see the knowledge of God's judgment on 9/11, and its deliberate prophetic nature allowed me unique insight into what was happening around the world in relation to biblical prophecy. The endtimes were coming into sharper focus. Through this understanding and by means of amazing confirmations, the Lord made clear my mission had not ended with our warning premiere in New York City. Though few would want to hear what I had to say, I could see it was more important than ever that people knew the truth about God's judgment on America and its profound consequence for the future.

PART 2

9

GOD'S CALL

Before I formed you in the womb, I knew you.   —Jeremiah 1:5 NKJV

AFTER THE ATTACK, the Lord enabled me to see how my whole life had been ordered by His hand to write about His judgment on 9/11 and its enormous prophetic implications. While I quickly saw this meant I could not write about them under a pseudonym—for either privacy or protection—I knew it was still necessary to write, despite the danger. First, my testimony was based on actual events. There was no way to get around this fact and still bear credible witness to our warning and God's judgment. Second, showing how He had prepared me for this testimony by careful design over a lifetime would further substantiate my claims. The Lord had left a trail of evidence to show He had chosen me for our mission long before the attack. Finally, my case for 9/11's role in the endtimes depended on knowing the truth of God's purpose in the attack and its intentional connection to the book of Revelation. This made my testimony as a watchman on the wall before 9/11 essential to the case (Isa. 62:6; Ezek. 3:17–19, 33:6), and who would listen to what I had to say about the endtimes without it? My voice would be just one more among many others. But the Lord had made it all of a piece to give me a platform. He had even called me to be a writer years before my conversion to train me for this very purpose.

DELIBERATE DESIGN

As providence so ordered it, my life began where the main attack would strike. During World War II, my sailor father met my pretty mother in her nursing uniform one day in New York City and soon swept her off her feet. Already engaged, she broke her engagement to elope with my father. But learning that Dad had lied about his background, she nearly ended their marriage but discovered she was pregnant. As a result of their chance encounter in New York City, I was born a year after the war, at the beginning of the baby boom, in the freest and most prosperous nation in history, at the peak of its power and success. Ancient Heraclitus said, "War is the father of us all." In my case, it was literally true, and *even doubly so*, for not only were my parents brought together by the Second World War, but if not for the deadly influence of the First World War on my mother's family (to be explained later), I wouldn't exist. How pregnant with purpose these things were to me after 9/11, like dual witnesses of God's great sovereignty spanning generations. To evidence deliberate design, He hadn't chosen *just any* watchman to deliver His warning to New York before the attack, but one who was directly conceived of it, *and that as a by-product of war, and, as I would come to learn, called to it long before his birth.*

After my brother, Michael, arrived, we moved to the big postwar housing development at Levittown. There, we were the typical young family enjoying the country's optimism and economic boom. We lived in a cute, new Cape Cod house in a brand-new neighborhood, and Dad bought a flashy, maroon Studebaker with a white convertible top. On weekends, he drove us to Jones Beach to swim in the ocean and play in the sand. We also had the first TV on the block.

Then, overnight, it all changed. On the way to school, a neighbor's son ran up to show us a newspaper with a picture of Dad in handcuffs on the front page. He had fallen in with older men to forge checks when his business failed. Dad went to prison, and Mom suffered her first nervous breakdown. This separated our family, and Mike and I were sent to live with a series of relatives, eventually ending up in a Chicago military school in first and third grades, respectively, where I experienced recurring nightmares of air raids by our adversaries from the war that had ended just nine years earlier.

Though Mom had been encouraged by her father to let us go, once she recovered, she moved to Chicago, rented a small hotel room, and came to get us every weekend. How different things would be had she not come back. The next year she was hired to be nurse and housemother at a private school in the old McCormick family mansion. Seventeen of us boarded there in the vast, one-hundred-room residence designed by Stanford White, celebrated architect of the "Gilded Age." Mom's job included sometimes walking all seventeen of us like one big family to a theater we kids proudly boasted was near where the old Capone mob had carried out Chicago's bloody St. Valentine's Day Massacre to consolidate his power.

At the end of that year, Mom married one of the teachers; and though Mike and I were still under our uncle's guardianship, she smuggled us away from Chicago to a beautiful, tree-lined village, nestled along the Ohio River in Pennsylvania, the place to which the Lord had called us in His plan (see Eph. 1:11, 2:10). Right on the river and surrounded by wooded hills, it was a boy's paradise. The town was home to the descendents of some of Pittsburgh's great industrial families and had a rich history. Our stepfather had been hired to teach at its exclusive private school. Though it seems nearly impossible to imagine, when we arrived, a few people were still living who had been born during the Civil War. A century before, one of the town's leading citizens was even "the father" of the national Republican Party that had been "born in Pittsburgh," which led to Lincoln's election and the war that ensued. David N. White, publisher of the *Daily Pittsburgh Gazette*, had editorialized that all the abolitionist groups in the country should form a new party to end slavery. He also wrote prophetically, "It may cost this nation a war."

In time that war came and cost him his own son. His name was memorialized on a monument in the cemetery overlooking our new town, standing like a tall Ebenezer to God's help in ending our sin in the terrible judgment of war and preserving the union for His future purpose (1 Sam. 7:12–14; Acts 17:26–27). But I had none of this understanding then.

Ironically, our first year we saw the movie *The Girl in the Red Velvet Swing*, about the assassination of Stanford White, to whom we felt especially connected having just lived in one of his elegant mansions. White had been slain fifty years earlier in a fit of vengeance by a wealthy Pittsburgher in what newspapers called "The Murder of the Century." The architect had seduced Harry K. Thaw's wife as a young star and the most photographed woman of her day. Furthering our sense of connection, the killer's family had had an estate in our new town at Thawmont. But it was only after 9/11 that the actual location of White's murder meant anything special to me. Like some distant echo of a greater wrath to come, the flamboyant architect had been shot dead in New York City atop a building of his own design—*Madison Square Garden*—predecessor to the very place God would send us with warning of a judgment on the city that would point to Mystery Babylon's fall in the book of Revelation at the end of time.

Despite high hopes for our new family, Mom's second marriage lasted only six months. But in God's good plan our stepfather had led us to this town and introduced us to the Episcopal church that would play such a major role in my life and work. Walking from our apartment on Straight Street every Sunday morning, we began attending church for the first time. As I sat in the sanctuary during service, I felt a peace unlike any other time in the week. I now believed in God and that He cared for us, and I took to heart everything I learned. Though most of my classmates hated church, I thought their attitudes were perfectly understandable. They were just kids who had lived their lives in a privileged and protected environment. They had never experienced all that we had encountered in our few short years. When Mom wanted to move away to California, the rector told her no; she needed to remain in this place for the stability of her children.

Being fatherless, having a different last name than my mother, and having moved so often, I was acutely aware of the uniqueness of our family circumstances. I had also attended seven different schools before fifth grade. Then I went to private school in fifth; transferred to the public school in sixth; and filled with trepidation at soon encountering the bigger, older students, I went to the junior high in seventh. But in eighth grade, for the first time in my life, I attended the same school two years in a row. Seeing so many familiar faces was a foreign experience. To my complete surprise, in my first class a girl who was widely regarded as the most popular in our grade for her good looks, fine figure, and outgoing, vivacious personality, sat down next to me. While I half-expected her to move away, she immediately recognized me as a friend and seemed genuinely pleased to see me again. After this chance seating, we talked together daily, though she went steady with a ninth grader. Before long I couldn't take my eyes off her and could think of nothing else. When her boyfriend told me to keep away, I made a wisecrack and paid him no attention. In God's wise plan, this youthful relationship would profoundly influence the direction of my life and calling: first with becoming a writer, and later, even with marriage—both of which would have to do with 9/11.

As it happened, that summer Mom married a third time, and we moved from our small apartment on Straight Street to our stepfather's big house on Sycamore Road—a place that would have a special prophetic purpose. Though this marriage was tempestuous and unhappy from the start, Mike and I each had our own rooms for the first time, and we grew to love this house as our home. Set on a hill a mile from town, the white-frame, three-story structure had a panoramic view of the Ohio River valley and was surrounded by gardens, tall sycamore trees, and woods where we could hunt, trap, and explore. Yet, in twenty minutes, we could walk to town, school, and church. I soon made my two closest friends on the way in Siebert, whom I knew already from Mr. Harvey's Sunday school class, and Casey, his neighbor who was transferring to our ninth grade from the Catholic school. Best of all, I was thrilled to discover the aunt of the girl in my class lived right above us on the hill, and this girl I liked so much drove up our winding road with her mother every single weekend to visit. Of course, I was constantly on the lookout for her from my window. After 9/11, however, I would see far more to the providence of growing up there in our family home on Sycamore Road. It was witness to God's long-term plan and my calling to deliver a deliberate warning to New

York before His deadly judgment. The *sycamore* would be linked twice to 9/11 through both prophets Amos and Isaiah (Amos 3:6–7, 7:14; Isa. 9:10). But, I would know none of this for years to come.

In school, I settled into patterns of behavior that would hardly reflect a person the Lord would use as a "watchman on the wall." I could never stand up and speak before class without blushing in utter confusion and embarrassment. I dreaded it more than anything. My mind went blank, and I couldn't think. Nonetheless, I was no wallflower. I was usually first to answer any questions, especially those about geography and current events. Curious and inquisitive, I read everything in front of me. If told something was impossible or unsolvable, I was instinctively drawn to seek a solution. And as far back as I can remember, I was always able to make complicated things easy for others to understand. At the same time, my familiar role in class became entertaining everyone with a steady stream of puns and jokes. Even when I tried to keep decorum, I couldn't help finishing a teacher's sentence with a funny quip. Such wit just popped out spontaneously, and the class would laugh out loud. Neither could I resist showing off with pranks and daredevil stunts, like headstands on a coke bottle, holding my breath for minutes at a time, or jumping out a window to rattle a substitute teacher. I had boundless energy and could never sit still. When Mom heard of my classroom antics, she said, "That's not like you at all."

On the other hand, when our world affairs teacher told how Christians were persecuted for their faith in different parts of the world, and how we in our country would never be willing to endure persecution, I went to him after class and said I thought I would be willing to die for my faith. "Really?" Mr. Simpson asked with surprise. Rick Armstrong said, "Knowing Jim, I believe he would."

The following year, when the Supreme Court ruled prayer in public school to be unconstitutional, I went straight to the principal and asked if we could pray on our own in the high school auditorium before class. He said no, and I simply took his word for it, ignorant of the issues at hand. But every night, no matter how tired, I prayed for my family and friends before sleeping. During the Cuban missile crisis four months later, I prayed especially for the protection of the girl in my class and imagined what I would do to help if the Russians did attack with nuclear missiles. The next year, barely six months after Bible reading in public schools was banned, Kennedy was assassinated. But back then I made no connection between these things and a lifting of God's favor. Though I wondered what it was about our country that made us so uniquely free and prosperous in the world, I had no idea it had anything to do with the blessing of the God we were now choosing to reject and His unique purpose for our nation (Ps. 33:12).

Finally, sports played a huge role in my life. Despite the fact I stood six foot one and weighed only 128 pounds, I was naturally fast and athletic. I loved all sports and avidly competed in football, basketball, baseball, wrestling, and track. Invariably underestimated and embarrassed at being so thin, I always surprised people and was among the best at any sport I tried. In football, I even relished making contact, throwing myself headlong into bigger opponents and holding on until others arrived. I also had a knack for anticipating what quarterbacks would do. After Coach saw me intercept three passes in one JV game, he had me temporarily replace an all-state-mention halfback to motivate him on defense, but I never lost the position. I overheard a teacher tell a coach I was the best defensive player he had ever seen.

Nonetheless, in God's wisdom, as much as I wished and prayed to be, I was never the big, handsome, muscular athlete that I thought would win the admiration and affection of the girl in class I cared so much about. Though I dated others, she consumed my thoughts! I looked at her all day in class. I called her weeknights, and we talked until my stepfather complained. On weekends I walked to town just to catch sight of her passing in a car or out with a friend. I went to the YMCA on Saturday nights for a chance to slow dance a few times. On summer nights she wasn't out, I would visit to go for a walk or sit on her porch. For those few hours, oblivious of passing time, I felt what seemed the contentment of agelessness, until having to go would jolt me from the illusion. I would have gladly married her at sixteen! Knowing Mom had married three times, I didn't think it lightly. But this was my own childish desire that the Lord would use to direct me to accomplish His good purpose. He had a better plan than I could see, and this would help to serve it.

A WRITER

One November night in my junior year, I came to a turning point that would unexpectedly change the direction of my life. I almost took my life that night when this girl I cared about so deeply firmly rejected me. We had been in the same class every day, all day, starting on five years. In fact, she was the only girl to remain in my section that whole time. *How could that be an accident?* I had thought, never giving up hope.

That night on her porch, just after our successful football season, I had the courage to tell her for the first time how I felt. In response she said she thought of me only as a friend and made her lack of romantic interest absolutely clear. Then she went inside and closed the door.

Though I wasn't thinking at all of God, He mercifully preserved my life that night for His own purpose. While I knew the Ten Commandments and had both heard and read them regularly in service, I didn't connect their application to suicide. I knew nothing of Plato's *Phaedo*, where Socrates reasoned with Simmias against the idea; neither did I recall Hamlet's fear of retribution in the hereafter. None of these things stopped me. Standing at the highway's edge and staring into the blue-black sky, I finally concluded I had nothing more to lose. It was as though I were dead already. I could go on living as if I were dead, yet if I did, who knew what might happen in the future?

But I had never experienced such resignation, hopelessness, and depression. This girl had just broken up with her boyfriend and hadn't rejected me for someone else. I was the problem, not her boyfriend. Her rejection was final. After that I avoided talking to her and poured out my complaint in a bitter poem about love. Then I wrote another and another as the days went by. Almost daily, no longer paying attention in my classes, I wrote poetry. I loved starting out with a blank sheet of paper. Over time, I wrote hundreds of poems in all varieties of forms that I shared with friends. Before long I could compose a sonnet out loud in iambic pentameter with rhymes.

That summer I taught myself to type and wrote several short stories. Then I began a novel called *The Castle of Sand*, filled with careful symbolism about a character named Peter Rew who built his hopes on a foolish dream (see Matt. 7:24–27). When our minister, Sam Odom, preached one Sunday about not burying your talents, his message made a deep impression. Wasn't writing my talent? Planning to apply to college that year, I thought God was calling me to study writing for a career. I was sixteen. I had never considered the possibility before. Immediately I began reading a wider range of authors and was hungry to learn about their lives. Thinking of myself as a writer like Fitzgerald or Hemingway gave me a whole new self-concept. It also helped make sense of why I always seemed so unconventional and never quite fit in. In our home we had talked about art and books as long as I could remember. My dad had attended the Ringling College of Art; my brother, Mike, had long been recognized for his exceptional artistic ability; and Mom loved books. Here I thought was an area of creativity where I could excel. The art teacher, Mrs. Chandler, even took an interest and had me give dramatic readings to school assemblies. Though I wasn't a fine artist, she appointed me Art Club president, saying, "But you have special ideas."

Then, that fall of my senior year, our stepfather walked out and left us with a coal furnace we couldn't maintain. With no heat at home that winter, I finished writing my novel after school in the cafeteria. At night, the three of us slept in sleeping bags in the kitchen, with the oven on. We could do little in the rest of the house until spring, when we moved back upstairs. One morning, after my alarm failed, I awoke late to notice Mom's door still closed when she would normally have left for work. After knocking and getting no answer, I opened the door to see her in bed, with yellow foam oozing from her mouth. Shocked, I ran to call a neighbor. Once the ambulance arrived, paramedics rushed Mom to the hospital, where they pumped her stomach because of an overdose of pills. The doctor told me if I had found her any later, she wouldn't have lived. When Mike came home to find there were just the two of us, he was deeply upset, but I tried to reassure him that God had made me late that morning to save Mom's life. We weren't alone. God was watching over us.

For the next few months, while Mom was hospitalized under psychiatric care, Mike lived with former neighbors and I stayed with my friend Casey, whose parents took me in like a son. Not long before, I had followed Casey's lead and applied to the same college, where I planned to study English literature and creative writing. Though our family had never set money aside for college, with a simple faith and naïve idealism, I had just expected to go and never worried much about it, assuming things would somehow work out. As it happened, when our rector at church learned I had been accepted but had no money to go, he called me to his office: an anonymous member wanted to help me start my freshman year. With a bounty of adolescent ignorance, I thanked our rector and took it all for granted. I would be able to attend college in pursuit of my goal to study English and become a novelist of the first rank. As mentioned previously, I had been influenced to think in this direction by a sermon the year before, and now I could go with the church's help. It was an investment by the church that would bear no immediate fruit.

Setting out for a new world that fall, I left behind the beautiful old Episcopal church where I'd been head acolyte and youth group president, and never missed a Sunday since fifth grade, except when sick or away at camp. But while I had a sincere faith in God, I possessed little biblical knowledge and no real grasp of the Gospel. I had no question God existed. Countless times I had felt His presence at night, walking home in the dark. I had seen Him at work in our family. I had prayed regularly and asked for forgiveness when I sinned. I even had a genuine sense of destiny and God's direction to be a writer. But I was totally unprepared for the secular worldview I encountered on campus, shaped by men such as Nietzsche, Freud, Marx, and Darwin. My professors constantly belittled Christian faith, especially in my English classes. Before long, I was skipping Sunday services at the local church with its anemic little congregation. Working two jobs to help with expenses and books, I slept six hours a night, and sleeping in Sundays was a welcome relief. But I had no spiritual input and little understood what was taking place, personally or on the large scale.

Home again that summer, I began dating girls I knew from high school. But one day, a girl I had never seen before caught my eye in a local restaurant. Wasting no time learning who she was, I asked her out just before she left that fall to study in Boston. Apparently somewhat of a tomboy when younger, by graduation from the private school in town, she had matured and developed into the most attractive girl in her class. During the year we continued to see each other on college weekends, wrote letters, and spent hours on the phone. How glamorous she looked as a debutante in her dark-green velvet gown at the coming-out ball in Pittsburgh that Christmas!

Over the next summer, we were constantly together: double-dating with a good buddy, driving her father's fast GTO, or proudly cruising around on my beautiful old BMW motorcycle. In time, our relationship grew to be the closest I'd ever had, and we became secretly engaged. After that, we happily consorted in every location we could find, from couches to carpets, front seats and backseats, her room, my room, fields, parks, and yards. Some nights I slipped upstairs with her and quietly climbed out her second-story window at dawn before her parents awoke. When her mother wondered how her daughter once had poison ivy where she did, we thought it humorous. We were enlightened and felt no guilt about our behavior. Moral restraints were old-fashioned. I no longer had any sense of the holy God's hatred of sin to help me check my behavior (Isa. 59:2).

When my fiancée's father was diagnosed with cancer that fall, we were stunned by the news. I prayed daily, but despite all our prayers, he died in January. It left me deeply confused. A successful attorney in his mid-fifties, he was the only one in his family who attended church. Still, our prayers made no difference. To me his death seemed senseless and helped undermine what little faith I had left. When his daughter said he believed in heaven and wasn't afraid to die, I thought it was just wishful thinking, an excuse to avoid facing death's finality. By my senior year, I no longer prayed or went to church. I had become an atheist and was proud of it.

Due to my increasing immorality, this unbelief and hardness of heart was convenient. That summer I had followed my fiancée to Europe for several weeks during her unsupervised six-month tour of Europe given by an aunt. When I got her pregnant shortly after returning, I drove her for an illegal abortion some months later with no qualms of conscience whatsoever. My fiancée came out in shock and bled for weeks. I wasn't even able to help her pay for the procedure when she asked. With the effects of her emotional pain, our relationship slowly deteriorated just when old dreams were being reawakened in my heart. I then broke off our engagement, untouched by either her grief or counsel that I was being foolish and would regret it.

Had it not been for the financial support from our church, and my sense of obligation for it, I would have dropped out of college too. I had generally hated the experience and never felt I fit in, but feared not having another chance if I quit. Bored and unhappy, I wanted to get on with a second novel. At the same time, Marshall McLuhan's radical ideas about electronic media and the ultimate demise of books had also influenced my thinking. After writing a novel and making a mark, I would move to Hollywood to make films and lose myself in production, sex, and drugs.

How far I had fallen! Only four years earlier, I had possessed genuine faith and a sense of destiny, but these were gone. My life now appeared meaningless. The Vietnam War had added to this view, even though my brother served there with the Marines. To avoid the draft, I joined the Army Reserve upon graduation. However, injured in a good-bye football game before training, I was discharged twenty-three days later. Suddenly, I found myself free for the first time to write as much as I wanted. My ambition to be a "writer" was now no longer some distant, far-off goal.

To support myself, I worked construction, at one point as union labor on the U.S. Steel Building, the tallest structure in Pittsburgh. At night and on weekends, I wrote in my room. For breaks, and to escape the gnawing loneliness and emptiness I felt, I would race my motorcycles at high speeds through our winding country roads. When drunk after summer parties, I often raced in the cool dark of night for the sheer exhilaration. It was only by God's grace I wasn't killed.

A year later, on the weekend of my twenty-third birthday, a carload of us drove to the Woodstock festival in John Benz's yellow Pontiac convertible, joining friends and my brother back from Vietnam with his friends. At dusk, the gathering of hundreds of thousands looked like some vast pagan army encamped in biblical times. Random tents and twinkling fires covered the hillsides as far as the eye could see. Music and marijuana wafted about the evening air that had an almost tangible pungency and presence. Brief as our time there was, it had a marked effect on me.

Beginning to experiment with LSD and other drugs, I decided writing was pointless and planned to set out for a new life of filmmaking and hedonism in California. But before leaving the next spring, I crashed my motorcycle on the curve in front of our house on Sycamore Road, delaying the trip. Even as I healed, my buddy Cee Mitsak offered to ride with me for the summer. Cee always called me "Crazy Amos," after an old baseball player, due to my odd athletic ability to make impossible catches while missing the easy ones. Finally, he and I rode off on two Royal Enfields in June 1970. We ran out of money in Boulder, Colorado, and had to stop our trip. (Three years later, as a new believer, I realized the Lord had twice blocked me from making it out to the West Coast. Not long after, I read the book of Amos for the first time and couldn't help but wonder if the providences of my nickname, growing up on Sycamore Road, and being a writer were meant to be signs that in the future I would write about prophetic things. They seemed to be echoes of this prophet named Amos, a writer and tender of sycamore trees, who wrote, "Surely, the LORD God does nothing without revealing his secret to his servants the prophets" [Amos 3:7].)

Stuck in Boulder, I took a construction job and began writing again in the spare time I had after work. Within a year I returned home and built a tree-house cabin up in the woods across the street and lived there a year to give full attention to writing my book. One night, when the temperature dropped to seventeen below zero, I learned that four people froze to death in their homes. I had gone to a bar with John Benz and returned late to a frozen tree house that tinkled like glass. Hugging my dog in a sleeping bag, I survived. But that summer, a plague of carpenter ants that marched out of the woods to my tree house finally drove me out. Still, I had not finished my book. Renting an apartment in town, I delivered beer part-time to write the rest of the day. About that time, a girl from the bar accused me of using her, not caring about anyone but me, and being the most self-centered person she ever knew. What had become of me?

Two months later I was jolted by an article in a popular psychology magazine and couldn't write for three days. The piece, titled "Madness and Creativity," claimed that several of the writers I most admired hadn't been geniuses at all. They'd suffered from mental illness. This thought terrified me. Mom had been hospitalized multiple times for manic depression. Had I inherited the propensity? How would I know if I were mentally ill? Would I be honest enough to face it?

By then I had been working on my novel for six years, and it was still unfinished. Two or three times I had started over. Lost in a sea of memories and emotions, I was trying to keep my life on paper. My old friends, like Casey, Galey, Eaton, and Slaminko had long settled down and had families and careers. While I had been involved with a dozen different girls since college, I still lived alone, drove a beer truck part-time, and had yet to complete my novel after years of trying. What if I never finished? What if I did and it failed? What if I *were* mad? I was twenty-six and gambling my life on a course of action that lacked assurance of completion, let alone success. Unawares, I had been prepared for a burning bush experience that would radically change my life and direction.

CONVERSION

On the third day of this crisis, the Lord graciously reached out to me. As I rolled a beer keg into the last bar on my route, an older waitress with a dark smudge of ashes on her forehead interrupted me. Saying something kind, she rubbed black ashes from her forehead to mine. Then I continued to roll the keg, to hook it up, thinking about what the waitress had just done. Vaguely, I remembered that my best friend in high school would receive ashes on his forehead before Easter. When I asked about it, Casey had explained what they meant and that it was a way of seeking God.

As it happened, I was then reading two books: *The Divine Comedy*, because of Dante's unrequited love for Beatrice, and Dostoyevsky's *The Brothers Karamazov* for a similar reason. *Hadn't both these great writers believed in God?* I thought. *Maybe He does exist. If He does, maybe He will help me. Maybe I should seek Him.* Recalling that Casey had given up something as a way to seek God in Lent, I wondered if I should give up something to see if He existed. Immediately, it occurred to me that I had been unable to write for days. Writing was what mattered most to me. If I gave that up for this time of Lent and God did exist, maybe He would help me. What did I have to lose other than a little time? For some reason, I thought the duration would be twenty days, not even a month. I could make twenty days. After that, I could start writing again. Then, the number forty came to mind as I thought about how far off Easter was.

Forty days! I couldn't forgo writing for forty days! I didn't know what to do with myself after three days. I surely couldn't sit still *forty* days. That was far too much time for me to lose. But back at the distributor's, I was surprised to see on the calendar that Shakespeare's birthday was the day after Easter. My friends all knew he was my literary hero. His birthday, April 23, was my lucky number. The timing of this date *had* to be propitious. Of all the times to start again, I would begin writing on Shakespeare's birthday! Surely that was a portent to me of good luck and success. With that, I gave up my writing for forty days to seek God and His help.

With no writing to do that night, I decided to paint my mother's room at our home on Sycamore Road as I had promised and long put off. As I worked, my mind raced anxiously. A distant phrase kept running through my thoughts, "*from ashes to ashes, and dust to dust.*" What if I died without finishing my book and just faded into oblivion? To clear my mind, I went to change the music on the radio. Maybe I would hear some song to help me sort things out. When I turned the dial, the first words I heard were "*Commit your life to Christ!*"—repeated three times.

I froze in thought. What did these words mean? Though I remembered that Christ was connected to God, I had drifted so far for so many years, I didn't recall anything about Him—neither His life, nor His death and resurrection. But there I stood, suspended in a spiritual blink of time. I vaguely knew enough about Eastern religions to grasp intuitively that if the God of the West were a fiction, the others were monstrous lies that no one could fathom. Moving on, I thought, *What will all the people who know me (and my goal to be a writer) think if I just give up and quit?* It occurred to me no one really cared about it anyway, and it didn't matter what they might think.

Then I thought about writing for history and posterity. In a flash, I realized two things. McLuhan had said fewer people would be reading books in the future. Was it worth the risk of wasting my life to write for an audience that wouldn't read as much? Even if untrue, knowing we had fought four wars in the past century, I thought civilization would certainly destroy itself with nuclear weapons within the next hundred years. There would be no libraries or institutions left to recognize and promote great literature. Should I keep gambling my life away and cutting myself off from everything else to write for a posterity that almost surely wouldn't exist?

With a mental image of me following this Christ through a maze, with no idea where it would take me, my heart said yes, even if it meant quitting my book. Instantly a string of words popped into mind from Sunday school: "*Yea, though I walk through the valley of the shadow of death, I will fear no evil: for thou art with me*" (Ps. 23:4 Book of Common Prayer). Perplexed by these words, I recalled in a moment where they had come from. It was something called a *psalm.* Then I remembered there was a number, the *Twenty-Third* Psalm! I was amazed. It was my lucky number, echoing Shakespeare's birthday! This number and these words spoke to me of favor and destiny. Could these things be coincidence? It must be another sign I was on the right path, and with that came a flood of thoughts. There must be a God! He must care for me. He would help me with my writing. Settled with a strange peace, I found another station and went back to painting my mother's room. That was Ash Wednesday, March 7, 1973, in our family home on Sycamore Road.

Oddly enough, the next night, Mom encouraged me to put off painting to watch a rare presentation of *Hamlet* on TV, knowing how much I would enjoy it. As I watched, a line I had never noticed before jumped out: "There is providence in the fall of a sparrow." These words Hamlet uttered seemed to describe exactly what was happening to me, but I had no idea that the inspiration for these words came directly from the Bible (Matt. 10:29). As it was, over the next forty days, something clearly providential happened every single day to help confirm to me the reality of God's existence. I even started the forty-day period upon seeing that Shakespeare's birthday fell the day after Easter.

What I did not know, and what would have meant nothing to me then had I known, was that during those same forty days of Lent when I laid my writing down to seek God's help, *the World Trade Center officially opened in New York City.* This timing was no happenstance. Incredibly, the God of providence—who has even the fall of a sparrow in His hand—had called me aside at that very time to prepare for a mission, decades away, that would involve *the fall of two great towers.* In the future, the Lord would send me to New York City as a watchman on the wall before 9/11. He would then ordain remarkable providences confirming that He had sent us with His warning before the attack and that I should write this book. But from the forty days of Lent in 1973, it would be a full forty *years*—like the Israelites wandering in the wilderness (Deut. 1:3, 2:7, 8:2–5)—before my book would tell how God's sovereign hand was at work in the fall of two towers being readied for His judgment even as they opened.

10

GOD'S PLAN

For we are God's workmanship, created in Christ Jesus to do good works, which God prepared in advance for us to do.

—Ephesians 2:10 NIV

THOUGH MY NEW LIFE IN CHRIST had no apparent direction for the longest time, God was at work in amazing ways that would become clear only after 9/11.

WRITING AGAIN

On Easter 1973, for the first time since college, I returned to the Episcopal church where I had grown up. With a ponytail and dressed in old work clothes, I sat in back, humbled by the things I heard and had long forgotten: "*Our Father, who art in heaven, hallowed be thy Name*"; "*God spake these words, and said; I am the* LORD *thy God: Thou shalt have no other gods but me*"; "*Ye that do truly and earnestly repent you of your sins, and are in love and charity with your neighbors . . .*"; and "*Hear what comfortable words our Saviour Christ saith unto all that truly turn to him.*" Hearing these old, familiar words, I knew they were true, and it shamed me. What an ignorant, arrogant fool I had been in all my selfish ambition!

On Shakespeare's birthday, April 23, the day after Easter, I walked to my apartment after a new job I had started that day at the cemetery on the hill overlooking town. A thousand thoughts, memories, and fears flooded my mind as I anxiously planned to begin writing that afternoon for the first time in some forty days. How would it go? Would I have a breakthrough?

As I passed by a shop with an open Bible displayed in the window, I stopped to look. A verse was underlined: "*and he will give you the desires of your heart*" (Ps. 37:4 RSV). It was as if these words were directed right at me on this special day when I was to start writing again. It seemed like a magical sign and promise just for me. Instantly I took it to mean God would help me and I would accomplish what I had sought to achieve for so many years. I would complete my novel, and it would succeed!

More important even than my book, I also thought it must apply to the girl I had cared about since boyhood and thought about every day as I wrote. After high school, she had moved away with her family. But near the end of college, I had seen her again with old friends on party weekends and had a visceral reaction each time. Once, a group of us had all stayed at the same motel. Another time, we stayed at Cee Mitsak's, and she invited me to come visit her, which I did, but to no avail. I even broke off plans to marry my fiancée over these hopes rekindled in my heart. While this girl had happily married, this verse seemed to promise my greatest desire would somehow still be granted. The next three nights in a row I actually dreamt about her, with the most realistic dreams, in a way that had never happened before, only confirming my hopes. I was thoroughly elated. Despite her marriage, I would somehow be involved with her again.

However, this selfish fantasy was soon rudely interrupted. My step-father, suffering from Parkinson's, had suddenly threatened to divorce my mother, who took care of him. I went to the pastor at church to talk about their problem, never imagining what he would say. He told me

God hates divorce, and divorce is never His will. Hearing this unexpected counsel, I instantly applied it to my own wishful thinking. It broke my heart beyond imagining. How could it be true? It meant an absolute end to the dream I had nurtured in my heart half my life. For I could readily see that if I were to be a true Christian, I must never interfere in the marriage of this girl on whom I had pinned my hopes and dreams for so long. I must genuinely want her marriage to succeed. I must pray for the couple's well-being and long lives together. Anything less and I might be guilty of coveting, or worse. In a moment's time, my very deepest dream was finally gone for good.

Within weeks I began to realize the whole purpose of my book was profoundly wrong too. The Lord was exposing my sinful desires and ambitions to His holy light. I had been filled with bitterness and resentment for the way things turned out. With the past I cared about so strongly slipping through my fingers like sand, I tried to cling to it and preserve on paper the intensity of the passion in my heart. I struggled to find a solution to the dilemma, but couldn't. I was like the man Jesus described who, trying to save his life, would lose it. Confessing to God that I knew my writing was wrong, I finally gave up. And after gathering five years of handwritten manuscripts, I dumped hundreds of pages into the garbage and threw them out. I was devastated.

In a matter of months, the Lord had stripped me of the two things that mattered most. I had built my life and thoughts around these twin idols. If I couldn't have one, I had thought I could at least have the other. Now I could not so much as dream about them without danger. How would I even go on living? What was the purpose of my life if I could never have the very things I wanted most? Daily, I prayed at the cemetery, begging God for help as I rode about the graves, cutting grass. Surrounded by acres of markers that were a constant reminder of dying, I saw no answers. I had no understanding yet about eternal life or heaven or any concept that my life was meant to serve God's purpose. I had been living for my heaven on earth.

In addition, I had no practical idea what to do with myself. I was a writer. That had been my identity and how I thought of myself for a decade. What was I now? What would I do? I had no real skills but writing personal stories. Who would hire me for that? While I had always been able to do a variety of things well, almost anything I tried, I was master of none. My whole life I had had a mix of gifts—academically, athletically, and creatively; yet despite all that promise, I was nearly twenty-seven and knew nothing to support myself but manual labor. What was wrong with me that I was so out of place? Why didn't I ever fit in as others did? But, I was ignorant of the fact that God had a plan for my life before I was born (Jer. 1:5–10), and even then was preparing me for it in a future I could not see.

To encourage me, two cheerful friends from church began to check on me almost daily. They called on the phone or dropped by to visit. They kindly helped me with stacks of laundry and the mess of my small apartment. They took me to meetings, events, and activities, and prayed with me, taught me Scriptures, and counseled me when I was discouraged and confused. I expressed amazement when they told me things like Christians were to refrain from sex until marriage and were to practice the principle of tithing. I thought, if you loved someone, how could God expect you not to have sex until you married? It seemed totally unreasonable. I had no grasp of the true purpose of sex or its spiritual meaning. And God *couldn't* want me to give away 10 percent of my money to the church. In my whole life I had never had enough as it was; how could I be expected to give away some and get by on less? But the very week I decided to obey this command (if that's what God really wanted) I received a 10 percent raise. Being a new believer, I saw this small providence as a demonstration of the reality of God's faithfulness and power meant to encourage me. After reading George Mueller's story about dependence on God in prayer for provision, I sometimes gave away what little I had. I gave for hungry people suffering from famine in Africa or to outreach ministries asking for help. Though I might have no food left in the apartment and no money to buy more, it seemed I was invited out at those times to every meal. I never went hungry. All of it was training for the future.

With help and direction from my new friends, I also began reading the Bible. I had never read more than a page or two before. As a writer, I was amazed by the power of its words. Their authority shook me to my core. While I had not wanted to grow up, the Bible told me to put away childish things (1 Cor. 13:11). In turning to Christ, I had been called to die. The life I had lived, with its wholly selfish dreams and ambitions, was now to be gone forever. Something radically different had taken its place.

In Christ, the Scripture said, I was "a new creation. The old has passed away; behold the new has come" (2 Cor. 5:15–17 ESV). Elsewhere it taught that this world was passing away. Only God and His Word would never change. "The grass withers, the flower fades; but the word of our God will stand for ever," it said (Isa. 40:8 RSV). How awesome and profound these thoughts were! What a powerful effect they had on me. Had I been allowed to have what I wanted most, I would have thought I needed nothing else. But they would all perish, and so would I. Yet God is eternal. Another Scripture said that in His presence is "fullness of joy," at His right hand "pleasures for evermore" (Ps. 16:11 RSV). He was to be more desired than all His creatures (Ps. 45:2). And though I had not been seeking Him, the Lord had sought me out to save me when I was a stranger "without hope and without God" (Eph. 2:12 NIV). My whole view of life was upended by His Word that I now loved. Though I had no idea then, in the future He would lead me to commit it to video in a revolutionary way.

SPECIAL VOWS

In short order I made three critical vows as a new Christian. Of enormous importance to me, I pledged not to write another book until I had read through the Bible to learn what it had to teach me. Who was I to write anything while I was ignorant of what God taught in His Word? All the themes I had written about were profoundly wrong. I no longer trusted my own thinking. And what would I write now anyway? I knew nothing else but my own thoughts. But little did I know how long this hiatus would be, or that my writing would someday involve biblical prophecy.

Second, having discovered that God hated divorce, I also read where Paul wrote that the best gift was to follow his example and not marry. Without a mate to please, you could devote your life to God's service. Since I had loved a girl much of my life and not married, I wondered if perhaps I should vow to remain single. I also feared my family's history of divorce and the awful mess I had made of my own engagement. I soon learned even Christian leaders like John Wesley had failed in marriage. What hope did I have? Furthermore, I was now seeing a number of attractive single women in church and forming friendly relationships. But I questioned if I could ever truly love again and feared slipping into a relationship because it was easy. When I shared my concerns with an older Christian, he cautioned me that I didn't want to vow not to ever marry. Then he told me of a well-known Christian leader who had given his youth to the Lord in a vow, and God had greatly blessed his ministry. Maybe I should consider that. So I did; I vowed to give my youth to God in service. I wouldn't marry until the middle of my life, which I took to be thirty-five (the age of Shakespeare's maturity!). In the meantime, I could grow while devoting myself to serving God with all the focus and perseverance I had previously used so selfishly. I didn't know what else to do with myself, and this seemed best.

Third, I vowed to remain in our town for five years. I had read in the book of Acts where Jesus told the disciples to wait in Jerusalem to be filled with the Holy Spirit. Once empowered, they would be His witnesses to the whole world, in stages (Acts 1:4–8). Instead of running off to pursue work or a career somewhere else, I knew I needed time to learn and grow and be changed. I also hoped to reach friends I had grown up with, though I failed terribly in my zeal. But step-by-step and stage by stage, I would move out in obedience to the scriptural command, until somehow, in the future, I would be spreading the Gospel to the world, as commanded in Matthew 28:18–20.

As it turned out, my three naive vows profoundly affected my life's direction and work in ways I couldn't possibly foresee. Though it would be years before I would write, I became a diligent student of God's Word in preparation. Upon completing my vow to remain single for a season, the Lord would bless me with a wonderful Christian wife, in spite of my past. I got to know Betty while remaining in our town, where the Lord had called her from the mission field. Had we married earlier, we would have had a family and could not have carried out our work. In the future, we would produce the Bible on video with our team, finishing the New Testament the week before 9/11. In God's providence, she would have an astounding connection to Ground Zero, providing amazing evidence of God's hand upon our mission and confirmation of His judgment. And because I'd vowed to move out in stages in the power of the Holy Spirit, until somehow I would help to spread the Gospel even "to the ends of the earth" (Acts 1:8 NIV; see also James 5:7–11), that would happen in God's grace in ways I couldn't begin to imagine.

GROWING IN CHRIST

In the meantime, no longer writing after work, I threw myself into every activity, study, and fellowship the church offered. Nonetheless, I wondered over and over, *How can I really be a Christian?* I didn't know the simplest things others around me understood. I constantly questioned my acceptance by Christ and whether God truly loved me because of my failures and sins. What if my faith wasn't sincere? I had already fallen away once.

On several occasions I broke down in the Sunday service, sobbing at the thought of some shameful thing I had done or people I had hurt. In the wretchedness of my heart, I had felt no remorse at all about the abortion of my own baby. My fiancée had suffered serious physical problems after the procedure; yet, with love and a sense of honor, she'd refused to press me into marriage. And in spite of the anguish and pain I had caused her, and the trust of her family, who had opened their hearts and home to me, I had selfishly gone my own way. Worst of all, I had not loved God. As a result, I hadn't loved others as I should have. I had known better and could have done so much good. I struggled to forgive myself for the failure of my character and what I had done, even while I learned more about God's forgiveness, my fallenness, and the basic Christian doctrines about regeneration, justification by faith, sanctification, and other teachings (Jer. 31:34; Rom. 3:21–26, 5:1, 8:6–7).

Our two co-rectors at church were John Guest and John Howe. I recognized John Guest immediately. He was the tall Englishman who had once offered me a ride as I walked to town in the rain with my dog, Earl—whose wet body fogged his VW windows. From his accent, I had thought this man must be the new minister in town that I'd heard about, and I told myself, "If he says a word to me about God or church, I'll punch him." He had said nothing, but he'd asked people to pray for the young man with a ponytail who lived in a tree house with his dog, and there I was, a year later, sitting in his church, humbled by God's grace. It was all His providence at work.

A charismatic evangelist and dynamic leader, John had settled in Pittsburgh at the encouragement of Reid Carpenter and others in support of the Reverend Dr. Sam Shoemaker's high vision that Pittsburgh be more famous for God than steel. Shoemaker had been instrumental in the birth of AA and other ministries. Speaking at his funeral in 1963, Billy Graham had said: "I doubt that any man in our generation has made a greater impact for God on the Christian world than did Sam Shoemaker." In 1951, to the surprise of observers, this eminent preacher of the Gospel had been called to leave a prestigious position in New York City to follow God's lead to Calvary Episcopal Church in Pittsburgh. The nation's ninth largest city at the time, Pittsburgh had been the industrial Silicon Valley of its day—the first capital of oil and then of steel. There Shoemaker had prayed on Mount Washington, where a young George Washington had stood two centuries earlier, overlooking the confluence of three rivers, and had seen the location's strategic potential. In a 1955 *Time* magazine article, Shoemaker spoke of his hope "for Pittsburgh's role in changing the U.S."[1] Later, John Guest was inspired by his vision, along with others, and helped launch a number of initiatives, including the Pittsburgh Leadership Foundation, Coalition for Christian Outreach, and Trinity Episcopal School for Ministry. Through John and their influence, Shoemaker's prayer for our city's role in national revival would later directly impact our vision to produce the Bible as a means to that goal. Amazingly, the Lord would then send us with this project and a warning of prophetic judgment to the very city Shoemaker had been called to leave exactly fifty years before 9/11—a judgment having profound biblical significance for the city and the country (Rev. 18). Of course, I knew none of that yet.

To join him as co-rector, John Guest had called John Howe, a first-class leader he knew from InterVarsity Christian Fellowship. When I moved across the street from the vicarage, John and Kari Howe took a special interest, praying and fasting for me as I struggled with depression, guilt, and uncertainty about the future. They led a warm and authoritative Bible study fellowship on Sunday nights that I wouldn't miss. John's teachings on Daniel opened my eyes to the power of prayer and the reality of God's sovereignty over human history and the kingdoms of men, as demonstrated in the affairs of Judah, Babylon, Persia, Greece, and Rome (Dan. 2:20–45).

Not only did I benefit from their gifted preaching, but the two Johns brought other world-class preachers and teachers to our pulpit as well. John Stott and J. I. Packer from England; Bishop Alfred Stanway from Australia; Peter Moore, founder of a new ministry to prep school students, based in Massachusetts; Bishop Festo Kivengere from Uganda, suffering then under the bloody persecutions of Idi Amin; and others. It was a rare, rich education for a brand-new believer like me.

I also took advantage of every other learning opportunity I could. Friends drove me to hear R.C. Sproul weekly at his new Reformed study center in Ligonier. As I sat on the floor, I questioned how this theologian could talk so easily to the crowd gathered in his living room and could answer the questions thrown his way. After a year, R.C. designed a personal tutorial for me to gain a broader understanding of the Bible. At the opposite end of the theological spectrum, I attended the Pittsburgh Charismatic Conference each year. Founded by Russ Bixler, a visionary pastor pioneering the local Christian TV station where I would work, the conference brought in Protestant and Catholic teachers and speakers from around the world. When people asked if I was evangelical, charismatic, or reformed, I had no idea what the terms meant and was suspicious of tags. All I said is that I was a Christian and wanted to believe what was true.

When the cemetery laid me off, I was hired by Dave MacKenzie from our church to join his small Christian handyman company that employed a ragtag collection of well-intentioned, unskilled young workers. Before long, he rented my services to the church to assist the janitor. At first, I was embarrassed—a twenty-seven-year-old college graduate who'd once had ambitions of being a great novelist—to be seen scrubbing the floor on my knees as prominent members passed by. But then I thought if this was what the Lord wanted me to do the rest of my life, I would do it. I was reminded of the words I had read in Psalm 84:10: "I would rather be a doorkeeper in the house of my God than dwell in the tents of wickedness" (NKJV). Nonetheless, in my eagerness to learn, I tied a full-size cassette player to my hip with a cleaning rag to listen as I cleaned. That way I could play teaching tapes from the church library six to seven hours a day. Though sometimes confused by the wide-ranging, inconsistent theologies I heard, I still grew in faith and knowledge.

Not long after, I moved back to our Sycamore Road home and helped Mom care for my stepfather, who was rapidly deteriorating with Parkinson's. Coming in late after long days of meetings and work, I knew Bill must be washed and dressed for bed, and he was always grateful. After that, I went to my room, aching to sleep, but would get on my knees, compelled to pray for family, friends, revival in our country, the Jews, and the unreached Gentiles—Chinese, Buddhists, Hindus, Muslims, and tribal peoples of the world. I often dozed off with my head on the bed.

Busy as I was, it took two years to read through the Bible carefully. I carried it with me everywhere. I couldn't wait to open it and read whenever and wherever I had a moment. Two passages in the Old Testament made a particular impression. The first was Nehemiah 1:4. As I studied Nehemiah and prayed for the spiritual renewal of our country and its "broken walls," I fasted to such a degree that friends commented on my thinness. The other was Isaiah 6:8. After his conversion, Isaiah had seen the Lord, exalted in His holy temple, asking, "Whom shall I send?" Isaiah replied, "Here I am. Send me." While painting our old stone basement, I had listened to a stirring sermon from the church library on this passage by Dr. Alec Motyer, principal of Trinity College, the new Anglican evangelical seminary in Bristol, England. Considered one of the world's leading experts on Isaiah, Dr. Motyer had preached with a powerful, reverent authority and sobering accent that gripped my heart. After listening to his sermon, I began to beg God to send me and use me in some way. But, burning with zeal though I was, what could I do that would make a vital difference for His kingdom? I was a janitor without practical skills and could see no possible opportunity. And introverted as I was, I could not speak like the preachers I heard in the pulpit with such distinctive gifts of presence, eloquence, and confidence. Yet, God was at work, preparing me in His own way. As an Episcopalian, I was free, oddly enough, to read the Scriptures for their true and obvious meaning, without the bias and preconceptions of many denominations. Ours imposed no viewpoint. In addition, I had been trained in English to recognize literary genres and to analyze the meanings of words. Regardless of what others claimed or the commentaries said, I couldn't help but be dominated by *the text of Scripture itself.* I was unable to escape its plain meaning, regardless whether some scholar or theological expert taught otherwise. God's Word was inspired, and it spoke to me. I now trusted it above the ever-changing opinions of fallen human beings. Still, I had no idea where the Lord was leading or how these things would play a part. But long years later, in a remarkable way, with my wife and our team, He would literally *send* me, just as I had prayed in our dark basement on Sycamore Road. Incredibly, unlike anything I ever expected, it would be to New York City, with a warning like Isaiah's in the same passage that had impacted me years earlier—"until the cities lie ruined" (Isa. 6:11 NIV)—and in its future connection with Isaiah 9:10.

NEW RELATIONSHIPS

Remaining in our town, I formed important new relationships at church. After a men's Bible study invited me to join, John Guest asked one of its older members, Bob Crock, to mentor me, and we became close friends. When Bob invited me to join his family on their vacation, his wife, Marnie, asked her friend Betty Buckingham. Betty was John Guest's secretary, and Marnie her main volunteer. After a week's vacation at the Thousand Islands, Betty and I drove back together on our own, talking the whole way. Once the Crocks returned, we met weekly at their house for dinner and a Bible study and continued our relationship.

Seven months later, Bob hired me to help write Christian educational materials for a new product line in his company. It was where I first learned about the challenge of selling products to the wider church as a diverse and fragmented market. The following year, the company paid for me to take a course at the brand-new Trinity Episcopal School for Ministry, where Bob was board treasurer. Begun at John Guest's initiative, the seminary was founded to help bring biblical renewal to the Episcopal Church. I immediately signed up to take practical theology, the only course taught by Bishop Alfred Stanway, who had been recommended by John Stott to be the founding dean. During Stanway's twenty-year tenure as a renowned missionary in Central Tanganyika, twenty thousand churches had been planted under his leadership! The bishop was noted for frequently quoting core principles from the Church Missionary Society: start small, while intending great things; follow God's leading, and put money in a secondary place; and under God, everything depends on the quality of the people chosen for the task. Listening to his amazing stories of answered prayer, I felt like someone who had wandered in a vast, dry desert and suddenly stumbled on an oasis.

Betty Buckingham was the first person the seminary hired. While the bishop located a house, she had set up files in her living room, and I delivered a typewriter from Bob's company to help get her started. Growing up in California, Betty had come to faith in college there through Inter-Varsity Christian Fellowship and then gone directly into Christian work. When John Howe called her to join the church staff, she was serving in Costa Rica with the Latin America Mission. John had known her when she worked for one of the rising stars in InterVarsity. When she came to our church, her closest friend said she thought Betty would meet her husband in this place.

Somewhat shy and prim with a sometimes sharp tongue, Betty was a wholesome late-bloomer with a wonderfully bright smile, strong opinions, and the most vulnerable, expressive eyes. As she walked, I couldn't help notice her attractive figure and legs, set off by her short skirts, as had been the custom in Costa Rica. An intelligent, well-read Christian, she was excited by vision. Betty had been a fine arts major who loved artistic crafts, but had sensed a call to ministry after conversion. She then served with InterVarsity in California and Philadelphia, the American Bible Society in New York City, and the Latin American Mission (LAM) in Costa Rica. In the process, she had grown into a mature believer with a deep faith in God's promises and a heart for missions. I was attracted to her and drawn by her sacrificial Christian life. In addition to helping lead the young adult fellowship, she and I spent hours together outside work, often had dinner together, talked on the phone daily, and communicated easily about everything. Still, though the Lord seemed to affirm our relationship time and again, it was awkward because of my vow not to marry for years.

Nonetheless, Betty came to believe God had given her a distinct promise from Scripture that we would marry. Her best friends thought it a mistake to think so, but she persisted to believe it was true. It was a promise from Habakkuk that would prove full of meaning for our lives beyond anything she could have imagined. It was to a *watchman* on the rampart and spoke of *writing the vision* and *making it plain*, and that *the revelation awaited its appointed time*, and *to wait for it*, for *it will surely come* (Hab. 2:2–3). All these things did come true . . . in time.

After four years of friendship, Betty pressed me in frustration for a decision. Was our relationship going anywhere? Would I marry her? If not, we could no longer go on as friends. It was too painful. I didn't know what to do. I hoped to marry her, but I wasn't prepared to break my vow or make a decision to say yes then. I also knew it would be unfair to leave her hanging on in uncertainty. I was now only thirty-one. Fasting and praying on a personal retreat, I received no guidance of any kind to break my vow or marry. Though I hoped it wasn't true, I felt obligated to tell Betty no. She was crushed. Severing our relationship, she stopped speaking to me, even in church. But had we married then and had a family, the work God had for us together in the future would have been impossible.

Only months later and within weeks of each other, Bob Crock, my best friend as well as my boss, and my stepfather both died unexpectedly. Not long after, the new president of Bob's company ended our project. Mom then sold our large Sycamore Road home and moved to a smaller house in town. Unemployed and deeply confused, I fell seriously ill for the first time in my life and was unable to go out for months. It had all happened as I approached the end of my five-year vow to remain in our town. All the relationships that might have kept me were ended.

INNER-CITY MINISTRY

Once healthy, I explored job opportunities, going to seminary, and world missions. While recuperating, however, I had read John M. Perkins's book, *Let Justice Roll Down*, and was affected by his message from Amos 5:24. A black Christian community developer, Perkins called for reconciliation and bridge building through the Gospel, across racial, social, and economic lines. These ideas sounded entirely new and foreign to me, but I wondered if God might be calling me to cross-cultural, inner-city ministry. Perkins likened outreach across the racial, economic barriers to reaching out to Samaria, which clearly fit my vow from Acts 1:8 to step out in stages as I grew in faith and experience. Strangely enough, his message from Amos that so influenced the direction of my life would be yet one more providential link with that prophet who wrote, "If there is calamity in a city, will not the LORD have done it? Surely the LORD God does nothing, unless He reveals His secret to His servants the prophets" (Amos 3:6–7). Amos's call for repentance and right judgment in Israel gave early warning of the very same judgment Isaiah would later foretell about the nation's coming destruction (Isa. 9:10). Though I couldn't know it then, the Lord's hand was strongly at work for the future.

As it happened, our church had committed to help renew the ministry of Emmanuel Episcopal Church in a historic building on Pittsburgh's North Side. During race riots a decade earlier, it had been partially fire-bombed. Designed by the preeminent architect H. H. Richardson and finished a month before he died, the church was recognized as one of the city's most important structures. This landmark building also featured an elegant marble façade and altar with a plaque from the same Thaw family whose son would later kill Richardson's most famous student—Stanford White—in an act of vengeance atop old Madison Square Garden. It was a story I knew well from childhood. Ironically, we would one day use shots of this Thaw façade in *The Book of Revelation* production months before we knew it would be released at Madison Square Garden. After 9/11, I saw these connections tracing all the way back to our days at the McCormick Mansion in Chicago as a web of providence that witnessed to how the Lord had been working all along to accomplish His own good pleasure and will (Eph. 1:9–11).

To help rebuild the local congregation, John Guest had invited a tough, ex-alcoholic street preacher from Canada. When the new vicar arrived, I was asked to drive him around the North Side to get acquainted. Then I moved there and was hired to be his lay assistant. Within months, John Perkins was invited to lead a series of meetings and stayed in my room. I also had my first contact with the new Christian TV station Russ and Norma Bixler had launched when I arranged for Perkins to be a guest. I had been so influenced by his book; now his visit encouraged me that I had made the right decision to move to the inner city.

In this new job, I worked eighty hours a week and earned five hundred dollars a month. I paid rent for my room in the vicarage, gladly tithed, and did almost everything one could do in urban ministry. I led the youth outreach, Sunday school, and Bible studies (the vicar said I knew the Bible better than the priests in the diocese). I trained with a Christian literacy group to tutor reading, practical experience that would influence our production of the Bible. I also did street evangelism, passed out tracts in bars, visited homes and hospitals, delivered food and clothing, managed a halfway house, painted and cleaned the church, and wrote proposals. I spent hours interceding at the altar in the dark for the children and families I cared so much about and asking God to make Pittsburgh a blessing, as Shoemaker had prayed. After working on Saturdays, I then phoned forty homes after dinner to arrange rides for morning Sunday school. If I didn't call, the kids wouldn't come. After that I cleaned the church by midnight and then hitchhiked ten miles to borrow the van from my former church to pick the kids up on multiple trips in the morning.

The singular variety to this schedule was a bimonthly private tutorial for two years with Dr. Sada Anderson, an African-American English professor at the University of Pittsburgh. I had a chance encounter on the street in the city one day with the wife of the minister whose sermon had led me to pursue English and writing in college. After asking about my writing, Polly told me about Dr. Anderson and soon provided an introduction. A strict and demanding teacher, Sada encouraged me to keep writing, but wanted me to focus on the modern essay instead of fiction—a huge change for me. In that regard, the one topic that most truly interested me was the Second Coming in biblical prophecy, yet Sada pressed me to write essays from experience. How amazingly providential this would prove to be, because God was graciously preparing me to do both.

As it was, I lived in my small room for three years, possessing only a chair, the table where I wrote, the daybed of an old friend, and a radio. Sometimes people from my suburban church saw me sweeping the sidewalk as they drove to downtown jobs. "What are you doing with your life, Jim?" they asked, thinking I was crazy to keep on with what I was doing. I could only answer that it was what I thought God wanted. I didn't know what else to do.

But cleaning the basement men's room one day, I cried out in loneliness, "Lord, I can't take it any longer. I've got to get married." I was thirty-four. That same day, the vicar asked me to call the seminary for information. When I did, I ended up speaking with Betty Buckingham for the first time in years. Having just prayed about marriage, our unexpected conversation had my total attention. Soon after, I saw her at a party of old friends. Again, my heart was drawn to her. Once I worked up courage to call her, Betty was cool and guarded. Gradually her barriers came down, and she offered her apartment while she was at work as a place for me to write on my day off—oddly enough, the same one in which the first English teacher to ever encourage my writing had lived. With that hopeful sign and on that pretext, I saw her weekly. Then we started dating.

At last, I came to visit with daffodils one spring night, to propose. I told her I loved her and asked her to marry me. She said yes, and we joyfully married at summer's end. By then we had known each other eight years. To the surprise of family and friends, God had answered what she had believed was His promise to her that we would marry, and He had honored my vow. Our wedding was held at Emmanuel three weeks past my thirty-fifth birthday. In spite of my past, the Lord had graciously blessed me with an attractive, bright, godly wife who loved Him and me. After 9/11, He revealed the remarkable providence that had brought us together in witness to our calling and His judgment (Eph. 2:10).

Starting out, not many wives could have adapted easily to our humbling circumstances. Betty gave up a well-paying job at the seminary to live on my meager salary. When it rained, the ceiling in our apartment leaked into pots on the bed. Our "bathroom" sink was in the hall. The bedroom had no heat. Every few weeks we shared a single hot fudge sundae at McDonald's to splurge, and I saved two months for a haircut. Betty's attitude was testimony to her faith and character, and the experience would prepare us for our future work together.

Employed at the church three more years, I was let go when its ten-year funding ended. I was then thirty-eight. I had been a Christian eleven years and had been let go from five straight jobs. Again, I wondered what was wrong with me. What in the world was I meant to do? Where would we go? In all my time at the church, the vicar had rarely complimented my work. He had almost never agreed with me and often belittled my ideas. He repeatedly said I would never be a leader, and if I tried to go to seminary, he'd oppose me. But what a blessing this turned out to be.

On the day I was let go, we learned a friend was looking for a couple to house-sit for a client in an exclusive suburb for a year without rent. As quickly as my job had ended, we had an unexpected sabbatical where I could seek direction and write résumés. In studying personality, I discovered I was an introvert by design, not by deficiency, accident, or upbringing. How freeing and affirming this knowledge was! I wasn't extroverted, like most in leadership, but I wasn't an introvert because something was wrong with me. God had made me who I was for a reason, and that gave me new faith and confidence. He had created me as a unique person with a global view. He had gifted me to see possibilities and things in the future, qualities He must want to use.

As I explored options in business and ministry, even tent-making, as the apostle Paul had once done by example, the more I looked, the less it seemed I was led to a job in business. While I had lots of ministry experience and a range of aptitudes, I had few marketable skills. When different friends suggested I apply to be a writer at the growing Christian television ministry in Pittsburgh, the idea didn't appeal to me, but at the second suggestion, I thought I should follow through in obedience to what the Lord might want. So I wrote to the general manager, Oleen Eagle. With nothing to lose, I told her how I had set out on a motorcycle to be a filmmaker in Hollywood, how I had lived in a tree house to write the great American novel before I turned to Christ, and how I eventually ended up working with kids at our inner-city church. She called me for a meeting at their facility on a hilltop in a small town called Wall. After a warm interview, I heard nothing more and assumed there was no interest.

Concerned most of all about outreach to Muslims, Betty and I flew to Pasadena to visit the U.S. Center for World Missions, founded to focus attention on the world's remaining unreached people groups. Ralph Winter taught that this mission would require intentional, cross-cultural outreach. As I knew from reading, Muslims had been among the world's most unresponsive peoples to the Gospel for centuries. Now God was breaking down barriers. But we found no feasible opportunity. Yet, the Lord had a future task for us that would have been impossible then and incomprehensible had I known it. In a most unexpected way, it would also be connected with Muslims and Islam. The next step in my vow from Acts 1:8 would begin to equip me with the skills, connections, and vision I would need.

11

CORNERSTONE TELEVISION

For the revelation awaits an appointed time; it speaks of the end and will not prove false. Though it linger, wait for it; it will certainly come and will not delay.

—Habakkuk 2:3 NIV

 RADICAL CHANGE OF DIRECTION, MY new job in Christian television was clearly God's will.

NEW JOB

The day Oleen Eagle called, we were down to our last fifty dollars. All Betty's savings were gone. We could go no further without a source of income, so that morning we knelt together, holding hands, asking the

Lord to make a way. We had done the best we could and could go no further without a job. A few hours later the phone rang. Oleen was calling, six months after my initial interview with WPCB-TV. Would I come in for a two-week assignment to write a fund-raising appeal for their new station in Altoona? Though it wasn't the type of writing I was hoping for and the duration was disappointing, the job answered our prayer and immediate need. We might still get involved with world missions when the project was over.

As it turned out, my assignment was a test, and they kept me. Russ Bixler respected my years of work in the inner city and had asked Oleen to hire me. While I had to learn how to write appeals, he patiently encouraged me. After six years of isolation in inner-city ministry, I also found the showy, fast-paced television environment required a major adjustment on my part. At the same time, I discovered I had an innate ability to grasp the ministry's large numbers and financial situation better than those working in that area, gifts and experience that would prove essential in the future. Someday I would need to raise and manage money for our Bible project.

Two years later, when the head of the development department retired, I asked for the job, and Oleen gave me the chance. She also sent me for professional training. To everyone's surprise our fund-raising began to increase. Besides writing appeals, I directed telethons and prepped talent. I threw myself into the work, and it came so naturally. In my first telethon, I estimated projected income within five hundred dollars of the actual amount. No one had done that there before. The numbers just spoke to me. At the same time I enjoyed drawing out the talent, standing by the camera for hours, and giving energetic encouragement and direction. During one break Russ laughed and said, "You communicate more information in less time than anyone I've ever known."

Exposed to the work of various ministries, I also began to learn information about our Christian heritage I had never heard. It was infuriating to see this precious heritage being lost and purposely suppressed in the culture war that was waging for the soul of the country. Though we retained a Christian majority, America seemed to be the only place on Earth where Christianity was not growing. Worse, this stagnation was occurring despite the combined efforts of hundreds of thousands of churches, thousands of bookstores, countless other ministries, and numerous radio and TV stations. All this effort only seemed to prevent us from slipping further faster. Turning the tide appeared impossible. Nonetheless, our ministry sought to expand aggressively and "to go and make disciples," using television. Early on, the Lord had impressed a promise from Isaiah 49:22 upon the Bixlers that He would use the ministry in a unique way to reach the nations with the Gospel. Under Russ and Norma and Oleen's leadership, we were easily the most creative TV ministry in the country.

Still, I was convinced if there was to be any hope for another great awakening in the United States, something radically different was needed. That all the different churches would suddenly change overnight seemed an unlikely expectation, however; and what was being done by ministries and organizations like ours, despite our best efforts, was clearly failing to turn the tide.

THE BIBLE

Then two things happened in my fourth year at what was now Cornerstone TeleVision that laid the groundwork for a vision to produce the Bible on video. The first was Chris Bueno's *The Indestructible Book* video that recounted the stories of John Wycliffe and William Tyndale and the origins of the English Bible. I had never known about the price these men had paid to translate the Bible into English for the common man to read. Through their efforts, England had become *the people of a book—the Bible*. As a direct result, our country and its institutions were shaped and molded by God's Word. In the fifteen years since my conversion, I had gradually drifted from a habit of reading through the Bible yearly and had lost sight of Scripture's primacy. With a renewed vision, I became focused on its power and priority. The Bible's divine message had not only changed lives, but its teaching and principles had transformed nations, cultures, and the course of history. If it had happened in our country before, I thought, why couldn't it again?

The second thing occurred as I prayed for direction in the new year and came across an essay in *Halley's Bible Handbook* about *the most important thing* a local church could do for its community: make it *a Bible-reading community* that read through the Bible every year. And here we were, a *regional TV ministry*. What could be more important than to encourage our region in the practice of daily Bible reading? I told Arlene Williams, our telethon coproducer, that I wanted to make this the theme of our fall telethon. Then she encouraged Oleen to attend a national meeting to promote 1990 as *the Year of International Bible Reading*. After Oleen returned, I shared an idea about how Ron Hembree could make his daily program a series taking viewers through the Bible in a year, reading fifteen minutes a day with his commentary. A dynamic Bible teacher, Ron had led one of the country's largest megachurches. When we implemented this program, it doubled our mailing list and donor base.

But Ron decided to produce it on his own. I was heartsick. I told Betty I'd never have another idea like it. Talking to Russ, I lamented the difficulty of getting people to read the Bible. How could we lead enough people to read it to see revival? "People just don't read as much anymore," Russ said matter-of-factly. "They watch TV."

In the meantime, we discussed the idea of a new production. Rather than a commentary about the Bible, perhaps we could have the Bible read aloud dramatically by an actor. TBN had produced something similar, but I doubted such a program would make the kind of difference that was called for. How many people would actually sit and watch it?

GOD'S PREPARATION

It was then that a series of providential events took place to prepare me for a new vision. In need of a car we couldn't afford, I suggested to Betty, "Why don't we give away what we have and see what God does?" Ironically, we gave our limited savings of six hundred dollars to CBN for its Arabic television ministry to reach Muslims in the Middle East. Within weeks, a robber broke into our house, stealing the few special possessions we owned, including our first color television and my new winter coat. I was furious. When insurance helped pay for a nice used car, I became more philosophic. But after the robbery, we thought it was time to move from Pittsburgh and be closer to the station in Wall. Then we considered being closer to my mom as she got older, though it would mean traveling farther to work. I had no idea we would leave Cornerstone in the future.

About then, a dear friend saw me on air and requested I come visit her in the hospital. When I told Mom, she mentioned the hospital was about to demolish two blocks of houses. After our visit, I noticed an empty lot across the street and had an idea. What if we could move a house that was to be torn down? When I ran the idea past a good friend who was a realtor, she suggested I call her next-door neighbor—the hospital administrator. I did, and he agreed to a quick tour of ten houses. In short order, we picked out one, and he said it was ours for a dollar if we could move it. Though we had no funds left and just one credit card, we worked with eleven organizations to move the one-dollar house—an enterprise fraught with challenges, difficulties, and expenses. Oleen said, "I wonder what God is preparing you for." Then, the week before we moved the house, Pat Robertson visited our ministry for the first time to participate in our tenth anniversary telethon, and I had the opportunity to tell him how our house move came about, starting with a special gift to CBN for Islamic outreach. As it happened, it would be in this new house that I would have the vision for the Bible on video, where we would complete most of the production, and where the Lord would lead me through His Word to foresee the attack on New York City. Then, after 9/11, I would be struck by the irony that Pat Robertson was one of only two well-known preachers to publicly link the terrorist attack to the loss of God's protection and His judgment on America, before being pressured to retract the truth.

Not long after our house move, the ministry hired a top-flight consultant on the Focus on the Family board to discuss "developing world-class leadership in your organization." He gave our team his role preference test to find how we could each best contribute. Soon the consultant gathered us together in Oleen's office. "I don't normally do this," he said, "but I want to draw your attention to someone." He pointed to me and said, "When Jim Fitzgerald tells you something, I want you to listen to him. God has uniquely designed Jim to take new and original ideas and find a way to make them work the first time. He has a gift of practical wisdom." Then he explained how people with my role preference were relatively few in number. In private, he shocked me even further: "I told Russ and Oleen they shouldn't make any major decisions without the three of you being in agreement." I had never been affirmed like this in all my years of work. He told me I had presidential gifts and needed mentoring to develop leadership skills. I had worked in the background so long his ideas sounded totally foreign. But his counsel changed my life.

Next came the Persian Gulf War in February 1991. Cornerstone decided to pray live nightly on air for our troops. God had clearly led us, as a sacrifice would soon be made by our community. WPCB-TV 40 was the station of license for Greensburg, whose Quartermaster unit suffered the most US casualties in the war when a random missile struck behind the lines. We had also learned in the war's buildup that Saddam Hussein watched the US news live via satellite. I thought immediately about its implications and said to Russ, "This means we could broadcast our programs around the world on satellite." He smiled benignly at my enthusiasm.

But two months later, in the spring telethon, we reached our goal early for the first time in the ministry's history. Having an extra day was an unexpected opportunity. "I think we should raise money tonight to buy a satellite uplink," Oleen said. I was stunned. After the Gulf War, we had continued to debate the idea of a satellite uplink to reach across the United States, but I thought there was no interest. Now Oleen was suggesting we raise the necessary $250,000 in one night, which seemed impossible. It equaled a quarter of the telethon goal that had taken us two weeks to raise.

"I don't think it's possible," I said.

"If God wants us to have an uplink, anything is possible," said Oleen. "What would it take to do it?"

"To raise $250,000, we would need a number of major gifts," I said, "like a gift pyramid. We would need to have at least one pledge of $25,000. There would have to be other large gifts, a few $10,000; $5,000; $3,000; and $2,000 pledges."

Oleen said we shouldn't ask for gifts below $1,000, and we all agreed. Then she asked me to explain the plan to viewers. Within minutes that night, the opening pledge was $25,000. In an amazing outpouring of support, we raised the entire $250,000 in a single night. One local pastor had come to proclaim that God was not yet done with America: the Lord had not forgotten all that America had done to spread the Gospel in the world. That night was April 19. In the midst of a culture war, I thought it providential and fitting to reach this goal on the anniversary of the start of our War for Independence. With an uplink, our ministry could reach all of North America from our base in Wall, to be a catalyst for revival. Surely, God had heard our earnest prayers.

Then in our fall telethon, we reached our goal early again. This time we had three days to spare. I thought it offered the perfect chance to kick off our planned building campaign. "Why not introduce the capital campaign?" I said eagerly. Russ disagreed. Our two-week telethons were the most physically demanding time of the year, all of us on our feet for hours, with our schedules overturned. But I thought these three days were an opportunity we couldn't afford to miss, so I decided to fast and pray. Yet, the three days slipped by without accomplishing anything further. The lost opportunity discouraged me greatly. The telethon ended late Saturday night, and Betty and I drove home at four in the morning to collapse exhausted into bed. The three days of fasting and prayer appeared to have been pointless.

But I was completely mistaken.

12

VIDEO BIBLE

As the rain and the snow come down from heaven . . . so is my word that goes out from my mouth: It will not return to me empty, but will accomplish the purpose for which I sent it.

—Isaiah 55:10–11 NIV

THE DAY AFTER OUR TELETHON, I had an unexpected idea: a completely new way to produce the Bible on history's most powerful tool for communication.

NEW VISION

I first envisioned what would become the *WatchWORD Bible* project on Veteran's Day, November 11. Originally, this was called Armistice Day to commemorate the end of World War II, the "war to end all wars."[1] To make the point symbolically, the treaty had been signed at the eleventh hour on the eleventh day of the eleventh month to convey the idea that more wars like it would spell the end of humanity. To have the vision for the Bible on video on this date was like a sign that underscored to me the urgency of the time and the lateness of the hour we had to spread God's Word, the most important weapon in our spiritual warfare (Eph. 6:12–17). I didn't know it then, but 1991 was also the year Osama bin Laden turned his ire against America for having its infidel armies in Saudi Arabia fight Muslims in the Gulf War. But I knew nothing about him then. Ten years later I would, when his anger would lead to 9/11.

After waking up late that day, Betty and I attended evening worship at our old church. During the service, words to the songs were projected on a big screen in large, white letters superimposed over the picture of a fjord. At home after the service, I sat numbly in my chair, too drained from our late-night telethon to do anything except sit before the TV. Our regular programming was back on. As I watched the program, I prayed with silent desperation in my heart, "Lord, what can we do?" Our nation had been in steady spiritual decline for decades. Wasn't there anything we could do to make a difference? In television we possessed the most powerful communication tool ever made, yet what was being done around the country by Christians was failing to make a sufficient difference to turn things around. Clearly, more of the same was not the solution. If we were to see revival, something radically new and unconventional was needed, I was convinced.

Praying and thinking, I went to look something up in *Halley's Bible Handbook*. There I came across old notes from three years earlier in the article about *the single most important thing* a church could do. The idea of a church making its community a Bible-reading community had been the seed for our one-year Bible reading program with Ron Hembree. However, now we had a satellite uplink. We could reach the whole continent. What could be more important than doing everything we could to try to make the country a Bible-reading nation again?

From our recent experience I knew simply encouraging people to read the Bible was not sufficient. Others had tried to promote Bible reading for years too; nonetheless biblical literacy declined. Most people didn't read as much anymore. They watched TV. And what if we had an actor read the Bible on TV? I asked myself again. How many would sit and watch someone read the Bible aloud on a daily basis? Certainly not enough to spark a national revival.

I then recalled Reid Carpenter's involvement with Campus Crusade in raising money for the massive New Media Bible project more than a decade earlier. The producer had envisioned filming dramatic reenactments of the entire Bible, yet only two of the sixty-six books were ever produced. One, *The Gospel of Luke*, had been sold to churches across the country for a thousand dollars each. Our church had purchased a copy on 16-millimeter film and played it a few times. *The Jesus Film* had been created from this movie and was reaching vast numbers, but *Luke* had long since come and gone. Millions had been spent on this Bible project before it stopped.

As a brand-new Christian interested in writing books and making movies, I had been excited by the vision of filming the entire Bible. This effort by Campus Crusade for Christ had made a deep impression on me. However, their experience also convinced me it was unrealistic to consider reenacting the whole Bible. It would be impossibly expensive and time-consuming to film all sixty-six books on location with actors. If those behind the New Media Bible had been unable to accomplish it, with all their connections and powerful backers, what hope would we have? Furthermore, the concept itself was problematic. Filming each book of the Bible, as a word-for-word drama, would make the videos long, drawn out, and less effective. It would also be enormously cost-prohibitive to support the acting, costumes, and staging for such a massive undertaking in a way to make it convincing. And what would one do with all the portions of the Bible that were not narrative stories? Many of the books were not stories. How could they be produced? Without a story or characters, they couldn't be reenacted. And who was I to even contemplate such a project?

At that moment, however, a new idea popped into my mind. Earlier that evening, projected on the big screen at church, the lyrics of the songs we had sung were superimposed over a beautiful picture. What if the words of the Bible were superimposed over relevant video scenes and came on and off as they were narrated? The fonts could be artistic in design to please the eye. Beautiful scenes of appropriate video under the text could hold viewers' attention and support the meaning. Music and sound effects could complete the production. In this way people could read the Bible as they heard it. Reading and hearing at the same time would increase comprehension and memory. It could be more effective than reading a book. If people could read the Bible easily on TV and in a way that held their attention, it could draw a host of new people to read God's Word, people who might never otherwise read it. In this way the Lord could speak to them through His Word, and they could be changed. What could be more important?

I also knew that for the past thirty years we had been through the most intensive period of Bible translation in history. New, easy-to-read versions were available everywhere, and were cheaper than ever to own. Yet, despite this proliferation of inexpensive, easy-to-read versions, Bible reading still declined and biblical illiteracy grew. All the new versions, notes, and covers had not appreciatively increased Bible reading. But a well-produced TV Bible could attract a whole new audience. TV was easier to watch and more entertaining; and best of all, every book in the Bible—even the Epistles—could be produced in this way with word-for-word text on-screen.

Furthermore, whenever God's Word was rediscovered and shared with the common man, revival followed. It was true in the biblical accounts and throughout history. God's Word always brought personal renewal and national change when spread abroad (Josh. 8:32–35; 2 Chron. 24:14–33; Neh. 8:1–8). Again, I recalled how England had become the people of a book through the work of Wycliffe and Tyndale. Wycliffe's itinerant Lollards had carried handwritten Bibles from village to village, reading them aloud to the people. By translating the Bible into the language of the common man and printing hundreds of thousands of illegal copies, Tyndale had hoped to make the plowboys in England know the Scriptures as well as the pope. America had been shaped as a direct result by their work. Couldn't this happen again? We would be taking God's Word to TV where the people were—"that by all means [we] might save some" (1 Cor. 9:22 ESV).

For several hours, I counted pages in the Bible and thought through our experience with Ron Hembree's program. I was amazed to realize the entire Bible could fit into a yearlong series of daily half-hour programs. Viewers would be able to read the whole Bible each year by simply watching for thirty minutes, once a day. Anyone could do that. The average person watched hours of TV every day. In this way, television would make the reading effortless and the various elements would help hold viewers' interest. If there was to be any hope for multitudes of new people to know God's Word and read it regularly, I thought there could be no easier way. People in Africa, Asia, Europe, and South America could watch it by satellite. Many could understand it in English, the new world language. Millions and millions of people could read the Bible in this way.

The idea had come to me the day after my fast. It would be more feasible and practical to produce than drama and more effective to watch in terms of time and learning. It could increase Bible reading around the world and help spark renewal. I laughed in amazement and said in my heart, "Lord, if this is Your will, I'll devote my life to it."

The very possibility of this idea filled me with hope. This production would not be *about* the Bible; it would be the Bible itself, word for word. If producing God's Word effectively on video wouldn't be a powerful tool for revival in our day, I thought, what ever would be?

AN IMPOSSIBILITY

Sharing my new idea with enthusiasm at the ministry, I was totally unprepared for the negative response I received. Our producers said it couldn't be done. In terms of technology, it was impossible to put that much text on video as I wanted. Even if I could, they said no one would ever want to read the Bible on TV anyway; and I'd never be able to raise all the money.

But I couldn't believe it was true. I knew God wanted people to read His Word. I was also convinced there must be a way to produce the Bible on video. Otherwise, I saw little reason for a radical increase in Bible reading in our media culture. People owned multiple Bibles that gathered dust on their shelves because they were seen as too difficult and time-consuming to read. And if people didn't read God's Word, how could they be changed by its message?

Refusing to take anyone else's word for what could or couldn't be done, I pressed ahead. If this new way could help even a few to read God's Word, I thought it would be worth it. What else could I ever do that could be more worthwhile? I also knew that if God had designed me to do new things for the first time, I had to be willing to risk failure. If I played it safe the rest of my life, I would be guilty of wasting this gift and leaving unfulfilled the reason I was created.

Coming to a settled conclusion, my next step was finding the right translation. For that, I wanted to use a modern version that could be easily understood by the widest range of people, from educated adults to inner-city kids or those speaking English as a second language around the world. In return I was sure a publisher would provide production funding in order to promote its translation on TV. As I would learn, I was totally naive about the whole business!

Just months later, I was sharing my new vision with Ron Hembree at the annual National Religious Broadcasters' Convention in Washington, DC, when an agent from Thomas Nelson Publishers introduced himself to Ron and sat next to me. He said Thomas Nelson had commercial rights to publish a new, modern translation from the American Bible Society, called the Contemporary English Version. ABS had translated it at a fifth-grade level for children and adults, and it was designed to be easily understood in oral reading. It had also received an imprimatur and could be used by Catholics as well as Protestants. I was delighted by this news I thought I was meant to hear. When I got home, I immediately called the CEV project manager, Jerry Trousdale. He was intrigued by my enthusiasm and flew from Nashville to learn more, meeting with Oleen and me to talk about the idea. Jerry told me with a laugh he had never met anyone more focused.

After this meeting we produced two short pilots over the next year as "proof of concept." To everyone's surprise they proved my idea of reading the Bible on video actually worked and was compelling. Our savvy fund-raising consultant then suggested we could sell videos once it was produced to generate revenue. But when I asked if the ministry would help fund the project, I was told it couldn't. Cornerstone had been built through years of sacrifice and never had sufficient money for its work, let alone taking on a project like the Bible. So before traveling to meet a producer in California in January 1993, I began a partial fast for twenty-one days to pray for guidance. On the last day, I received a remarkable answer and left on the trip in peace. Upon returning, I asked Oleen if I could pursue the project on my own. Reluctantly, she agreed.

Asking to undertake a project of this magnitude was the biggest step I'd ever taken in my life. My heart was pounding, and my hands perspired.

Was it really God's will? What if I was wrong? But I had asked, and Oleen agreed. I'd now accepted the challenge of somehow seeking to produce the whole Bible on video. Until 9/11, I would have no idea how truly I'd been led.

THE CEV TRANSLATION

Receiving Oleen's permission for the project, I wasted no time and right away set out to license the CEV translation from the American Bible Society, asking Jerry Trousdale to arrange a meeting with their leadership in New York City. ABS agreed to meet in February 1993, and I drove from Wall with two others to the Broadway offices of the world's largest Bible society to discuss the project. Our pilot videos impressed them, and they were clearly taken with the idea. Jerry told me later he had never seen so many of their top brass in a meeting.

Returning home, we quickly submitted a proposal. ABS responded by saying they would give no production funds, but would grant the CEV license. After 9/11, I would reflect on the remarkable timing of that meeting to start our project. In God's providence, we had met with ABS in New York City to license the CEV translation *one week before the first World Trade Center bombing by terrorists, on February 26, 1993.* Having already released *The Book of Revelation* at Madison Square Garden in 2000, we finished the CEV New Testament *one week before the second terrorist attack on the World Trade Center, on September 11, 2001.* Spread out over eight years' time, the start and completion of the production had formed a pair of perfect bookends with the attacks—in amazing witness to God's prophetic purpose for our work and warning

Immediately after our meeting in New York, I founded Watch-WORD Productions to enter a contract for the CEV license. By late summer, however, the ministry said my work on the project was becoming a diversion. In spite of the previous permission, I was given a thirty-day ultimatum: either drop the project, or give up my job as vice president with a newly vested pension and leave to do the video Bible on my own. Having worked at Cornerstone nearly nine years, I didn't want to leave, and Betty worked there too. I cared deeply about the ministry and its mission. I had been given the opportunity to learn about production, fund-raising, marketing, and management there. I also had the chance to observe a range of denominations, churches, and ministries. My idea for the project itself was the fruit of working under Russ and Oleen's mentoring. But after praying through the month of September, we tendered our resignations. They hadn't thought we would quit and believed we were making a big mistake, but we decided not to turn back. In hindsight, it was essential we leave the nest, though I had no idea what we were in for.

With $10,000 in seed money from Thomas Nelson Publishers, money from friends, and most of a home equity loan, we had quickly spent $50,000 on a dynamic three-minute CEV pilot at the Westinghouse studio in Pittsburgh and our trip to ABS in New York. The project estimator at Westinghouse had given us a quote of $2 million to finish just the *Gospel of John*. Then we had to leave the ministry and go on our own before we could build a foundation of interest and financial support. Only my severance remained. But believing the Lord had called us to produce the Bible on video, we chose to step out in faith to pursue this vision. I also thought if I stayed at the ministry to play it safe and keep my job, I would be guilty of not using the gift God had given me to do new things for the first time. As it was, Betty and I had come to the place in our lives where we were willing to risk losing everything to try because the need was so great and the opportunity so significant. We knew something of this magnitude was needed to help spark a revival in the country. At our ages, we also didn't naively assume success. I had just turned forty-seven and had been a Christian twenty years. But in September eight years later, 9/11 would clearly prove the project was no whim. The Lord had led us to undertake it.

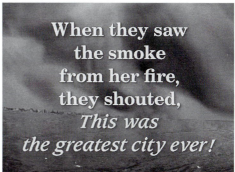

LEFT: The marquee at Madison Square Garden on July 9th, 2000, where *The Book of Revelation* was released at The NY International Independent Film and Video Festival
RIGHT: *WatchWORD Bible* Revelation 18:18

UN Headquarters on the East River in New York City by Ad Meskens

World Trade Center night view © Q. T. Luong

Madison Square Garden © Getty Images

Madison Square Garden

Madison Square Garden © Corbis

LEFT: *WatchWORD Bible* Revelation 1:8c
RIGHT: Manhattan with the World Trade Center towers © skypic.com

ABOVE: Empire State Building © Robert J. Fisch
RIGHT: Author in Rome with the Coliseum in view

TOP: Parthenon on the Acropolis in Athens
ABOVE: Ruins at Philippi

Philippi ruins

Ruins of the ancient library at Ephesus

Damage to the USS *Cole* after the attack (US Government photo)

God will bless
everyone who reads
this prophecy
to others,
and he will bless
everyone who hears
and obeys it.

LEFT: *WatchWORD Bible* Revelation 19:14

RIGHT: Scott and Joyce at our main production computer

The second plane approaches © 2001, The New York Times Company

South Tower collapses © AP / Photo by Det. Greg Semendinger/ NYC Police Aviation Unit

New York skyline with Twin Towers before 9/11 © Balthazar Korab Ltd. / Artifice Images

OPPOSITE: Second tower hit © 2001, The New York Times Company

Attack at the Pentagon © AP Photo

THE Atlantic MONTHLY

OCTOBER 2002

The conclusion of
AMERICAN GROUND
BY WILLIAM LANGEWIESCHE

Plus:
THE NEXT
CHRISTIANITY

*The modern world arose from
the trauma of the Reformation.
Brace for a Second Reformation—
a global convulsion that will
shape the coming century*
BY PHILIP JENKINS

Ruins at Ground Zero © AP

LEFT: Dead at Gettysburg
RIGHT: Statue of Liberty with fallen towers in the distance © Daniel Hulshizer / AP

TOP: McCormick Mansion, Chicago
© Irina Hynes
ABOVE: Kennedy Cabinet Meeting – Cuban
Missile Crisis (US Government photo)

Old Main on campus © Midnightdreary

LEFT: Emmanuel Church, North Side © Timothy C. Engleman
RIGHT: View from the cemetery © Anne Hennessey

1970 Royal Enfield

American fighter jets over Iraq in the Persian Gulf War (US Government photo)

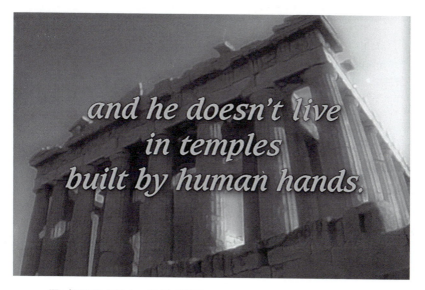

WatchWORD Bible Acts 17:24c (CEV)

Scene of wreckage from the first Trade Center bombing

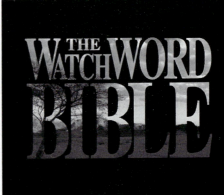

LEFT: Our company logo
RIGHT: *WatchWORD Bible* logo

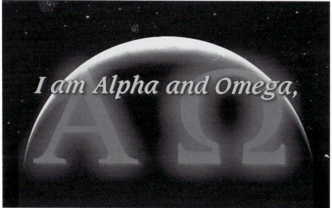

TOP: *WatchWORD Bible* Luke1:52 (CEV)
ABOVE: *WatchWORD Bibl*e Revelation 1:8
(CEV)

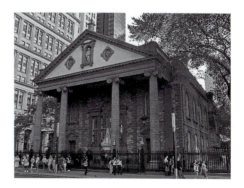

St. Paul's Chapel © Jason Klobassa

The early Dutch settlement at New Amsterdam

LEFT: United Flight 175 approaches second tower © Corbis
RIGHT: Infomercial interview

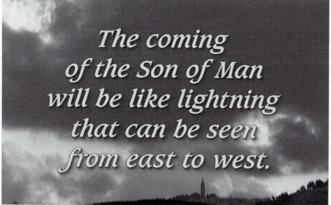

*The coming
of the Son of Man
will be like lightning
that can be seen
from east to west.*

TOP: North Tower implodes © 2001, The New York Times Company
ABOVE: *WatchWORD Bible* Matthew 24:27

A small team: Helen Jean, Betty, Jim, Joyce, and Scott

Nations and kingdoms will go to war against each other.

LEFT: The State Flag of Israel
RIGHT: *WatchWORD Bible* Matthew 24:7

Temple Mount, Jerusalem, from the air with the Dome of the Rock

Aerial view of the White House (US Government photo)

President Bush aboard USS *Abraham Lincoln* (US Government photo)

TOP: President George H. W. Bush (Bush 41 –
US Government photo)
ABOVE: *WatchWORD Bible* Revelation 6:2a-b

And its rider
was given the power
to take away all peace
from the earth,

WatchWORD Bible Revelation 6:4c

President George W. Bush speaking before Congress (US Government photo)

LEFT: Flag of the former USSR
RIGHT: Flag of Saudi Arabia

Then I saw a black horse, and its rider had a balance scale in one hand.

WatchWORD Bible Revelation 6:5c

WatchWORD Bible Revelation 6:8b

and they could kill
its people
with swords,
famines,
diseases,
and wild animals.

WatchWORD Bible Revelation 6:8d

ABOVE: The *Mayflower* at sea
RIGHT: The Battle of Vienna

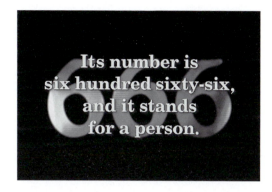

LEFT: Presidential Seal
RIGHT: *WatchWORD Bible* Revelation 13:18

The Embarkation of the Pilgrims, US Capitol Rotunda

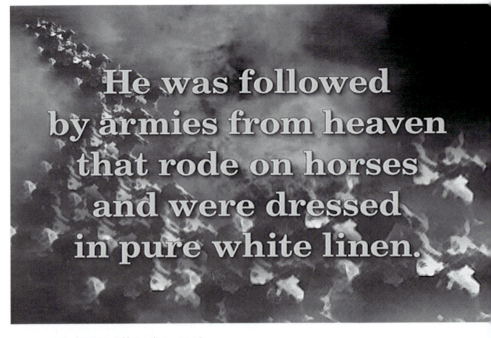

He was followed
by armies from heaven
that rode on horses
and were dressed
in pure white linen.

WatchWORD Bible Revelation 19:14

At the sound
of a loud trumpet,
he will send his angels
to bring his
chosen ones together

LEFT: *WatchWORD Bible* Matthew 24:31
RIGHT: President Barack Hussein Obama (US Government photo)

WatchWORD Video Bible iPhone App (Acts 17:24c)

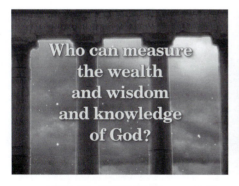

LEFT: *WatchWORD Bible* Romans 11:33
RIGHT: Contemporary English Version (CEV)

LEFT: Japanese
RIGHT: Arabic

»Ich bin Gabriel.
Ich habe meinen Platz
in der Gegenwart Gottes.

Now I want you
to know, brothers,
that what has
happened to me
has really served
to advance the gospel

LEFT: German
RIGHT: Philippians 1:12 (NIV)

13

WATCHWORD BIBLE

All scripture is God-breathed and is useful for teaching, rebuking, correcting and training in righteousness.

—2 Timothy 3:16 NIV

N EARLY 1994, we began full-time production of a dynamic videobook that we named *The WatchWORD Bible*.

NEW TESTAMENT PRODUCTION

Based on overly optimistic projections that it would take only a year to produce the New Testament, I developed a business plan to raise investment monies for phase one in our long-term goal for the whole Bible. Due to the nature of the project and my ministry experience, I originally planned to form a nonprofit organization. However, a major Christian foundation counseled that if the videos would be as good as I claimed, we should form a business and sell them. They said it would be a better way to operate, and more organizations should do the same. In that case, I thought the English version could become a financial engine to help fund future world language productions. Our lawyer suggested creating a business trust, and I raised our first money in the new year from family and friends.

We hired a small staff, and our team then set out with genuine excitement to produce the Bible as the first-ever "videobook," using powerful, cutting-edge workstations with computer graphics and editing software that were just coming into their own. Joining Betty and me in a small rented office in Pittsburgh, our team consisted of three gifted believers who each had a master's degree and special talents. Mark was an experienced producer who left Cornerstone to direct production and take software training with us at Softimage in Montreal. Joyce was a talented calligrapher who had never yet worked on a computer and agreed to create the titling. Betty's cousin Janet, with top-notch computer and artistic skills, quit Intel to join us as our in-house computer expert. We laughingly called ourselves "chip monks" who were converting the Bible to digital video to reach a new generation with God's Word. For our company logo we purposely chose black and gold colors and incorporated the city's name to reflect our commitment to Shoemaker's vision for Pittsburgh "to be as famous for God as it is for steel."[1]

Despite our eagerness and enthusiasm, however, we immediately faced serious problems at almost every point. I hadn't understood the shortcomings of the computer technology we leased and just took people's word that it would work, though what we wanted to accomplish wasn't really clear to them because no one had done anything like it before. As I discovered too late, every frame of uncompressed video had to be loaded into a powerful workstation as a separate file. We had almost three million frames to produce, yet we could load and process only nine hundred a day, thirty seconds total. Any changes or mistakes and we had to process it over again the next day, a pace that would take a dozen years. Clearly, we were headed for disaster—about which I had an unforgettably vivid dream. Enormous volumes of material had to be produced at the detail level of a complex thirty-second commercial. With detours and setbacks, it took two years to finish only four chapters of John's Gospel, at a cost of almost five hundred thousand dollars, half of which was debt with my personal guarantee. I had raised investments, leased expensive workstations at seventy-five thousand dollars each, and then desperately borrowed money I never should have without a certain way to pay it back.

Finally releasing four chapters of John's Gospel in a twenty-five-minute video called *In the Beginning*, we sold three thousand VHS copies and ran out of money. One by one, our staff left. We may have quit, too, except for our commitment to the vision and the fact that we now had investors and owed money we could never repay unless successful. For the next seventeen months, Betty and I drove to our empty office to pray and seek financial help from investors, publishers, ministries, and donors from across the country, with absolutely no interest from any quarter. No one could see the value of what we were doing; it was not God's time. During those months, I often walked from our office to pray by the ruins of old Fort Pitt at the forks of the Ohio. Instigated in part by George Washington and a rash encounter, the bloody conflict started there between the British and French over two centuries before had turned into the first true world war. It had determined the ownership of the continent, and as a direct result, the nature of America's unique future role in world affairs and missions—events I was to learn after 9/11 would prove of great prophetic significance to the endtimes. Praying there, I continually asked God to somehow make a way for His Word to spread from Pittsburgh through the *WatchWORD Bible* around the globe, just as the waters flowed from this meeting of three rivers to the gulf and then into the ocean.

To find something profitable to read during time when I could do nothing else at the office, I scoured our bookshelves for a title. Having often seen Betty's old copy of Martin Luther's *The Bondage of the Will*, I wondered what it was about. John Howe had encouraged Betty to buy it before we met. I joked that her books had come to me as a spiritual dowry. Thinking I finally ought to read a classic by Luther, I took it to the office. Almost overnight it transformed my thinking; my lack of theological clarity vanished entirely for the first time since becoming a Christian. I constantly interrupted Betty with Luther's pithy arguments and my new insights. In his debate with Erasmus about the helplessness of the human will, Luther had written, "You have not worried me with those extraneous issues about the Papacy, purgatory, indulgences and such like—trifles rather than issues . . . You, and you alone, have seen the hinge on which all turns, and aimed for the vital spot."[2] I could hardly believe the wonder of what I read and the forcefulness of Luther's writing. The beauty of the truth I was discovering filled me with joy and enthusiasm that bubbled over into my own creativity. I began writing poetry again, which I hadn't done since high school.

Next I wrote a two-hundred-page manuscript, my first such endeavor since vowing twenty-three years earlier to stop writing until I read the Bible. Now I had something to say. It was a long-form essay about the bondage of the fallen human will to three powers greater than itself. Luther had written eloquently about sin and Satan as two powers greater than the human free will. Reformed teachers, on the other hand, talked almost exclusively about spiritual death and its consequences. Luther's perspective of bondage to sin and Satan was largely missing from their arguments. Yet when all three powers were taken together—sin, Satan, and spiritual death, the hold of these three upon the human will became so much more convincing to me. Under their dominion, we were powerless and unwilling to turn to God unless He first stepped in by His grace to save us and set us free. Had that not been my own experience? But why had I never heard of Luther's argument before? Why had I never been encouraged to read one of the greatest Christian books of all time? The Father of the Reformation had taught the bondage of the human will was the hinge on which the entire event turned, yet in all my studies I had never once heard his key point expressed. Much was made of his five "Solas": *Sola Scriptura, Sola Fide, Sola Gratia, Solus Christus,* and *Soli Deo Gloria*; but here in Luther's own words was *the central issue,* and I had never even heard of it. Of course, I knew the five doctrines of the "tulip" acrostic and *total depravity,* but that abbreviated teaching did not communicate with anywhere near the clarity or forcefulness of Luther's argument.

As if a light had come on, I now possessed a whole new understanding of our fallenness and the absolute nature of God's sovereignty. I could suddenly see through much of the hodgepodge of contradictory teaching I heard in the Church. It seemed to me the vast bulk of Protestantism had slipped back to a pre-Reformation view of the doctrine that was its basis and heart. *Though I couldn't know it at the time, understanding this doctrine would later prove to be essential to my grasping the reality of God's sovereign hand in 9/11 and that event's prophetic significance for the endtimes.*

In the meantime, through months of discouragement and seeking help, the Lord kept us going in countless ways, large and small. We would find groceries on the porch. Mom shared food money from her pension. Our dear friends, the Skebas, replaced our car and faithfully sent monthly gifts. An animator friend paid to use our idle equipment. Others helped us make mortgage payments. Driving to church, we might be running out of gas, but someone at church would slip money into my pocket and we'd make it home. Then, just when we were about to lose our home and the equipment, Betty offered her recently available seminary pension to help hang on. It could pay our various creditors only two more months, but then the tide turned. We received a small grant, and other funds were soon invested or given by friends wanting to help. This turnabout coincided with the release of a revolutionary new video editing system, the four-year development of which had been funded by Bill Gates.

Having learned from our mistakes, I now took no one else's word for anything and did my own technical research. I knew this new Softimage DS editing system would produce more quickly and do all we had needed from the beginning, but it would cost as much as our house. Ironically, we were able to order the system from New York City when the dealer there offered to lease it to us himself personally in spite of our poor credit.

THE FOUR GOSPELS

To reduce expenses, we worked in the house we had moved nine years earlier and hired just two staff. Joyce returned, and her talented son Scott became our editor. As it happened, they both trained in New York City in the very first class offered on the new Softimage system, just two years before we would return to the city for the film festival. When they got back, we began work at an intense pace. We also recorded the narration in Pittsburgh on weekends with Don Wadsworth, a gifted professor of voice at Carnegie-Mellon's world-class drama department. Then Brian Hanson and Grace Kang were commissioned to write the underscore, making financial sacrifices to create hours of inspiring original music, written scene by scene.

Working first thing in the morning until late in the evening, we finally completed producing the four Gospels by spring 1999. Two of them had never been produced before. By then, it had taken more than seven years from when I first envisioned the Bible on video.

During production, the schedule had been so demanding I wondered if I would survive. Prior to beginning each day's work, I needed to select twenty to thirty clips from our database of more than 140,000 shots. I then had to load the appropriate video clips into the computer before the staff arrived. At that point, Scott and I would sit side by side all day creating the right look for each scene. He then worked hours more compositing the text. As it was, even when running out of money, I could raise funds only at night or on weekends. When I told people about our project, they often asked if this was all we did or if it was part-time. They had no idea of the work involved. Betty created storyboards, logged the masters, paid the bills, and did the company administration and paperwork. Joyce edited the narration for pacing, designed the titling, and fixed images in her broadcast paint program. Scott created the video effects, edited the tens of thousands of elements together on the timeline, and selected appropriate music where necessary. But, with our new equipment, we made real progress. When we finally finished the four Gospels in May 1999, I felt a profound sense of peace and accomplishment. If I were to die now at least the Gospels were produced. We hadn't been crazy after all. The Lord had enabled us to come this far. In time I would see just how surely He had led us in undertaking the project. In a year, He would send us to New York City with His warning of an impending judgment; and fourteen months later it would strike.

THE BOOK OF REVELATION

Having exhausted our existing footage library and lacking resources to shoot footage we needed for the book of Acts and the Epistles, I decided to change course. In June I had wrestled with the expensive decision whether or not to upgrade our editing system to access the newest generation of special effects. It proved to be a choice of enormous consequence. Once the upgrade arrived, Scott experimented for two weeks to discover the system's capabilities. Upon seeing his wildly creative sample, I realized we could actually produce *The Book of Revelation* using our current footage with special effects. I had always planned to produce it last, due to its natural place in the New Testament. Its powerful symbolic imagery would also be the most challenging to create, and we would be at our best by the project's end. But, unable to acquire new footage, we couldn't proceed with Acts or the Epistles. Furthermore, with all the talk about the potential Y2K threat in the year 2000, the Millennium seemed an appropriate and providential time to produce *The Book of Revelation*. I even thought releasing this prophetic book at this unique time in history might gain us attention and the support we needed to complete the rest of the Bible.

Though several investors wanted me to stop production and focus on sales to be sure a market existed, I thought if we let our staff go now and paused for marketing, we may never start again. Also, we weren't producing typical standalone "dramatic reenactments," but rather a series of *videobooks* that went together. For that reason, I thought the New Testament stood a far better chance of succeeding as a whole than as four individual videos that might easily get lost in the market and kill the project permanently. Two of the Gospels existed as dramatic reenactments already, but no one had ever produced the entire New Testament. Most of all, I believed the Lord had given me a vision to produce the whole Bible; and as long as we were able, I wanted to complete as much of it as possible. Nonetheless, we still sold twenty-five thousand videos over the next three years with our limited resources.

Deciding to proceed with *The Book of Revelation*, financial constraints led to budgeting just three months for its production. Even that was longer than we could afford. But once underway, I saw it would be a mistake to compromise the quality. Somehow I had to raise more money for a longer production, believing it was the right thing to do and that God would make a way.

It was a huge commitment. The five hundred complex scenes required eight months to create and render. Improvising as we went, we could create only a few each day. It took Brian Hanson ten months to write twenty-two compositions for the underscore. During the months of production, however, we had deeply immersed ourselves in John's sober prophetic message. In this way the Lord had prepared me to hear His warning through a verse in Revelation 18 about an imminent judgment upon New York City and to share it with Scott, Joyce, and Betty before we went to the film festival. Then, with hearts full of heaviness and dread, we premiered *The Book of Revelation* in the media capital of the world at the Millennium. Fourteen months later, with devastating violence, 9/11 struck the city.

14

THREE CONFIRMATIONS

Write the vision and make it plain . . . , that he may run who reads it.

—Habakkuk 2:2 NKJV

UST AS THE LORD gave me *three witnesses* of our warning before
9/11, He provided *three confirmations* after the attack to assure
me of His will and that our mission to New York City was no
coincidence (Deut. 19:15; Matt. 18:16). Like some uncertain Gideon
in need of special guidance, I was greatly encouraged by these three
remarkable signs. In the context of our mission, their distinct *nature,
timing,* and *number* formed an undeniable pattern that could not be
ignored. Through the difficult years ahead, they would bolster my resolve
to write boldly about God's judgment on America and its great prophetic

purpose—despite what others might say or think. If I was wrong about 9/11, why would He provide such striking confirmations that would just mislead me further? Because these three providential confirmations were public knowledge beforehand and couldn't be made up after the fact, I also knew they would help silence skeptics and others believing I simply made up my claims after the attack.

FIRST CONFIRMATION

The Lord's first confirmation came to light immediately after 9/11. It staggered my imagination. Though I wasn't meant to discover this sign until after the attack, the Lord had provided an amazing link *to exactly where it would strike* before it happened.

Waiting for us in the mail upon returning from the film festival in July 2000, we found a letter from Janet Dibble, Betty's cousin who had helped us start the project, offering a copy of *The Dibble Family History*. The fruit of forty years' labor by Betty's mom, Ada Dibble Buckingham, with Janet's diligent help, this three-hundred-page, leather-bound book was soon to be published. Among a list of ten highlights, her letter stated that their early Dutch ancestors had owned property near Wall Street at the founding of Manhattan. We called Janet to order the book and thought nothing more about it. When the *History* arrived, it sat unread on our shelf.

After 9/11, when I first tried to write about our mission to New York in 2000, I sought to include my family's long connection to the city. I wanted to show that in sending us, the Lord had chosen someone to deliver His warning who was a product of the city, with three generations of relationship as further evidence our mission was no accident. I also didn't want to write as some outsider who knew and cared little about the city, but as someone with a deep, loyal attachment. My maternal grandfather, Dean H. Travis, had been a successful banker there on Wall Street. I remember seeing his distinguished-looking picture in the *Wall Street Journal* when I was a boy. Mom had been born in the city in 1923, and though her family moved away when she was a girl, she always considered herself a New Yorker. During World War II, she returned to the city to train at Lenox Hill Hospital, following in the footsteps of her father's sister who had trained there during World War I before dying in the great flu epidemic of 1918–19.

While in New York, my mom, Dolores, met my future dad—she had often told me the story. Having survived the sinking of his ship in the Caribbean, Jim Fitzgerald, a handsome young sailor from Chicago, was stationed at the Brooklyn Naval Yard. Though Mom was already engaged, my dad won her heart with his charm and attention. They soon eloped and married in the Little Church Around the Corner. Her father was furious, but by then it was too late. After the war, Dad attended art school in Sarasota, Florida, where I was born. Then our family returned to Flatbush in New York City. Two years later, we moved out to Levittown, where Mike and I grew up as Yankee fans like Dad, himself an excellent ballplayer. No doubt our world would have continued to orbit around New York had he not gotten into trouble and gone to prison, which led us to leave.

Writing about my New York roots, I thought I should include Betty's brief connection to the city too. As a young woman, she had worked for a year at the American Bible Society. In fact, I recalled that she had been employed there just as construction began on the Twin Towers under Rockefeller leadership. Suddenly, I remembered the story of her early ancestors in the *Family History* and had a surprising thought: Where was the property her family had owned near Wall Street at the city's founding in the 1600s? Had it been anywhere near Ground Zero?

"Betty," I asked, "would you get your family history and look up where your ancestors owned that property near Wall Street?" Though the book had been around a year, we had never opened it. In a moment, Betty was back upstairs. What she read sent shivers down my spine. *At the early founding of New York City, her Dutch ancestors had the lease to what would later become the World Trade Center property.* I was dumbfounded by this fact of providence. Betty's direct ancestor, Dirck Jansen Dey, had acquired a previous portion of adjacent land from its original owners, and then the lease to the Duke's Farm or King's Farm from Governor Andros. Some of their land had remained in the family nearly a hundred years.

One section of her ancestor's extensive landholding had stretched 309 feet on Broadway and 800 feet to the Hudson shore, where Dey Street was named after the family. Part of the street still existed, though most of it had been covered by construction of the Trade Center when Betty worked in the city for the Bible Society. In addition to the fact of her ancestors' ownership, a section of the property had been used for the building of St. Paul's Chapel—the very Episcopal Church that miraculously survived 9/11. Indeed, Trinity Church had used the old Dey lease from Governor Andros in court to prove their later ownership of all this most valuable property. And after George Washington's historic inauguration as the first president of the United States of America, it was to St. Paul's Chapel on this former Dey land that he, John Adams, and members of Congress walked to worship when New York City was our first capital. (It is this St. Paul's Chapel that would figure so prominently in *The Harbinger* by Rabbi Jonathan Cahn, and his application of Isaiah 9:10 to the 9/11 attack and the nine signs mirroring the pattern of God's judgment on an unrepentant Israel.) Standing in the shadow of the falling towers, this small church was spared destruction miraculously by a lone *sycamore tree* cut down that day by a flying steel girder. As Cahn pointed out, one of the symbols of God's judgment that the Israelites refused to recognize was *the sycamores cut down*. I can hardly say how incredible it was for me to learn of this connection to the attack. Due to the famous reference to sycamores in Amos 7:14 and the amazingly relevant connection to 9/11 in Amos 3:6–7, I had already seen this tree as a providential witness to God's particular calling on my life even from childhood. I had grown up in our family home on Sycamore Road. The Lord had called me there to lay my writing down and follow Christ—even as the Twin Towers prepared to open in 1973. For two or three years, I had prayed there over and over that God would "send me," as Isaiah had prayed to be sent—little realizing that he was sent with a word of judgment to his people (Isa. 6:8–11). Then, almost three decades later, the Lord sent us to New York with warning of an imminent judgment whose major symbols would include, of all things, a *sycamore tree*! This was the symbolic tree destroyed on 9/11, and that on land once owned by Betty's first ancestors.

I had sat in awe at what I saw to be the imprint of God's providential hand on this information about Betty's family's direct connection to the Trade Center property. How could it be possible? Believing in the God "who works all things according to the counsel of his will," it was almost too much to comprehend (Eph. 1:11 ESV). The Lord had sent our little team to New York City in 2000 with warning of a surprise attack that took place fourteen months later on land that *her family* had owned at the city's founding more than three hundred years before.

Who could make up such things? They were all a matter of public record. We had shown *The Book of Revelation* in New York City on July 9, 2000. We had photographed the marquee at Madison Square Garden that day. It had publicized my name and our production of *The Book of Revelation*. The notice for *The Dibble Family History* had been waiting in our mail the day we returned from the film festival. Janet had helped Betty's mother with the book for eighteen years and had agonized over it the final five months as if birthing a baby. She had finished the last of the work in June with a sense of urgency, the letter went out in July, and the book was published a few months later, between our premiere and 9/11. When the attack happened in the year after our premiere, it didn't hit just any random part of the city. Ground Zero had been purposely targeted because it was an iconic, world-famous piece of real estate symbolizing our economic power. Now we learned it was the land that had belonged to Betty's family at the start of the city.

Without some direct link to our warning, this connection would be merely an interesting bit of information to share with friends about 9/11. But, in light of *our warning the year before* and *the timing of the notice and publication of this news* after decades of work, I saw it as God's clear confirmation of His hand on our mission before the attack. Why else would He bring such an amazing fact to our attention afterwards when He did?

Furthermore, the Lord could have chosen anyone for this mission. But He had chosen Betty and me, and now we learned that her ancestors had owned the target—in fact, had owned it at the start—centuries before the city had built up its reservoir of judgment (Gen. 15:16). Any lingering doubts I had about a possible coincidence with our mission were swept away. What God had shown me through His Word and providence in July 2000 had been no coincidence, no product of my imagination, no delusion. The Lord *had* sent us to the city to deliver His warning in advance of 9/11. He had just now provided confirmation by means of a most amazing providence. Furthermore, the scope of time involved in this connection showed that the God of history had ordered these events for His own purposes over centuries. Hadn't He clearly demonstrated in this remarkable connection the truth that His judgment on 9/11 was no impulsive act or random occurrence, but one purposed in His foreknowledge even from the city's founding? Hadn't the Revealer of Secrets just shown evidence of His eternal counsels and His immutable decrees (1 Cor. 2:10; Eph. 2:10)?

With sudden clarity, I also saw through these things how the Lord had brought Betty into my life for a purpose far beyond ourselves. We had met almost thirty years before in the church where I grew up. I was from the East and she was from the West. In God's providence, neither of us had ever married, though both were older. Our marriage might have seemed a happenstance, yet here in this extraordinary sign I saw how God had woven our lives together like threads in a great design. He had been weaving this pattern for centuries in special witness to His work.

Our ancestors on both sides had arrived at the founding of the colonies. Two of my mother's direct forebearers, Richard Warren and Francis Cooke, were Pilgrims who sailed into Massachusetts Bay and signed the Mayflower Compact in 1620. Over succeeding generations, her father's family ended up in Cairo, New York, by the Catskill Mountains, where her father married her mother. His banking career took them to New York City. Mom later married my dad there, divorced, remarried in Chicago, and relocated us near Pittsburgh, remarrying again and moving to our stepfather's house on Sycamore Road.

Betty's early relative, Dirck Jansen Dey, appeared in the records of New Amsterdam in the 1640s when he married in the Dutch Reformed Church. His family was among the first few hundred colonists to live in a unique island city standing between Europe and the vast inner continent of America. Dey had been a soldier who obtained more than sixty-three acres of land outside the city wall and became wealthy running the ferry to Staten Island. His great-grandson, Theunis, had later provided headquarters for General Washington and his army in 1780 at his mansion in New Jersey, where Hamilton, Lafayette, Knox, Lee, and Arnold were all present. Theunis's grandson was the mayor of New York City when Washington was inaugurated first president, and Theunis's great-granddaughter would later marry into the Dibble family. Betty's Dibble ancestors had arrived in Massachusetts in 1632 with the Puritan migration. From there the Dibbles moved on to Connecticut, helping the Reverend Thomas Hooker found Hartford; and then, through the centuries of our country's westward expansion, they traveled across its northern tier, first to upper-state New

York, where Charles Dibble married Theunis Dey's great-granddaughter, then on to Michigan, Minnesota, Idaho, and lastly, California.

Betty's father, Philip, had emigrated from France to Canada and into California. His own father had died in Algeria, North Africa, serving as a surgeon with the French Foreign Legion before World War I. His German mother had then smuggled him away to Canada as a baby to escape his father's family. Later, Philip grew up in California, then met Ada at Berkeley, where they studied architecture. They married and had two girls, Katharine and Elizabeth, my future wife.

While praying on Catalina Island after college Betty thought she heard a voice tell her she would be going to Pennsylvania. She left California not long after and got a job with IVCF in Philadelphia, then left that for a job in New York, and after that to work in Costa Rica. She returned to Pennsylvania when John Howe called her to join the staff at our church.

For my part, having broken my engagement after college and later failing to reach California, I returned home to finish writing my novel. Two years later I was converted during a crisis and, shortly after that, made a vow to remain single until the middle of my life so I could grow in faith and devote myself to service. Soon after, I was hired as a janitor at our church, where Betty had just come on staff from Costa Rica. Immediately, we became good friends. Eight years later, at the end of my vow, we married. A decade later, we set out to begin the New Testament project.

Then, after almost twenty years of marriage, the Lord suddenly sent us together with His warning of a surprise attack on New York City. Through His Word and the timely ordering of events, He had led *me* to see what would happen soon. Incredibly, when it took place, it occurred on land that had belonged to *her* ancestors. Clearly, God had brought us together in His perfect time for this work He had ordained. The year I left my tree house, He had brought Betty from Central America to our small town to become my future wife. In time, we would be two witnesses that 9/11 was not a senseless act of terror, but a deliberate divine judgment of immense prophetic significance. Even Betty's birthday seemed to underscore her providential connection to the attack and to testify that she had been born for such a purpose—to deliver God's warning to New York City before an attack the president had called in his diary "the Pearl Harbor of the 21st century."[1] Of all the possible dates, providence had so ordered that her birthday was December 7, the date of the infamous suprise attack on Pearl Harbor. How could things like that be random accidents in light of everything else?

Without question, the remarkable sign of Betty's heritage strengthened me immeasurably. It was one thing for me to express an *opinion* that 9/11 was an act of judgment and a prophetic sign, but I wasn't offering an opinion. I would claim in writing before the world that God had sent us in advance with His warning of an attack that would destroy buildings with fire and smoke and kill many people. Some would be angry. Others would be hurt. Many would refuse to hear it. How could I possibly claim God sent 9/11? How could I know it was punishment for our sins and a warning of the endtimes? I knew most Christians wouldn't accept these things either. Many would reject the concept of God's wrath outright. Others would believe it impossible that He would reveal such a thing through His Word and send warning to a city in advance. But it was all true. The Lord had brought judgment upon New York City through a prophetic attack just as He had led me to see through His Word and the circumstances of providence. While I knew no amount of evidence would convince skeptics, I was now convinced it was God's will that I write what I knew to be the truth, and the evidence of His hand at work would help those with open hearts and ears to hear it.

SECOND CONFIRMATION

Two weeks after our mission, the Lord provided a second confirmation—a sign of *how* the attack would happen, though again I didn't understand it at the time.

Just weeks after we returned from the film festival, as I've written, I fell in a freak accident and broke bones for the first time in my life. Experiencing such a painful, unexpected accident right after our mission made me question if God was punishing me for what I had said and thought about an impending judgment upon New York. Oddly enough, on the same day on the opposite side of the country, Betty's mother fell and broke her ribs too.

However, as I read through Ezekiel just days after 9/11, I came to chapter 4, where the prophet, exiled in Babylon, was told to lie on one side for many days, and then on his other side, as a sign to the Jews of the method God would use to judge Jerusalem. With a flash, I recalled my fall after our premiere. Had it been meant as a witness in my own body of what would soon happen to the towers in New York? I wondered. Had God used my odd flying tumble to serve as a physical sign of His judgment, just as He had done with Ezekiel? The Lord had said to him, "I have made you a sign to the house of Israel" (Ezek. 12:6, 11, 24:24–27 NIV). Having sent us to deliver His warning to New York, had the Lord then used my unexpected fall—and Ada's—to actually confirm to me His imminent judgment and even its method?

Though I couldn't claim with certainty that our two falls were meant to be providential signs of God's method of judgment on 9/11, I could hardly think otherwise. Shortly after our mission to New York City and the publication notice of Ada's *Family History*, with its connection to the Trade Center property, both of us fell and badly hit our sides on the same day. Now reading this passage after the attack, in light of these things, it seemed so unlikely that our two falls—like mirror images of *how* the attack would occur, with two falling towers struck in their sides on the same day—were one more coincidence. I had never broken a bone in my life, even as an active athlete and a motorcycle rider, and was always proud of my agility and balance. Though I'd been angry with myself over the painful, foolish mishap and anxious about the Lord's possible displeasure with me, after reading the passage in Ezekiel I was convinced of God's purpose in the accident. He had spoken to me through His Word about the attack, and was continuing to do so to prepare me to write about it with conviction and credibility. What I had to say would be painful and unpopular. I was further reminded that God had commanded Ezekiel not to fear the people's faces but to faithfully tell His message (Ezek. 2:6, 3:9). He was strengthening my faith for the work ahead and He had much more to teach me.

THIRD CONFIRMATION

Being demonstrably less certain than the first confirmation, the second didn't have its full effect until supported by a third: a concrete, undeniable fact, impossible to make up or dismiss out of hand, that pointed to the *exact day* when the attack would occur, though once again I didn't recognize it before 9/11.

As previously mentioned, we had agreed to produce the Arabic New Testament to air on SAT-7 throughout the Middle East, North Africa, and Europe when I met with their leaders in Beirut, Lebanon, in 2000. This production would be our next project after English and our first adaptation. To help fund this Arabic production and similar projects, we formed a nonprofit organization, WatchWORD Worldwide, several months after 9/11. Then the Lord led us in an amazing way to Ishak, a godly, gifted believer who had emigrated from Egypt to Canada and had dreamed for years of producing Christian programs to air in Egypt. He joined our team in 2002.

It was after a visit to Ishak and his wife, Linda, almost three years later, that I was given the third confirmation. We were eating together at a Greek restaurant when I shared with them how the Lord had spoken to me almost daily after 9/11 through the book of Ezekiel. Linda said she was reading it just then and asked me to send her the passages. When I returned home, I began noting references. When I came to where the Lord told Ezekiel to lie on his side, I was suddenly struck this time by *the sign's duration* (Ezek. 4:4–8). I hadn't reread the passage since 9/11.

"Betty," I yelled, before finishing it, "I'm rereading Ezekiel where God told him to lie on his side for 390 days as a sign of His judgment upon Jerusalem. That's about the time between when I fell and broke my ribs and September 11!"

I hadn't expected the attack to happen as quickly as it did, only fourteen months after our premiere. Now rereading the passage, I questioned if the number of days Ezekiel was to lie on his side could also be related in some way to my fall and 9/11. If so, I thought that could help confirm more conclusively that the accident *had* been a purposeful sign of the impending attack.

But I had called out to Betty before reading ahead and had forgotten that Ezekiel was to lie on his other side forty more days. In a moment, I could see the large first number proved too short to fit my conception, and the numbers combined were too long.

"Maybe not," I yelled back. "There's another forty days. That would be too long."

Together they totaled *430 days*; but having added them, I immediately had another thought. How many days had there been between *our premiere* and 9/11? At first glance, I was surprised to think the duration might actually be approximate. Could it possibly be close enough to mean something? Going to a calendar, I counted the days from our premiere on July 9, 2000, to the attack a year later on September 11. I stared at the number in disbelief. *It was 430 days, to the day!*

Is it really possible? I wondered with amazement. *The Book of Revelation* had premiered in New York City as a publicized event on a particular day. And of course, the date of 9/11 could not be better known. The attack was named after its date, and here the 430 days between our warning to the city and 9/11 matched Ezekiel's sign of warning to the day.

To me, that there were *exactly* 430 days between our warning in New York and the attack was too inconceivable to be yet one more "coincidence," and all the more because I had begun reading Ezekiel the day after 9/11. When I had read about his physical sign then, I wondered about the providential significance of the two simultaneous falls Ada and I experienced after the film festival. I had believed they were an accurate reflection of what had happened to the towers; yet I couldn't say with an absolute certainty that they were in fact a deliberate sign. But seeing now the exact number of 430 days in Ezekiel's sign as between *our warning and the attack,* I was amazed. The same number of days without a context would be a meaningless coincidence. But in light of everything else, there could be no mere coincidence *in the specific nature of our two falls* taken together with *the exact duration of 430 days before God's judgment.* These things now convinced me they were both intentional signs to encourage me further, confirming not only *how* God's judgment would happen, but *exactly when* as well.

Once again, I was incredulous at the Lord's working. He had woven these things together like a seamless garment—in a way that plainly showed His hand at work. He had also answered my prayer from three years earlier about the reason for my painful fall. It was another clear-cut confirmation to support the testimony that He *had* sent us to New York in advance to deliver His warning, and that *9/11 was a judgment of the greatest prophetic significance.*

THREE CONFIRMATIONS

Though I didn't perceive them at the time, the Lord had provided three providential signs between our premiere and 9/11 that formed an amazing pattern: pointing to exactly *where, how, and when* the surprise attack would take place. But I was not meant to see them before 9/11. Who would have listened anyway? What would have changed? But that was not their purpose. Rather, I was to see them after the attack to confirm that *the Lord had spoken to me through His Word and providence before 9/11* and that *He was still speaking to me after the attack*. To me this meant our mission hadn't ended with our premiere in New York City. The Lord wanted people to understand that He had judged us on 9/11, and He had done it in a way to reflect the fall of Babylon. None of this had been my own imagination. What were the odds that we would produce *The Book of Revelation* in its entirety for the first time, that it would be released in New York City at the Millennium—the year before 9/11, that I would tell our staff that God was sending us to warn of a surprise attack on the city "in a single hour" that would reflect Revelation 18 and the fall of Babylon, and that this very thing would happen in New York exactly 430 days later? What were the odds of all these things being mere coincidence piled upon coincidence—to be followed then by three distinct confirmations that in context formed an unmistakable pattern showing *where, how,* and *when* the attack would happen; and that along with everything else, the direct ancestors of one of those sent had originally owned the property that was attacked? It was not possible. I understood instead that the Lord was guiding me and strengthening my resolve to write about His purpose in 9/11 in the face of certain hostility, unbelief, and opposition from countless quarters. While most would dismiss these things, I believed my testimony would help bring repentance and faith to those with ears to hear what God was saying through it.

Yet, year after year the Lord provided me no opportunity and no open door. I burned to share the burden of what He had shown me, but it was impossible. After 9/11, we had to wrap up the New Testament production, design extensive packaging, get products manufactured without financial resources, and then begin marketing. Thankfully, a duplicator extended credit to create tens of thousands of DVDs and VHS tapes. Next, we created a website. Then CBN gave us a major break with a TV program that became an award-winning national infomercial. A media buyer in Phoenix provided funding and airtime. Another company in Virginia took our calls. We handled customer service and pursued other distributors and publishers and attended trade shows.

At the same time, I thought we needed to continue production. While we had our trained team and equipment, I wanted to finish re-creating and upgrading the background video as a base for other major New Testament languages and versions. As a way to help defray the cost, we simultaneously began the Arabic New Testament with an understanding we would receive matching gifts for every $100,000 we raised if we created a nonprofit organization for the purpose. But no sooner did I do this, commission the Arabic narration in Beirut, hire Ishak, and buy the equipment with money we raised, than I was informed the matching funds would not be possible. Now we had to struggle with the additional financial burdens of funding another production on top of marketing, because I had foolishly hurried ahead without a commitment in writing. Entirely confined by these activities, I had no time to even think or write about 9/11.

Nonetheless, despite being told our project would never work and no one would want it, we generated $5 million in sales revenue on our own over fifteen months through a national infomercial. One viewer said her whole town was talking about the *WatchWORD Bible*. Another said it was the subject of daily conversation on her commuter train to Chicago. The media buyer who fronted the money for airtime was surprised by its success. He told me he had learned from it. Marketers had said we should sell just one DVD to get people started. They said no one would order the complete set of twelve DVDs or twenty-four VHS cassettes for such an expensive new product. I disagreed and thought most would want the whole New Testament, and said it was our goal to help them read it. In spite of what the marketers predicted, well over 90 percent ordered the whole New Testament Many bought multiple sets. A few spent thousands of dollars ordering sets for their entire family. Hollywood had never produced a movie people would spend so much to own.

In all this work, we had had to learn two new things for the first time. First was *how to produce a videobook*, which took us a decade. After that, was *how to market a videobook*, which had not been done before either.

In the process, we had spent millions of dollars on production and marketing. Yet, fifteen years after my initial vision, we still weren't in stores and remained a best-kept secret. Furthermore, the funds we made were never quite enough to cover all the work, airtime, inventory, and ongoing productions. At one point our staff had grown to more than fifteen. Even my brother had come to help.

As it was, few knew the stress, frustration, and humiliation we went through year after year. On a personal level, I missed pay much of the time. Betty hadn't been paid in all her years of work. We had been unable to repaint our house since leaving our jobs, and most of the paint had peeled off in ugly strips. When our oven ceased working, we couldn't replace it. Our toilet had to be emptied with a bucket, and we couldn't afford to get it fixed. Many times I told the Lord I couldn't take it any longer and felt like giving up when it seemed impossible to go on. Twice, over the years, our advisors had pressed me to declare bankruptcy, but time and again, by countless acts of deliverance at the last moment, the Lord had made it possible to keep going just when it looked as though there was "no help" for me in God (see Ps. 3:2). Many had given just what was needed when our gas, phone, or electricity was about to be turned off. Several families had donated hundreds of thousands of dollars. Once we were threatened with losing the license to key background video in our production unless we paid $113,000 in back royalties within thirty days. We had been unable to raise the money over several years; how could we do it in thirty days with an ultimatum? But every day I prayed over Psalm 107, that the Lord would deliver us from our distresses. Then, as we prayed in the chapel after service one Sunday, a longtime friend wandered in and asked how things were going. I almost didn't tell her our situation until she said she hated it when people pretended everything was fine. So I told her. When she went home that day, she found a check from her daughter, sitting in her husband's mail, for a mortgage loan twenty years before for $100,000. She and her husband had long since done without the money, so they gave it to us for the bill, and it was paid in full the day it was due. That next Sunday we walked into service late, just as Psalm 107 was being read: ". . . *and he delivered them out of their distresses*"! (NKJV). While producing *The Book of Revelation*, I was praying about our desperate need when Betty came in to say she had just seen one of our close friends passing by and shared our situation. The Dickinsons called back soon after to say they would provide $25,000. The Castors had generously helped us keep our equipment at critical points. After starting the Arabic New Testament project, I was praying urgently after learning that the matching $100,000 wouldn't be coming and the situation was desperate. Later that afternoon, I received a call from the tenant of our former house in Pittsburgh, reporting it had caught fire. The house was ruined and the settlement was more than $99,000, which enabled us to keep going. Still, when things seemed darkest, and I was tempted to think the project had not been God's will, but only a foolish endeavor of my own imagination, what helped me most was remembering the Lord had used our production as His warning to New York before 9/11, and His providential hand had clearly been on the project from its beginning.

However, as the years slipped by, I wrestled with the fact that God had shown me these profound things about 9/11 and its significance for the future, yet I couldn't share it. Trying to make sense of this, I was again encouraged by reading Ezekiel. God had called him to be a watchman, given him a message of warning, and then commanded him not to speak about it: "Go, shut yourself inside your house . . . They will tie [you] with ropes . . . so that you cannot go out among the people." The Lord had added, "I will make your tongue stick to the roof of your mouth so that you will be silent and unable to rebuke them, though they are a rebellious house" (3:24–26 NIV). God had done this to Ezekiel until the time had come for him to speak, and I took instruction from these circumstances that seemed so applicable to my situation. As it was, I was unable to speak effectively about what God had shown me, and I hardly knew what to say when I tried. When I did have the rare opportunity, I was often speechless or sounded ridiculous. When I tried to write, that didn't work either. In my weakness, I would question again, why had the Lord shown me these things if I could not do anything about them (Amos 7:14)?

And who was I that anyone would listen to me anyway? I lacked the typical gifts of most Christian leaders. I wasn't a prominent preacher at a large megachurch. I wasn't a well-known teacher or prophet with an established reputation and following. I didn't lead a major ministry. Except for our production, I was entirely unknown. We were hidden away, working on our project. While I knew God had made me to see and do new things for the first time, most of what I did made no sense to those around me. Though I burned with intensity about 9/11 and what I knew, who would listen or believe what I had to say? I was often so introverted I could hardly speak up in a group unless I knew the people well. Sometimes I felt like an invisible man. On top of all this, we were constantly out of money, making it appear to others that God was not with us.

Yet, despite these things, I genuinely knew in my heart the Lord had called me to fulfill a unique purpose. I wasn't some strange person claiming a private vision about 9/11 out of the blue and after the fact. The Lord had called us to produce the Bible on video. After we finished the Gospels, He led us to produce *The Book of Revelation*. Then He showed me what would happen to New York and sent us there with His warning through our premiere. Then we finished the New Testament the week before 9/11. After that He provided remarkable confirmations. How could I deny the providence of these things? Why would God do such extraordinary things unless He planned for me to communicate them? Surely it wasn't merely for my personal benefit. He had also called and trained me to be a writer.

Then, in May 2006, the Lord made it abundantly clear the time had come to finally tell the story in earnest. It happened in a remarkable way. Based on the success of our infomercial, we signed a three-year retail distribution agreement with a Los Angeles company headed by a former president of Disney and Paramount. Our agreement garnered a small mention in *USA Today*. Though the Los Angeles deal eventually failed, I was suddenly relieved of most of my marketing and sales responsibilities. At last I thought I could devote early mornings, nights, and weekends to writing about 9/11. When I attended the Evangelical Christian Publishers Association Conference in Newport Beach, California, just two days after the deal, I took my laptop so I could immediately start the book on the trip, which included a week with Betty's family. Arriving a day early, I had eagerly looked forward to outlining plans for a long-form essay as soon as we reached our room; but the hotel said the room was not ready due to electrical problems. After having us wait hours in the lobby, the hotel finally offered their only other available room, if we would take it, apologizing profusely because it was in a different building, a tower overlooking the ocean, and *the room number was 911*. Amazed by seeing God's hand of approval on my plans to begin the book on the trip, we gladly took it.

With a sense of His blessing, I finally began writing my testimony about 9/11—nearly five years after the attack—in room 911.

Just as it took us ten years to master producing the Bible *as a videobook*, it took more than ten years to master what I knew about 9/11 and its prophetic purpose. I wouldn't finish the book until more than a decade after the attack. However, while I'd been kept from writing about it as quickly as I wanted, I came to realize that, too, was the Lord's plan (Hab. 2:1–3). I was to write more than a testimony about His warning before 9/11 and my firsthand knowledge of His judgment. I would also write with insights gained from years of study, prayer, and reflection afterwards. Through this ten-year process, the Lord had enabled me to gain practical expertise in New Testament prophecy and eschatology, and their application to history and current events. As a result, I would offer irrefutable evidence—through Scripture, history, and providence—to show *that 9/11 was God's terrible instrument to begin the endtime judgments of the final generation.* In so doing, I would directly address the lack of teaching and misguided teaching so prevalent in the Church about endtimes prophecy. Furthermore, I would write these things when people would be better prepared to receive them—including the shedding of new light on America's unique and hidden biblical role in the endtimes (1 Cor. 14:8).

My sober message about the endtimes became a third of the book. I held back nothing for fear of what others might think—Christians, Muslims, or unbelievers. As Luther said, "Though we be active in the cause, if we are not fighting where the battle is hottest, we are traitors to the cause." In writing about the biblical implications of 9/11 and its role in the endtimes, I am fighting where I see the battle to be hottest. I also understand it puts me in danger. Yet, even playing football as a tall, underweight safety, I had acted this way. Reading plays quickly, I'd rush headlong into the line to tackle bigger opponents, holding on until help arrived. Only now the issues are life, death, and eternity. As I show, I believe Scripture reveals America is destined to fall in this generation, and our loss of power is precisely what will pave the way for an Islamic Antichrist to reign. Though the Church generally fails to recognize where we are in the biblical timeline, and those who do may lack the facts to prove it, I aim to prove beyond a doubt that the final endtime countdown began with God's prophetic judgment on September 11, 2001.

PART 3

15

FINAL GENERATION

I will stand my watch and set myself on the rampart, and watch to see what He will say to me.

—Habakkuk 2:1 NKJV

SCRIPTURE GIVES AMPLE PROOF that the attack on 9/11 was God's great catalyst to begin the endtime judgments of Revelation in the final generation of history, as we know it.

THE BEGINNING OF SORROWS

At the time of our New York premiere in 2000, I believed a prophetic surprise attack would come at some random point within a decade. After 9/11, however, I realized *the timing of an attack of this magnitude in the first year of the New Millennium* must have its own major prophetic significance. That such a stunning and audacious attack, with its unprecedented world-wide visibility and vast repercussions, should happen *when* it did was part of its message. What was God saying by the timing of this momentous prophetic attack? Why did this judgment come so quickly at the start of the New Millennium, surely the final millennium before Christ's return?

Furthermore, I knew it pointed to God's judgment upon the great city of Babylon in the book of Revelation. The Lord is not capricious. I believed He must be speaking through these things. Perhaps it had to do with the nearness of final events. I began to wonder if maybe we had entered into that prophetic season Jesus called just "the beginning of sorrows" (Matt. 24:8 NKJV), and if so, it meant the final generation before His return. These questioning thoughts led me to carefully restudy the Olivet Discourse. There I was amazed to see what appeared to be striking relationships between His teaching and world events (Matt. 24:1–51; Luke 21:5–36). In this teaching, I found five distinct reasons to believe *the time of sorrows* had indeed just begun.

Reason One: Jesus taught the endtime events before His return would be compressed into the period of *a single generation*. He said, "This generation will not pass away, until all these things are accomplished" (Matt. 24:34 WEB). In other words *all* the endtime events prior to His return were to happen during *a single generation*. Without His teaching, we could wonder if they might happen imperceptibly over a much longer period or perhaps much less, but Jesus made it clear. *All* these events would be limited to and occur during a single generation that He called "this generation."

I couldn't see how Jesus, in using the words *this generation*, could mean the generation standing before Him. In its context, the term *this generation* was more related to the events He described than to the disciples listening to Him at that moment. The term closely followed His description of the endtime events, and meant those people who would be living when they happened—"this generation" alive *to see them*. In doing so Jesus was teaching principally about the *duration of these events*. In this way, believers alive at the endtime could recognize the events and prepare accordingly. He could not possibly be teaching about *when* they would happen, because He wisely said in the same passage that even He didn't know "that day and hour" (Matt. 24:36 NKJV). Therefore, how could He have meant His disciples standing there? To think that was to believe Jesus contradicted Himself in the very same conversation. Sadly, even a man as intelligent as Gandhi said he couldn't believe the Gospel in part because of this Scripture. Gandhi thought Jesus claimed He would return during the lifetime of His disciples; but He didn't. Therefore Jesus's teaching was wrong and He wasn't divine. But Gandhi was entirely wrong about the meaning of the passage.

I also knew preterist scholars believe that Jesus's words *this generation* referred only to the generation of those listening to Him when He spoke. They say He was teaching His disciples solely about Jerusalem's destruction in their generation, not about the Second Coming. Yet the disciples distinctly asked Jesus about the destruction of Jerusalem *and* about the end of the world. Jesus then taught about *both* things, and most of what He instructed went well beyond Jerusalem's destruction.

For example, in Matthew 24:27–44, Jesus plainly taught about dramatic events before His glorious return. He described "the sign of the Son of Man" in the sky who would come "on the clouds of heaven" and the angels who "gather together His elect from the four winds." In this context, He even alluded to the fact that "heaven and earth will pass away" (NKJV). That these verses might *also* have a relationship to the destruction of Jerusalem was an instance of Scripture having multilayered meanings, but in these particular verses, Jerusalem's destruction was not primary. It was more than hyperbole. Jesus was describing His Second Coming in the final generation.

In truth, as Jesus taught about both topics in the Olivet Discourse, each had to do with the idea of *a generation*. He taught that *the endtime events would all happen in the future during a single generation*, and He also taught that Jerusalem's total destruction would happen during the lifetime of those listening to Him (Luke 20:20–24). In fact, if Jesus's crucifixion was as early as AD 30, Jerusalem was destroyed no more than forty years later. Its brutal and bloody destruction by Rome was God's punishment upon the Jews for rejecting their own Messiah, as Daniel and Zechariah had long foretold (Dan. 9:26; Zech. 12:10). Daniel had also prophesied the city's destruction as a consequence of this rejection. When it came, it happened *within a generation*, as Jesus taught, a generation in the Bible being typically *forty years*. This was the length of time the Israelites wandered in the wilderness, during which the old generation died away while the new generation arose to conquer Canaan. Therefore, when Jesus taught that *this generation would not pass away before all these things happened*, He was saying that all the events of the endtime will take place within a period of approximately forty years or less, for God *will shorten the time* (Matt. 24:22). These events will require *a process of time* over a period of years; they won't all happen instantaneously or imminently. Many things must happen in this time, but everything that *must* happen will happen in a single generation, as the Lord taught—the final generation before His return. Furthermore, the fact that the destruction of the Temple and the city came within forty years or less gives additional reason to believe that all the endtimes events will also be limited to a single generation.

Reason Two: Jesus taught that this final period of approximately forty years *will* be at hand when "the times of the Gentiles are fulfilled" (Luke 21:24 NKJV). Here our Lord foretold that the Gentiles would control Jerusalem until the time of the end of the world. In fact, the city was already under Roman control and was then trampled to the ground by their legions in AD 70. After that it was controlled by a series of successive Gentile powers until June 7, 1967, when the Jews took it back. This long period was "the time of the Gentiles." What a remarkable prophecy!

As Jesus also foretold, any Jewish survivors of the Roman destruction were taken from Jerusalem as prisoners of war and dispersed to other nations. After this, their descendants didn't return to the land of Israel in significant numbers for almost two millennia. Then a series of events in Europe, beginning with the First Zionist Congress in Basel, Switzerland, culminating with Hitler's Jewish Holocaust during World War II, made it clear these people needed their own homeland once again. Many looked to the ancient prophecies of the Old and New Testaments as their guide for the idea (Ezek. 36:24, 39:27; Zech. 8:7).

Amazingly, Israel regained its statehood in a single day on May 14, 1948, following a UN decree. Nothing like that had ever happened to any other people throughout all recorded history; yet, Scripture had foretold it (Isa. 66:8). The Jewish people would again be in their homeland to play a prophetic role in the endtime (Zech. 12–14). Jewish forces recaptured the rest of Jerusalem in 1967 during the Six-Day War.

Clearly, such prophetic happenings as the return of the Jews to their ancient homeland and Jerusalem's return to their control were signs that the last days were near. Though Gentiles were allowed to oversee the Dome of the Rock, Jesus had foretold that *the time of the Gentiles* would end.

Reason Three: Jesus taught that the generation of His return could be recognized *even as it began.* The Lord said this when the disciples asked about the destruction of Jerusalem and the end of the age. In response Jesus made numerous predictions of things to come. Then He said, "Now when these things begin to happen, look up . . . because your redemption draws near" (Luke 21:28 NKJV). By these words Jesus was teaching that His followers would be able to recognize the time of the final generation at its beginning. If this were not true, why would He say, "When these things *begin* to happen"? It was because they would be discernible *from their beginning.*

Nevertheless, despite Jesus's straightforward statement, many Christians believe it wrong to try to discern the time of the end. They believe that since we can't know *the day* or *the hour* of Christ's return, all analysis of any kind is misleading and a waste of time. Rather than risk being like those who were mistaken in the past, they prefer to ignore the subject of biblical eschatology altogether. Yet many of these same people believe that in AD 70 Jewish Christians escaped the destruction of Jerusalem precisely because they looked to this passage for *timing.* Why, then, do they think we can't also learn from these verses about the timing of Christ's return? Jesus was teaching about both things because the disciples asked about both. In fact, the fulfillment of the first should help us believe for the second.

Furthermore, if Jesus considered it important to teach His disciples specific and concrete truths about the end for inclusion in His Word, shouldn't we consider it important to study and pay careful attention to them? Paul wrote that *all Scripture is inspired and is profitable for teaching* (2 Tim. 3:16). Who are we to think otherwise? We resist heeding clear words of Scripture by overcaution, prejudice, and sloth. Paul also reminded us that these things *will not surprise us like a thief in the night* in the way they will surprise the unbelieving world (1 Thess. 5:2). Though we cannot know the day or the hour of Christ's return, the plain teaching of our Lord and others is that we *can know* and *recognize* the season when it comes.

Reason Four: Jesus taught that the final generation of history would end shortly after the Gospel was preached to the whole world. He said, "And this gospel of the kingdom will be preached in all the world as a witness to all the nations, and then the end will come" (Matt. 24:14 NKJV).

Later, after His resurrection, He commanded His followers *to go and make disciples of all peoples on earth* (Matt. 28:19–20). As I knew from Church history, Christians had worked to varying degrees of success ever since Pentecost to fulfill what the Church called *the Great Commission* (Acts 2:14–41). Now, after almost two thousand years of toil and tears, this glorious goal was actually within reach. Due to major developments in technology and travel, missionary leaders working in organizations like the Lausanne Movement actively strategized about how the Gospel could penetrate every last unreached people group on Earth in this generation.

One example was a vision called the Back to Jerusalem Movement, pursued by the Chinese underground Church. They recognized that the Gospel's advance in history had mainly been a westward movement around the earth. First Jerusalem received the Gospel, then Samaria, then Antioch, and from there, Paul was directed in a westerly direction that took him into Europe. Later, Europe took the Gospel to the Americas and Africa. In the last two centuries it made extensive headway in Asia. Now these Eastern believers sought to complete the Gospel's westward circumnavigation of the globe by evangelizing back to Jerusalem to close the circle in this generation. Another example was the work of Wycliffe Bible Translators, whose goal was to translate the Scriptures into the remaining languages and dialects of the world still without a Bible—perhaps a total of twenty-two hundred. Their prayerful aim was to complete this task by 2025.

Whatever obstacles still remained, Jesus promised that *the gates of hell* could not prevent the successful spread of His Gospel and the building of His Church (Matt. 16:18 KJV). Some from even the world's most resistant peoples were to be in His kingdom, for God had declared He will have a harvest from every tongue, tribe, nation, and people on Earth, including *Muslims, Hindus, Buddhists*, and all others. At last, the Church appeared poised to complete the Great Commission in less than two decades. When it finally happens, the Lord will not be arbitrary. The end will come quickly. In the meantime, the Lord has been patient and long-suffering, awaiting the full number of those who will be saved to come in (Rom. 11: 25; 2 Pet. 3:9). But once the Gospel has circled the globe and done its work, He will draw things rapidly to a close. The Gospel could reach the whole world *in this very generation.*

Reason Five: Jesus taught that the final generation would begin with a series of specific, prophetic events that He referred to as "the beginning of sorrows" (Matt. 24:8 NKJV). He used this term to summarize a future period marked by wars, rumors of wars, famines, pestilence, and earthquakes. After enumerating these signs He gave this warning: "See that you are not troubled; for all these things must come to pass, but the end is not yet" (Matt. 24:6 NKJV). Then Jesus taught that all these events were *just the beginning* of sorrows. In other words, though these dreadful events would be frightening, worse things were yet to come before His return, including the Great Tribulation (Matt. 24:9, 21; Rev. 7:15).

While some Christians equate this time of sorrows with the Tribulation period, as if they were the same thing from a different perspective, I didn't see how that could possibly be true. Jesus went on to describe in the next six verses that the Tribulation period began later with the persecution of believers (Matt. 24:9–14). Therefore, *the beginning of sorrows* couldn't be the Tribulation period, but only that specific series of events *preceding* the Tribulation.

In addition, the phrase Jesus used to describe this tumultuous period was actually a positive one. It spoke of *the initial labor pains* women experienced at the onset of childbirth. By using it, Jesus wanted His followers to know that, despite what things might look like when they happened, God was sovereignly at work for good. Believers were to recognize these events as the beginning of the birth pangs of His eternal kingdom. The pangs would come slowly at first and then gradually increase with frequency and violence to the end. But at last His kingdom would be delivered in all its fullness and glory.

Yet, many have discounted the possibility of ever recognizing this particular period of time as a sign of the end. They say we have always had wars, famine, pestilence, and earthquakes. How would this particular period of time stand out from all other times? But Jesus taught that His followers would be able to recognize this unique season from its very beginning, just as a mother recognizes the first signs of her labor (Luke 21:28).

That was exactly what happened with me in the months after the Lord's judgment on 9/11. As I wrote short pieces about its purpose and prophetic implications, I started wondering if perhaps we had actually entered into that time Jesus called "the beginning of sorrows."

In light of the shock of 9/11, it was easy to consider. Many were saying the world would never be the same again. We were about to begin a long war against a form of radical Islamist terrorism. It was a time of profound sorrow and pain for America and the whole world. In addition to these, *I knew for certain* the attack was God's deliberate judgment and a sign pointing to prophetic events in the endtime. But even so, how could I write with conviction that what Jesus called just "the beginning of sorrows" had truly begun unless I knew it to be a fact? I could make a loose claim, but how could I ever be certain? As I studied the Olivet Discourse, Jesus's description of this time appeared on the surface to be generally vague and immeasurable. One might know it only long after. Then a series of realizations began to sink in.

Neither America nor the world at large that witnessed the event had recognized God's judgment or purpose in 9/11. Neither had either group in any way changed its course of rebellion against Him in response. To me this meant that, as grievous as 9/11 was as a chastening for sin and a call for repentance, a program of more and greater judgments must certainly follow in the future. God had already brought judgment upon us in the attack. And though severe, it had been much less than we deserved in light of our sin and rebellion towards Him. But if our sin had reached such a stage that God was compelled to act in a judgment as severe and shocking as 9/11, what did that mean for the future if we did not take this measured judgment to heart and change our behavior? From our own history, I knew the Civil War had brought an end to slavery, and the destruction of that terrible judgment on our country had been commensurate with our sin. But even after the terrorist attack, we had not ended the grievous sins that led God to judge us in 9/11. Nor was this judgment, severe as it was, anywhere equal to the extent of our national sin of abortion alone. Without repentance, more punishment was surely due and waiting; and because there appeared to be little likelihood of a widespread repentance in the future, *I could see no end to the sorrows to come.* God's judgments would only escalate, with small chance we would learn their painful lessons. I could see no way out of it. We were also embarking on a long war against terrorism that could readily point to "wars and rumors of wars," the first of the sorrows Jesus described (Matt. 24:6 NKJV). Because of the unique and important position our country held among the nations, it seemed to me intuitively that the whole world was embarking upon a season of sorrows of great magnitude and duration from which it could never recover in the foreseeable future. Too, I knew the 9/11 attack was a deliberate judgment associated with the prophetic fall of Babylon, which took place at the end. How could this time not be the season Jesus described?

This was my conclusion after carefully studying Jesus's words on Mount Olivet. With the attack on 9/11, I was convinced we had entered the time He called "the beginning of sorrows," and therefore, the final generation before His return. But then I saw more evidence in Scripture that absolutely amazed me.

BEGINNING THE JUDGMENTS OF REVELATION

If *the time of sorrows* and *the final generation* had truly begun, I thought we must also have entered into the prophetic time the apostle John foresaw in his vision on Patmos—the time of the judgments of the book of Revelation. Again, in a vague sense, I thought this seemed possible. Yet how could I know for certain?

This thought drove me to review Revelation 6:1–8. As I knew so well from our production, the judgments of Revelation began with the verses we call *the four horsemen of the Apocalypse*. Though knowing these descriptions to be famously mystical and symbolic, I was immediately startled by what I found—having just studied Jesus's teaching about the beginning of sorrows. The four horsemen judgments described by John in Revelation 6:1–8 were exactly the same events described by Jesus in Matthew 24:4–8 (KJV). I had never observed the correlation—an observation that equated these two passages and linked them together. What struck me first was the order of events. Jesus and John described the same five things in the same order. Aside from the earthquakes mentioned by Jesus and not by John, these were all human-caused events. Jesus taught of wars and rumors of wars; John began with the first rider winning victories and seeking to win more. Jesus spoke next of nation rising against nation and kingdom against kingdom; John saw a second rider with a great sword removing peace from all the earth. Jesus then said there would be famines; John wrote that a third rider would bring famine. Jesus revealed that pestilence would follow famine; John declared a fourth rider would bring pestilence. Following both passages the next verses described persecution and martyrdom.

Discovering the relationship between these two passages surprised me because I was already convinced we had entered the time of sorrows. If the events outlined on Olivet were the very same as the first judgments in Revelation, this meant we *must* have entered into the season of the apocalyptic judgments—for *the beginning of sorrows* was none other than the riding of *the four horsemen of the Apocalypse.* Additionally, John had received his vision on Patmos around AD 90, two decades after the fall of Jerusalem. By the time John wrote his vision, the city had long since fallen, so he had to be teaching about the end of the world. Therefore, if Jesus and John were describing the same events in their two passages, this also supported that Jesus was teaching on Olivet about more than the future fall of Jerusalem. In addition, in His teaching about the beginning of sorrows, Jesus was speaking specifically of *Gentile nations and their actions,* not about the Jews; and *therefore so was John.* This fact was of key importance. It meant that *the final generation of forty years or less would commence with major Gentile events,* not with Jewish events, not even with the reestablishment of Israel as a nation in 1948, as many had incorrectly believed and were to be later disappointed. Without question, the birth of Israel was a critical precursor, but biblically, the final generation must begin with major Gentile events—*events like 9/11.*

I was amazed by these thoughts. Hadn't the Lord opened my eyes in the same way through His Word and its application to providence before 9/11? This time I was led step-by-step again to see we must have arrived at the season about which Jesus and John both prophesied. No wonder, then, that the Lord had pointedly spoken to New York City through the earnest production of *The Book of Revelation* at the Millennium. No wonder the 9/11 attack had been a sign that profoundly reflected the fall of Babylon. The time had come for the events of John's prophetic vision to actually begin in human history. We had entered into the time of the judgments of Revelation! I could hardly believe it was true, but what else could I think?

Furthermore, if the beginnings of both teachings were identical, I quickly realized their overall durations must be as well—*a single generation.* Jesus had taught this truth on Olivet. This meant that all the judgments found in Revelation, from the four horsemen through the return of Christ, must also be spread in order over the span of a single generation of forty years or so, and not be limited to only a seven-year period that seemed impossible for all the action to occur. According to chapter 6, these judgments would begin with the rider on the white horse setting out to conquer. They would end with the events of Chapter 19 when the Lord returned, riding a white horse, to defeat Antichrist before Jerusalem at the battle of Armageddon.

What I discovered next, however, nearly dumbfounded me. For it was one thing to equate the Apocalypse with the beginning of sorrows in a general theological way. It was quite another to be specific in time and place. If we had actually entered the time of the judgments of the book of Revelation, I thought there had to be at least the possibility for the appearance of the first rider of the Apocalypse on the scene. In addition, if this *was* the final generation, then it meant that all the major players had to be onstage and could now be identified. In the limited time left, there was absolutely no chance that unknown players could arise to play significant roles. Yet, all of this seemed entirely out of the question—until I looked.

16

FIRST HORSEMAN

Then I saw a white horse.   —Revelation 6:2 CEV

C AREFULLY ANALYZING SCRIPTURE AND PROVIDENCE, I was utterly amazed that the first rider of the Apocalypse—who rides a white horse, in search of victory and armed with a bow and wearing a crown—could be seen in the office of *America's president* fighting *the War on Terror*.

Of course, I didn't see this immediately. Despite what I had come to think *theologically*, I was *philosophically* unprepared to see the appearance of the white horse judgment in our time. I had a real problem with my own expectations and perception of our time. Conceptually, I couldn't accept that such an event as the white horse judgment could actually be near or even on the horizon. It was like my inability to perceive the nearness of 9/11 when the Holy Spirit first spoke to me through the Scripture. But here it was, much worse. John's images were fabulously symbolic and extraordinary. I had a hard time believing this storied prophetic event could now be near fulfillment. It was easier to imagine such a thing at some far-off point in the distant future. Besides, wouldn't we already know? How could such a momentous, supernatural, biblical, endtime event pass by unnoticed in our world of 24/7 news? Yet, if I were to claim we had truly entered the times of Revelation, being taken seriously would require me to be specific.

CORROBORATING SCRIPTURES

As I knew from our production, John wrote in quite specific terms about the beginning judgment in God's prophetic program. Now I also knew that Jesus and John described this period in similar ways. Jesus said it would begin with wars and rumors of wars. John wrote it would begin with the rider on the white horse, who went out armed with his bow to conquer and win more victories. Like two witnesses seeing the same event from different vantage points, each served to confirm the other. Taken together, they helped with interpretation as well, providing additional information. John's rich symbolic detail added insight to Jesus's words, and vice versa.

One example of why this double witness was important was that some believe the armed rider on the white horse represents Jesus bringing the Gospel to the world. They see this image as a reflection of Christ riding to victory on His white horse at Armageddon (Rev. 19:11–16). For my part, I always found this interpretation difficult to take seriously. To include Jesus "spreading the Gospel" in the judgments to be poured out at the end did not make sense to me; neither would the news of His ministry be a new prophetic revelation at the opening of the first seal. But, certainly this idea didn't fit with Jesus's own words on Olivet, where He described this event as *a time of war and rumors of war.* Obviously, that did not mean Jesus spreading the Gospel.

At the opposite end of the spectrum, others, based on their reading of Daniel 9:27, teach that the rider on the white horse must be the Antichrist, who comes to make a deceitful peace. But I couldn't believe this either. As John revealed, this rider didn't come with a pen to make peace, but armed with a bow to make war and conquer. They also believe all four horsemen judgments take place within a seven-year period under the reign of the Antichrist. But this scenario seemed impossible. In practical terms alone, the events entailed in the apocalyptic judgments would take far longer than seven years to work out. But here again, Jesus's witness on Olivet provided additional insight.

First, the events of the end would take a whole generation. Jesus also revealed that the beginning of sorrows took place *before* the Tribulation, and therefore, so must the four horsemen judgments. Since Antichrist wouldn't come into full power *until* the Tribulation, this meant the rider of the white horse *had* to be someone else. Finally, since the answer was sealed, how could we know who it was until it was *unsealed* by Christ?

Again I went to review Revelation 6:1–2. Perhaps I would see a clue in John's symbolism to help me understand. In these verses the Lamb opened the first of the seven seals, and one of the four living creatures cried, "Come out!" Immediately *a white horse* appeared. Clearly the color of this horse symbolized the ideas of *conquest* and *victory*. It had long been a custom for kings and generals to ride white horses in their victory parades. Upon conquering Gaul and Britain, Julius Caesar had famously entered Rome astride a magnificent white stallion. Beyond the idea of conquest and victory, I thought that white might also suggest a sense of *goodness* and *rightness* in the rider's cause. Wasn't Washington frequently pictured riding his white horse?

THE WHITE HOUSE

As I analyzed the various aspects and possibilities of this symbolism, an entirely unexpected thought popped into my mind about this image of the white horse and its rider—its application to America and relevance to current events! The symbol of our leadership and power in the world was a building called the *White House*. It was the official residence of the man who held the office of president of the United States of America. For *exactly* two hundred years, this building, named for its color, had been the preeminent symbol representing our nation's executive authority—ever since Jefferson's presidency in 1801. This seat and symbol of our unparalleled power was recognized by multitudes everywhere in the world. Could something this significant be incidental in God's providence as we approached the end of time? Following the collapse of the Soviet Union, we were now the world's first sole superpower since Rome.

Besides possessing great power, the United States was known for its idealism and relative goodness among nations in a fallen world. We had been a refuge and beacon of hope for millions and had rebuilt enemies and brought relief to needy countries and people. No doubt a tough adversary and competitor, the United States was a democratic republic with deep Christian roots that had sometimes struggled with and generally avoided the overt empire building of our European ancestors. (And, where we succumbed to temptation, divine justice brought severe chastisement, with painful defeats and losses at Pearl Harbor, in the Philippines, and in Cuba). We had had many opportunities along the way to keep the spoils of war and didn't. We could have done so after World War II, as Russia did, but we declined. We could have done so with Japan, but declined. We could have seized the Middle East oil fields, too, but didn't, and so on. And now, we were going to war with radical followers of Islam. They were a ruthless, decentralized, intelligent, committed, fanatical enemy. They had attacked our economic center and Pentagon without warning on 9/11. They had used passenger planes filled with innocent civilians as weapons in their jihad against our nation and way of life. In response, the most powerful leader of the most powerful nation on the planet declared we were embarking on a long war that could last twenty years. He called it a *War on Terror*. Any nation or people that supported terrorism would be our enemy. He portrayed this war as a struggle of good versus evil. This man was America's newly inaugurated president, who had recently won a hotly contested election at the Millennium. He occupied the *White* House, perhaps spared possible destruction on 9/11 by the brave passengers on Flight 93.

How could I have overlooked such a string of circumstances? Weren't they amazing? Suddenly, the idea of the white horse riding in our time actually seemed plausible.

PRESIDENT AND COMMANDER IN CHIEF

As Revelation 6:2 revealed, the rider of the white horse carried a *bow* and was given *a crown*. A bow obviously represented *weaponry* and *military might*. In particular, a bow might even symbolize military power exerted from a distance. The bow's great advantage was its ability to shoot at distant targets. A crown stood for *authority* and *victory*. It pointed to the *authority* of a ruler leading an army. This rider received the crown of victory because he had been *victorious*. In context, these victories clearly meant winning local or regionalized conflicts, not the world war that followed in verse 4. He also seeks to "win more" victories (v. 2 CEV).

In every single aspect, these details fit our situation. In the War on Terror, our recently elected president and commander in chief vowed "to lead the world to victory." Those were his words. "To victory" was repeated for emphasis.[1] Before long we were victorious. With unmatched hi-tech, long-range weapons and our allies, we appeared to conquer the Taliban in Afghanistan in a matter of months. It was a rapid, historic victory over a fierce enemy in difficult terrain. Many had believed victory in this rugged nation to be impossible. The once-mighty USSR had been unable to defeat this small country of Afghan warriors over a period of many years. No one in modern history had done it, not even the British at the peak of their global power. Following this first victory, the president soon sought another in Iraq. With overwhelming force and aided by our allies, we appeared to win this second war in weeks. Standing on the deck of the USS *Abraham Lincoln*, the president once again declared *victory*.[2]

America had won two quick victories back-to-back. We did it in unprecedented fashion with our mighty bow. Our long-range weapons and firepower were superior to all the weapons of the rest of the world combined, and the world wondered anxiously about the possibility of war with the other countries the president called the "Axis of Evil."[3] Though becoming bogged down in Iraq, would he seek additional victories before leaving office? North Korea was developing nuclear weapons. Iran continued its support of terror and sought to aggressively develop nuclear weapons in the face of strong Western opposition. Our president stated we could not permit Iran to become a nuclear power. Rumors of war were in the air.

How these things fit the words of Jesus on Olivet and the picture of the white horse rider with his crown and bow! Even our great symbol of the American eagle clutching arrows in its claws fit with the imagery of the first rider and his bow. If such monumental happenings at this unique time in history didn't fulfill the white horse prophecy, I wondered what ever would!

For his perceived recklessness, the president's political opponents referred to him as a "cowboy." His critics blamed him for fighting the war in Iraq, for its slow progress in bringing stability, and for its failures. *Frontline* even produced a special on the War on Terror in 2006 for PBS called *Bush's War.*

And who doubted there would be a war on terror without this president? If his opponents had won either election, the situation would have been vastly different. However, notable providence had put him in power, as I knew because of what the Lord had led me to see in November 2000. I had just returned from shooting footage in the Middle East only days before the election. What God's Spirit had made clear to me then came back to mind and further informed my understanding of this president who could be the rider on the white horse.

Less than one year before 9/11, the president was elected in a most extraordinary way. Despite all the best-laid plans, money, devices, and efforts of both parties, the outcome of the 2000 election was altered by *the decision of one poor mother* to escape Cuba with her son. She drowned bringing Elián Gonzáles to America. In the greatest of tactical blunders, Clinton's attorney general eventually arranged for this little boy to be removed from his family in the dark of night at gunpoint and returned to Cuba. The backlash among Hispanic Democrats in Florida was so great that many immediately changed their registration to the Republican Party. This unlikely switch by numerous Hispanic voters was sufficient to swing the incredibly close presidential election in Florida the other way. As soon as the results in Florida were known, I said to Betty that the difference in the election was Elián Gonzáles.

I had followed this whole affair closely and knew immediately that a relatively small number of disaffected Hispanic voters, so maligned by the press, had actually turned the national election. This was not merely my opinion. Asked months later if the Democrats had lost the election because of his scandal with Monica Lewinsky, President Clinton said no. He said it was because of Elián Gonzáles, shrugging as if to say, *Who could have planned for such a contingency?* Florida was a crucial victory. Though losing the national popular vote, by narrowly winning Florida the Republican candidate won the Electoral College. The Supreme Court had to be called in to confirm that George W. Bush was president.

His election had happened in such an unusual fashion—coming down to Florida and the small Hispanic vote as it did—that it showed God's hand at work in such a clear-cut, measurable way. That's why I was certain providence had put this man in office for its own special purpose (Dan. 2:20–22). Despite his flaws and failings, it was clear the president was a man of courage and determination. Few would have stood firm before the fierce opposition he faced, doing what he believed to be in the country's best interests and for the benefit of the world. In the War on Terror, he used the great power of his office to be a "terror to evildoers" (Rom. 13:3 ESV).

This president was also ridiculed for being an outspoken believer in Jesus Christ. He had been led to faith as a young man by Billy Graham during a family vacation in Maine. Years later, when Bush was governor of Texas, his mother, Barbara, said to him after a Sunday sermon about Moses that God might be calling him to the presidency.

It proved true. He eventually followed in the footsteps of his father, George H. W. Bush, the president who led us during the Persian Gulf War in 1991. A political dynasty, they were the first father/son presidents since the era of the Founding Fathers, John Adams in 1796, our second president, and his son, John Quincy Adams, in 1825, our sixth.

How remarkable all this was to me. In the context of an attack on New York City that pointed to prophecies in the book of Revelation, a Christian president occupied the White House, undertaking a long war against a radical form of Islamist jihadism that coveted world domination in the name of Allah. By his office, he was supremely obligated to resist the spread of this radical brand of Islam that sought to replace Western civilization and its Christian roots with an Islamic faith and rule. Surely, such endeavors would fit the scale and symbolism of the rider on the white horse.

Then I wondered further. In taking a courageous stand against evil, was it possible that this president of the United States—a follower of Jesus Christ—was meant to be *a reflection and sign*, albeit limited and imperfect, of the perfect Lord Jesus coming on a white horse at the end of time to defeat the Antichrist and his forces of darkness (Rev. 19:11–16)? Was such an idea to be seen in the symbolism of this white horse and its rider? Was that why some thought Jesus was the first rider? Was there something *good* about this judgment that was a sign foreshadowing Christ's return in ultimate victory? Was that why this president and his policy were so intensely hated? In fact, one of America's greatest theologians, Jonathan Edwards, had once preached a famous sermon from Ezekiel 19:12 on "strong rods"—those good, strong leaders in government given by God to be to their people "images or resemblances of the Son of God" and who are "their saviors from their enemies."[4] In Revelation 6:8, I saw further evidence for such a *positive view* of this first rider and his judgment. The brief summary that followed the opening of the first four seals included only the second, third, and fourth riders. Any mention of *the first rider's judgment* appeared to be missing from this list of terrible judgments. Did its absence indicate that the first judgment was distinct and different from the others, and not evil in its purpose or outcome, but good, hopeful, and even protective? Had God allowed for this judgment to take place for these reasons, though its goals of widespread freedom and democracy were hopelessly idealistic?

Considering all these things, I wondered, *What could one imagine that would more closely match* all the concrete details of the white horse passage *than what was happening in the world after 9/11?* When would we see the likes of such events in the decades of what could be the final generation? It didn't seem possible. Certainly, we must be witnessing the fulfillment of the first of the four horsemen described in Revelation 6:1–2. Weren't we seeing it in the president of the United States of America, residing in the White House, the seat of American might, and leading the greatest economic, military power on Earth in a War on Terror against Islamic terrorism?

How incredible it seemed that this prophetic judgment described by John more than nineteen hundred years before could actually be happening in our time. Until this point I had never read nor heard any explanation of the rider on the white horse that made plausible sense. Now these thoughts amazed me—the attack on 9/11 had called forth the first horseman! But then I thought, if America's president was truly the first rider of the Apocalypse, beginning the endtimes that Jesus and John both described, then other riders would also have to follow in close order. The first preceded a second, a third, and a fourth. Sure enough, no sooner had I looked carefully in the light of this first rider to see what I could see, than three possible horsemen could be seen upon the horizon, each in waiting with what appeared to be almost inevitable disaster.

17

SECOND HORSEMAN

Then another horse came out. It was fiery red.   —Revelation 6:4 CEV

OHN'S SECOND PROPHECY of *all-out global war* could be fulfilled
by a World War III—a cataclysmic, worldwide conflict early in
the final generation that paved the way for Antichrist.

From Jesus's words on Olivet, and from Revelation 16:12–16 and
19:11–21, it was clear John's picture of this global war could not be Armageddon. That historic battle was to be fought later, at the Lord's return.
Rather, as Scripture taught, the second rider would bring this devastating
world war *during* the beginning of sorrows and *after* the rider on the white
horse (Matt. 24:7; Rev. 6:3–4). In fact, the two judgments were closely

linked. The first would lead in some way to the second, which in turn would prepare the way for the next two.

The second judgment was described at the opening of the second seal by the Lamb. A voice from the four living creatures cried, "Come out!" Immediately, *a fiery red horse* came forth. It was obvious the symbolic color of the second horse represented *war and bloodshed*. But if that were all, there would be little in the color pointing to anything distinctive in human history. War had always been bloody, world war in particular. Fifteen million had died in World War I. More than fifty million perished in World War II. But surveying current circumstances in light of this Scripture, I quickly realized this fiery red color could symbolize more than bloodshed alone. Its cryptic language of *fiery* and *red* might possibly provide clues to the identity of the perpetrator or perpetrators of this world war that would remove *all peace from the earth*.

EVIL POWERS

Just as the color of the second horse had two aspects, I could see two relevant evil powers capable of instigating world war. Even as *white* could symbolize the United States, with its rule of law, free political system, and deep Christian heritage, *red* could point to a powerful ideological evil at the end of the age: *atheistic world communism*. Certainly this evil power could be represented by this symbolic color. The relationship between this evil ideology and the color red was enduring, tracing back to a bloody massacre in the French Revolution. Ever since, communists had proudly called themselves *Red* Communists and *Red* Chinese, and their uniforms have displayed the color to this day as a bloody badge of honor. Could God be speaking to us through the detail of this symbolic color identified so strongly with major *atheistic* powers at the end of time? John's symbol was inspired by the divine mind, knowing the end from the beginning. Was He speaking through this concrete detail?

In addition, the second aspect of color could point to another evil power. The color was described as a *fiery* red. This one-word adjective seemed to purposely speak of more than simple bloodshed, but suggested *eager, violent, even fanatical bloodshed*. The symbolic language might convey something of the nature of the coming war as well, with perhaps the use of *fiery* nuclear weapons. In light of current events, I thought how incredibly relevant these possible implications were. A fanatical, forceful Islam was again resurgent for the first time since its fateful defeat in 1683 at the gates of Vienna. Providentially empowered by oil wealth now at the end of time and animated by religious zeal, its radical leaders were bent on world conquest through jihad in the name of Allah. They were also developing nuclear weapons.

Furthermore, regardless of protests to the contrary, Muslims had used force to conquer enemies and spread the faith from the inception of Islam. Ever since the early seventh century, they had killed resistant "infidels" with fanatical fervor, and this bloody methodology enabled Islam to displace Christianity throughout most of the Middle East, parts of Asia, all of North Africa, and into Europe. Now, fiery Islamist leaders demanded the total capitulation of the Judeo-Christian West to Islam and the imposition of sharia law. To get their way, these radicals resorted to terrorism. And while not the majority, millions of ordinary Muslims around the world had rejoiced on 9/11 to see the blood of infidels shed for Allah's glory by their brothers.

What further amazed me was that the two aspects of the *fiery red horse's* color could be seen matching new alignments in the world. The main practitioners of a *fiery form of Islam* were joining in common purpose with the major practitioners of *Red Communism* in an effort to defeat the West. Though Soviet communism appeared to be a permanently vanquished adversary upon the collapse of the old Soviet Union at the end of the Cold War, a return to dictatorial governance was again under way in Russia. In addition, while many hoped that market influences would ultimately change the nature of China, it wasn't at all certain that would or could happen anytime soon. Worst of all, Iran, the nation at the heart of state-sponsored terrorism, was developing nuclear weapons. Russia and China supported its actions in duplicitous ways and provided material support to its revolutionary government. All these sobering developments fit the symbolism of the rider of the fiery red horse perfectly.

As this passage foretold, the second rider will be given *power to remove all peace* from the earth so that *people should kill one another* (Rev. 6:4). In other words, he will be given sufficient power to start a world war in which people will not just kill each other in limited, localized conflicts; they will kill each other *everywhere*. As it was, the danger of a world war starting in the Middle East was already being widely reported. In fact, some leaders went on record saying that World War III had begun. Biblically speaking, though, I didn't see how that could be true. During the War on Terror, the world remained largely at peace. The prophecy also taught that world war would follow the rider on the white horse. Therefore, I knew these two judgments could not be the same. That they were inextricably linked, however, might explain why some believed the larger war had already begun. But according to Scripture, there would be no doubt when this war took place. It would remove *all peace from the whole world*. If the next world war were not it, I wondered, how many more such wars could Earth survive, given the state of technology? Again, I thought, such facts strongly supported the idea that the red horse judgment pointed to the next world war and not to some other future war, and that this further indicated we had entered the final generation and the judgments of Revelation.

According to John's prophetic vision, whatever peace existed after the white horse exited the stage, it would be shattered in time by the fiery red horse judgment. The whole planet would descend into war. Death and destruction would be everywhere. No place on Earth would be safe, not even America. Yet, the world would never understand or believe this titanic conflict to be the riding of the second horseman of the Apocalypse or the judgment of God that it was. They would recognize it only as *World War III*. With all the world's weapons of mass destruction, such a war would be the fiercest, deadliest war in the long, sad history of our race.

But who exactly would launch this war? I wondered. Would it be the head of a single nation, as in the case of the rider on the white horse, or perhaps the leader of a terrorist group? Would this rider be a Muslim or a communist, or the two together?

EVIL RIDERS

Because the word *fiery* modified the *red* color of the second horse, it seemed this might reveal a shared leadership and responsibility for bringing about world war. In that case, neither party might act entirely on its own. Their actions would support each other. In President Bush's case, Britain's Tony Blair had been our ally in the face of stiff national opposition. Others had also stood with us, like Italy's Berlusconi and Japan's Koizumi. Nonetheless, as everyone knew, America's president had been the leader of the Western allies.

But was it possible to foresee who might personify the second rider or riders?

I had begun considering Osama bin Laden, who founded al-Qaeda with a grand vision to conquer America as the principal obstacle to Islamic dominion of the world. He had started the organization while impoverished and with few remaining followers. He foresaw a world united under sharia law. He then declared war on America in 1996 from a cave in Afghanistan. Only a small number in our government knew of him at the time; fewer had taken him seriously. But bin Laden had the audacity to plan 9/11 as a way to draw America into battle with the Islamic world, a holy war he was sure we wouldn't long endure. It resulted in our War on Terror.

Almost prophetically, bin Laden had referred to Bush's war supporters as ones who were betting on *the weak horse*. By virtue of its sustained commitment to the vision of world conquest, Islam, he implied, was *the strong horse*. An Arab who loved horses and an excellent rider, bin Laden had said people would naturally bet on the strong horse in a race.[1]

His words and actions at the time had made bin Laden a possible candidate for the second rider of the Apocalypse. He had prayed to Allah that he might live to see the world war he hoped to start; yet, I hadn't seen how he could be this rider. Hadn't he served his purpose in energizing the jihadist movement by establishing al-Qaeda and drawing the white horse into battle through the attack on 9/11? In these actions, he had played a crucial role. While his followers might strike our cities with dirty bombs and small nuclear weapons, in what he called an "American Hiroshima,"[2] there would be no state to retaliate against. I thought such attacks seemed unlikely to launch a total war of "nation against nation" that would "take all peace from the earth" (Matt. 24:7; Rev. 6:4 NKJV). For this reason, I hadn't seen how bin Laden could be the second rider. He hadn't been the leader of a state, and lacked the mobility and power that seemed essential to fulfill the role of the second horseman. Then his killing by Navy SEALs in a night raid in Pakistan in 2011 made it conclusive. Bin Laden could never carry out the role of the second rider.

But who else could?

As John revealed, the rider on the fiery red horse would be given "a great sword" sufficient *to remove all peace from the earth* (Rev. 6:4 NKJV). A "great sword," of course, meant a weapon of enormous capability, the use of which would lead to widespread global war—war waged on a massive scale that removes all peace on Earth, what we would call *total war everywhere*. Unlike the bow that could kill from afar, the idea of this great sword, combined with the loss of global peace, could encompass everything from the use of horrifying WMDs, including the possibility of nuclear, chemical, and biological weapons, to grim hand-to-hand combat. Without doubt this great sword and its aftermath would mean death to large armies in the field, countless civilians in cities, and great numbers of people around the globe, even in the United States.

In addition, though John had limited language to describe advanced future weapons systems, it seemed no happenstance that the weapon in his prophecy was *a sword*. If the bow was an appropriate weapon symbol for the rider on the white horse and the United States, it stood to reason the sword in the hands of the second rider might also have further implications. In respect to the history of Islam, hadn't the sword been the weapon of choice to conquer and subdue its enemies? The Islamic cavalries were famous for their use of scimitars in battle. Beheading helpless captives, they demonstrated a disdainful superiority, further terrorizing their foes and adding to the legend of the Muslim warrior's prowess. In fact, the practice was so distinctively Islamic that terrorists were still beheading captives—as they did with journalist Daniel Pearl. As much as the cross was the symbol of Christianity, it could be said Islam's *primary symbol* was the sword. Even now, it is prominently emblazoned upon the modern flag of Saudi Arabia, the birthplace of Islam and home to the pilgrim centers of Mecca and Medina.

If the symbol of a great sword did give actual insight into the identity of the rider of the fiery red horse, I believed three things would have to be true about its identity. It would need to involve a sovereign Islamic state possessing weapons of mass destruction sufficient to start a world war. This state must also have close relationships with communist powers like Russia and China. Finally, it should evidence a likelihood of initiating world war if provided opportunity.

It was readily obvious that one, and only one, such state existed:

Iran. This predominantly Shiite nation—whose state symbol was Allah's name with *a great sword* in the center—had been at the heart of Islamic fundamentalism and state-sponsored terror since the revolution of 1979. Iran was using money from its oil revenues to develop nuclear weapons. It had already been *given* access to nuclear technology by the United States, Pakistan, and Russia. And while the country's large population of young people didn't hate the West, its corrupt leadership had long declared war on us, inciting angry crowds to chant, "Death to America," and vowing to utterly destroy Israel. In fact, Iran's leaders had been on record for decades saying they were willing to see the nation destroyed if it would advance the cause of Islam. Ironically, it was centuries of constant warring between mighty Rome and ancient Persia that so weakened both that it paved the way for Islam's unlikely victories when its armies first burst forth from the deserts of Saudi Arabia.

Furthermore, acting like an Islamic John the Baptist, Iran's President Ahmadinejad had said it was his calling to initiate world war to make way for the coming of Islam's messiah, the *Twelfth Imam*.[3] According to Shiite belief, this Muslim leader had disappeared in the ninth century in order to return after a terrible war at the end of time. After this war, the Twelfth Imam, or Mahdi, would arrive to bring world peace under the iron rule of Islam. Amazingly, the Mahdi that Ahmadinejad looked for clearly fit the Bible's description of Antichrist.

While there had been a great likelihood of US attack on Iran to stop its nuclear development, our commitments in Iraq, combined with misleading intelligence that delayed our action, made it impossible. While Israel threatened to strike Iran preemptively in an effort to destroy its nuclear capabilities, such an attack was not certain to succeed. In the meantime, Iran continued its nuclear program and remained a viable candidate for starting a World War III.

In terms of other possible instigators, I had quickly dismissed President Bush from being one who could begin this world war and be the second rider. John's prophecy taught that the rider of the red horse followed the rider on the white horse. How could they be the same rider? Then the president's two terms were up, and he was gone from power.

Neither did I think the rider of the fiery red horse could be the leaders of communist North Korea, either Kim Jong-il, or later, Kim Jong-un. While they possessed nuclear weapons, these seemed meant to guarantee retention of power and to trade with other regimes. Despite North Korea's frequent threats and acts of brinksmanship, I didn't believe they would risk losing power by initiating a world war that could wipe their country off the map.

Nor did it seem likely that China's Hu Jintao or Wen Jiabao would initiate such a war. China was not yet in position to instigate a successful confrontation with the West. She still had too much to lose in trade and economic development. Nevertheless, she was building a massive nuclear navy that could someday reach our shores with missiles. Her top general thought parity with us might still be a decade or more away.

Neither could Saudi Arabia or Egypt start a confrontation in the near term that could lead to world war. Even if they both fell to radical jihadists, they lacked nuclear technology and would be powerless to start a world war with a "great sword."

Nor did it seem likely to be our tentative ally, Pakistan, where bin Laden had lived in safety for a decade. Perhaps the most dangerous country on the planet, it possessed an arsenal of nuclear weapons. Yet, these weapons had been developed primarily as a deterrent against India. While Pakistan had sold its nuclear technology to rogue states, it didn't appear to have aspirations to start a world war, unless it fell to the likes of the Taliban or al-Qaeda.

However, in Putin of Russia I saw a distinct possibility. The former KGB officer had consolidated great personal power. He had attacked Georgia and sent bombers to Venezuela and battleships to Cuba. It also seemed Russia would undoubtedly be the principal force in the red aspect of the fiery red horse. The Old Bear had long desired property and warm-weather ports in the Middle East. But would Putin and his cohort, Medvedev, start a nuclear world war with the West? They knew they couldn't withstand retaliation without great destruction. Forty years of cold war history had shown this to be true. Unless calculating for American weakness and lack of will, Russia seemed unlikely to initiate a world war by itself, but could be drawn into one with others out of necessity, ambition, or accident.

To my mind, this left only Iran and its leadership with the expressed desire, motivation, and potential *to instigate* a world war in the relative future. Iran's President Ahmadinejad had said he saw himself as preparing the way for the Mahdi by creating circumstances for a world war. On September 17, 2005, he had even shocked diplomats when he ended his first major speech at the UN with a prayer for the Mahdi's return.[4] Later, he claimed to be bathed in green light while he spoke[5] (see 2 Cor. 11:14). Furthermore, Iran was being enabled in its zealous ambitions by communist allies.

Finally, there was another reason to believe Iran could be the most likely instigator of this prophetic world war. In Scripture, it was the angelic prince of Persia who fought with Gabriel when the prophet Daniel fasted and prayed for twenty-one days, seeking revelation for the future of his people. The Lord appeared to Daniel, and the angel Gabriel then revealed the vision of what would happen in the latter days (Dan. 10:1–14). Many believe this revelation of the future went as far as the coming of Antichrist (Dan. 11–12). In light of this prophecy, how very appropriate it was for Iran to play a crucial role in these events, as the place where Daniel had had his vision about the end and where the evil angelic prince of Persia maintained dominion.

If a nuclear Iran did initiate war with the nation of Israel, then Russia and perhaps China would be snared into battle by self-interest. While many teachers believe a coming war would be the Bible's *Gog-Magog war* (Ezek. 38–39), I didn't see how this was possible. If the fiery red horse judgment would prepare the way for the coming of the Antichrist in what were the remaining years of this final generation, how could it be Israel's miraculous long-term victory over its enemies as pictured by Ezekiel? For this reason, I thought his prophecy more likely referred to Armageddon with the defeat of Antichrist and the great deliverance of the Jews at Christ's return. Nonetheless, Israel had to survive this coming war to fulfill its endtime role. Though Iran threatened to wipe the nation from the earth, Scripture taught that God would never allow that to happen. Furthermore, in His providence, the Muslim site of the Dome of the Rock remained in Jerusalem, making that city an undesirable target for an Iranian bomb in a way not true of a secular city, like Tel Aviv.

Now, I believed it was only a matter of time before this prophetic war would begin. It would happen when the Lord Jesus opened the second seal and called forth the fiery red horse. Then its rider would be recognized when he removed *all peace from the earth* with his great sword in this generation. If this rider were the leader of Iran or Russia or the two together, they could be joined by other Islamic nations and their communist allies. As a result, the rest of the nations of Earth would be drawn into a World War III with the certain use of terrible nuclear, biological, and chemical weapons. All that Scripture foretold of such a war seemed possible in our time, and in fact, more than possible—practically inevitable in ways that would leave the world vulnerable to the remaining apocalyptic judgments and coming of the Beast (Matt. 24:7; Rev. 6:4).

18

THIRD AND FOURTH HORSEMEN

Then I saw a black horse . . . Then I saw a pale green horse. —Revelation 6:5, 8 CEV

I̶T WAS NOT DIFFICULT to imagine how the third and fourth horsemen could ride in the wake of a global war in this generation with world-wide *famine* and *pestilence*.

DISRUPTION AND HUNGER

Revelation 6:5–6 revealed that the third horse of the Apocalypse would be the black horse of *famine*. It followed close on the heels of the devastating war brought by the second horseman. This war would lead to massive famine through the widespread destruction of the means of agriculture, the ruination of property, and the breakdown of distribution.

With such problems, one could see that basic foodstuffs would quickly become scarce and too expensive for all but the rich. Modern urbanization would accentuate these problems with millions upon millions of people now congregated in cities. They could no longer grow their own food and would be totally dependent upon others for its timely production and delivery. Brief disruptions and dislocations would cause riots and despair. Population centers would have little patience to bear the stress and strain of hunger. Nations already on the edge could be driven over the brink into mass starvation. Even a hi-tech nation like the United States could be quickly brought to its knees by a single low-altitude nuclear EMP attack over the heartland, creating an electromagnetic pulse that could collapse our entire computerized infrastructure and take years to recover, if at all. Iran and China were known to be working on such technology.

DISEASE AND DEATH

Revelation 6:7–8 taught that the fourth horse would be the pale green horse of *pestilence*. Weakened by war and famine, whole populations would certainly become more vulnerable to diseases. Travel by large numbers during war and the density of populations would also enable diseases to spread more rapidly.

As a result, the extent of human die-off could be more massive than anything the world had ever seen. During the Middle Ages a third of Europe's population had died almost overnight from the Black Death when crusaders returning from the Holy Land brought back the bubonic plague. During World War I, the Spanish flu had claimed 650,000 lives in the United States alone, including my mother's aunt, a young nurse. As much as 5 percent or more of the earth's population may have died worldwide, multiple times more than in the war itself. The worst pandemic in history, this lethal 1918 flu had foreshadowed what could come upon the earth in the apocalyptic judgments. An *avian flu*, it was an extremely contagious virus that perhaps developed in the circumstances of war, spread rapidly, and died away with its victims. This flu virus may have contributed to the nearly simultaneous epidemic of *encephalitis lethargica* that swept through the world in the years 1915–26. My mother's own mother may have died from the debilitating effects of this unusual disease when my mom was just nine, a tragedy that had a profound effect upon her life and mental illness. In doing my research for this book, I learned that two of the three family members in my grandfather's generation, his only sister and his wife, both died from the epidemic diseases created in the crucible of World War I. While serving in the Army, Grandfather had also gotten sick, but survived. Had he died, I wouldn't be here. Strangely, however, if his sister and his wife hadn't both died when they did, then my mother would have never met and married my father, and I wouldn't exist. But by God's grace I do; and by faith in His Word, I know my name was written in the Lamb's book before the foundations of the world (Jer. 1:5; Eph. 1:4; 1 Tim. 1:7; Rev. 21:27).

While modern medical science had made vast progress since these epidemics of World War I, many parts of the world still served as incubators for dangerous contagious diseases. In what was a possible foreshadowing of the pestilence to come, a strain of the avian flu had emerged in China and was slowly making its way around the globe by the migration of birds. In the process of time, it could evolve, transmit to mammals, and become more communicable to humans. Though every effort had been made to contain its spread, what would happen during a world war? Beyond this threat, the gathering of armies and lax moral discipline would lead to increases in sexually transmitted diseases like HIV/AIDS. Already at epidemic levels in Africa, killing millions, it would get worse in Asia and elsewhere. Less deadly sexual diseases (STDs) would spread as well, creating misery and suffering. Even previously defeated diseases, like tuberculosis, were appearing in new, drug-resistant forms that were becoming nearly impossible to treat.

As if all these scenarios weren't bad enough, some of the world's most advanced laboratories had dedicated decades to developing more deadly toxins to serve as bioweapons. Russia, China, and the United States had spent millions to create stores of killer microbes, pathogens, and poisons. During World War III, bioweapons such as weaponized anthrax would likely be released, to untold death and devastation. Able to be delivered inexpensively, such weapons could be spread by terrorist teams. Before the War on Terror, al-Qaeda had set up numerous bases for developing a variety of such weapons in Afghanistan. The knowledge of these things caused me to wonder if the *pale green horse* of pestilence might even point to the purposeful spread of disease in wartime by Islamic terrorists, an action that could continue to wreak havoc long after. As red could be said to be the color of world communism, green was the color of Islam. Ironically, such an outcome would echo the deadly plagues that ravaged Europe after the Crusades. In 2009, an entire cadre of jihadists in Algeria had died experimenting with bubonic plague as a weapon.

Considering the availability of weapons of mass destruction, the speed and ease of modern travel, and the ever-increasing number of large, concentrated population centers and their near-total dependency on outside provision, who could doubt the next global war would be followed by unprecedented famine and pestilence? All of it appeared possible in this generation. If we had already seen the riding of the first of the four horsemen, as I believed, then Scripture taught that these others were imminent, inevitable, and of dreadful consequence to the world.

19

TOLL OF THE FOUR HORSEMEN

They were given power over one fourth of the earth.   —Revelation 6:8 CEV

THE APOSTLE JOHN WROTE that in the devastation brought on by the apocalyptic judgments, *a quarter of the world's entire population would perish* (Rev. 6:8).

In the apostle's summary of these initial judgments, as previously noted, the first rider seemed to be absent from his list, perhaps confirming the positive purpose of the white horse judgment. But without question, the last three riders delivered God's wrath with great effect upon a human race in rebellion to its Maker. While each new judgment offered fresh opportunity for people to repent before the Holy One of heaven, when all was done, war, famine, and pestilence would combine to destroy a quarter of Earth's inhabitants.

Calculating what these numbers might actually mean today, I was stunned. The world's entire population when John wrote on Patmos was at most 120 million. The death of a quarter of these people would have equaled all Soviet losses in World War II—thirty million men, women, and children. But since the apostle's time, the earth's population had exploded and now approached seven billion. The death of a quarter of these human beings would be as many as *1.75 billion people killed in the next world war and its aftermath*. If the Scripture was true, it meant that an enormous number of people were destined to die in a relatively short period at the hands of the last three horsemen of the Apocalypse—far, far beyond anything in all recorded history.

From the time of Christ, *eighteen hundred years* had passed before the global population reached its *first billion*, which had happened about 1800. However, just two hundred years later, the population had swelled to six times that number, reaching *six billion* by the year 2000. Just eleven years later, the earth's population had reached *seven billion* in 2011. This increase of a billion people took little more than *a decade* to accomplish what had previously taken *eighteen centuries*. Beyond this billion, experts projected massive increases to come. Yet, in light of the judgments before us, I thought it seemed unlikely the earth's population would much exceed seven billion people. Lending support to this belief was the fact that *seven* was *the number of completion* in Scripture, as God had rested on the seventh day in the Creation account. For the human population to reach this uniquely symbolic number just as we approached the end of time seemed providential and prophetic in itself. As Scripture taught, Earth's population would decline precipitously after the apocalyptic judgments—falling from perhaps seven billion to just over five billion. In Revelation 9, John foretold that in a later judgment the world would lose a third of the remaining population, once again perhaps 1,750,000,000 people (v. 15). If true, in less than a generation, the earth's population would be cut in half, a season of destruction and human death on a scale beyond even Noah's great flood.

Trying to make sense of such numbers, I reflected again on the 1918 flu epidemic, which is believed to have killed as many as 100 million people. With world populations now four times larger, that number from

1918 could translate to 400 million today, and with the increase of modern travel and high-density urbanization, that number could easily double to 800 million. Global war with weapons of mass destruction followed by famine and other diseases could be seen to double that number to 1,600 million, or 1.6 billion. Even the benefits of modern medicine would break down under the cumulative effects of total world war, famine, and pestilence. Taken together, it was possible to see how these judgments could take the lives of 1.75 billion people in only a few short years. Nevertheless, whatever the actual count, Scripture warned that great numbers would die in the coming apocalyptic judgments. Each of these judgments would begin at the exact hour, day, month, and year that God had purposed. Nothing could or would avert them.

So there they were, the four horsemen judgments feasibly occurring in this generation, commencing with 9/11 as God's catalyst to call out the first rider to fight the War on Terror against a radical Islam. Of this judgment and its significance, I was convinced. If this was true, then, it meant the remaining judgments must also happen in our time. Indeed, as I looked, three other riders could be seen waiting their appointed times: an almost inevitable world war—most likely to be initiated by a nuclear Iran and Russia and their allies—with widespread famine and disease following the conflict. These would also lead to America's permanent loss of power and ultimately the Antichrist. But even as I thought and wrote these things, I knew they had to be subject to confirmation. As John foretold, a global war and its aftermath would destroy a quarter of the earth's population in the final generation. *If this happened in this generation*, then there could be no doubt where we were in history. This would be definitive proof that we had entered the season Jesus called "the beginning of sorrows" (Matt. 24:8 NKJV) and the first four judgments described in Revelation in what was therefore the final generation of His return.

Yet, no sooner had I wrestled with these conclusions in light of prophecy and providence than the Lord led me to what absolutely convinced me where we were in His endtime program. The Holy Spirit opened my eyes to see America's remarkable identity in prophetic Scripture and our connection to the coming of "the lawless one" (2 Thess. 2:8 NIV). Yet, had the Lord not first opened my eyes to see His terrible purpose in 9/11 and its prophetic implications for the endtimes, I never would have seen or believed it.

20

AMERICA'S HIDDEN ROLE IN PROPHECY

You already know what is holding this wicked one back until it is time for him to come.

—2 Thessalonians 2:6 CEV

WITH ITS FOUNDATIONAL CHRISTIAN EUROPEAN HERITAGE, the United States of America could be seen playing a key role in Paul's enigmatic teaching to the Thessalonians about the end *of the restrainer who holds back the lawless one*—who will be Antichrist.

THE RESTRAINER

Along with many, I knew from Revelation 13:7 that the Antichrist would someday gain control over America because this passage taught he would be given *authority over every tribe, tongue, and nation.* Such control would therefore have to include the United States of America, currently the dominant superpower of the world. Clearly, this meant that if the Beast was to rule the world *in this generation,* the United States could not long continue to be the great, powerful republic we had become over the past two centuries. I had already come to see how our full decline from power could be brought about by the apocalyptic judgments, if not before—the signs of our internal moral decay were everywhere about us.

Then, attending a conference in 2007 on "the de-Christianization of Europe," I had a flash of insight into Paul's much misinterpreted passage of Scripture that spoke directly to the coming of Antichrist. This supremely important passage teaching about the endtime was perplexing, for it was purposely specific and vague at the same time. In 2 Thessalonians 2:6–8 (NIV), Paul reminded the Church that "the lawless one" would not be revealed until two prior things occurred. The great falling away from Christian faith, which he called *apostasia* in Greek or *the apostasy,* must take place first. Then, second, the power that *restrained* the coming of the lawless one had to be "taken out of the way" in order for the lawless one to be revealed. It also seemed that these two conditions Paul described were linked together—that the falling away from faith would lead to the loss of power that restrained the lawless one from coming.

My sudden insight into this passage resulted from the information being discussed and explored during the conference: the decline of Christian faith in Europe over the past several centuries; the destructive effects of the radical ideas embraced there since the Enlightenment; the irreversible decline in native populations in all the European countries as a result of their ideas; the rapid growth and influx of Islamic immigrants into Europe with their high birth rates; the almost inevitable dominance of Islam there in the future; and how these same influences and developments were coming to the United States, which had its historic roots in Christian European culture and migration. In the context of these ideas and all that I had written about 9/11 and its prophetic significance, I recalled Paul's teaching to the Thessalonians about the great apostasy and the restrainer of Antichrist, and could see its remarkable application to these historic developments.

As I knew, Bible commentators throughout Church history had

long speculated as to *what* and *who* the restraining power was that kept *the lawless one* at bay. The early fathers believed that Paul referred to the Roman Empire and the emperor. They said that though Paul had told the Thessalonians in person exactly *what* and *who* the restrainer was, he couldn't write openly about Rome's fall or risk being perceived a traitor. For caution's sake, he had to write in veiled terms about Rome's future fall from power. However, when the Roman Empire ceased to exist and the last emperor was deposed in 476, the lawless one hadn't been revealed. How, then, could Paul have meant the Roman Empire, if it ended and the Antichrist didn't appear? Was Paul wrong? Was Scripture in error? Or had Paul meant some other power as the restrainer, such as the Church or the Holy Spirit, as many were now teaching?

During the Reformation, leading Protestants believed that the *Antichrist powers* had appeared—one of them being Islam—and there would be no *individual* Antichrist. Yet, despite their profound expositions of Scripture and the doctrines they so brilliantly applied to every sphere of life, these godly leaders were limited by their vantage point in time when it came to dealing with prophetic eschatology. In a providential precursor to the Reformation, Columbus had discovered the New World only decades earlier, and this would advance the Gospel as well as change the course of history in entirely unknown ways. Hadn't Pastor John Robinson famously counseled the Pilgrims and my own mother's ancestors as they embarked from Plymouth for the New World to be open minded—because "*the Lord had more truth and light yet to break forth out of His holy word*"?[1] While this could not be true of basic Christian doctrine, I knew it *had* to be true of prophetic eschatology, which dealt with the unfolding of events in the future, including nations not yet born. In fact, as I would see, these few poor Pilgrims would play a vital role.

My initial insight at the conference on Europe's de-Christianization was that a vastly transformed Roman Empire did in fact continue after 476. If seen from a broad perspective, it could be truthfully said that *Rome and its great influence* had lived on to this day in Europe and in Western civilization. (As I later learned, even Chesterton, in his *A Short History of England*, disagreed with Gibbon about the Roman Empire's fall: "The Empire did decline, but it did not fall. It remains to this hour.")[2] And, Gibbon himself wrote in the *Decline and Fall of the Roman Empire*: "Nor was the influence of Christianity confined to the period or to the limits of the Roman empire . . . By the industry and zeal of the Europeans, it has been widely diffused to the most distant shores . . . and by means of their colonies has been firmly established from Canada to Chili, in a world unknown to the ancients."[3]

The realization of these things meant to me the idea of the Roman Empire as the identity of *the restrainer of the lawless one* called for fresh consideration. By inference, I knew that Paul had believed *the pagan Roman Empire* would be radically changed from what existed when he wrote to the Thessalonians in his first Epistles. This inspired apostle had clearly foreseen Christianity's future victory over the dominating empire and its emperor. He had written to the early Greek believers about a future apostasy before Christ's return; yet, how could there be an apostasy without first *a widespread faith* to fall away from? I had grasped this insight about Paul's vision for Europe and Rome while in Turkey, near Troas. I had seen that as Alexander had conquered Asia to spread Greek language and culture in the East, Paul had been led in exactly the opposite direction to conquer Greece and the West with the Gospel, being blocked from going east, and then being called in a dream to go to Macedonia on the European continent (Acts 16:6–10). Directed to that place by the Holy Spirit, Paul began a ministry in Philippi that would cause a spiritual earthquake whose tremors eventually shook the whole Roman Empire (Acts 16:16–40). In Thessalonica, Paul and his followers were accused of "turn[ing] the world upside down" (Acts 17:6 NKJV). They did. After a trinity of centuries and ten cruel persecutions, the world's mightiest empire fell to Christianity and became Christian under Emperor Constantine. This Roman emperor was also the one who called the Church's famous Council of Nicea in AD 325.

But the story continued. Just five years later, this same emperor transferred the empire's capital to Constantinople, a city set on seven hills, like Rome, in today's Turkey. No dull, dry history, all of this was God's hand at work. This move to Asia would be extremely important in the future unfolding of His plan. While the empire based in the city of Rome did end in literal terms in 476, having moved its capital the previous century, the empire continued to exist in the East. This Christian empire lasted another one thousand years. During that period, it stood as *a restraining bulwark* for eight long centuries against militant Islamic advance into

Europe, until Constantinople finally fell in 1453. Nevertheless, even that loss was not the end of Rome, per se, for the old empire had been slowly reconstituted in yet another form on the continent.

In God's providence, upon the ruins of the former Western Roman Empire, Europe had gradually built itself a new identity. United by trade, a universal Latin language with its alphabet, and a common Roman Catholic religion, the continent had assumed Rome's mantle, but added the title *Christendom*, in response to Islamic aggression. No wonder God had directed Paul to this critical continent. A once-pagan Europe and its many peoples and nations—from Ireland in the west, to Russia in the east; from Scandinavia in the north, to Italy, Greece, and Spain in the south—were slowly transformed by the Gospel and understood themselves to be Christians. This happened over the course of centuries through the teachings of godly believers like Saint Augustine and countless missionaries, martyrs, and others, in obedience to Matthew 28:19–20. As a result of this transforming process, Christian Europe *resisted* Islam's bloody onslaught on three major occasions—from her west, south, and east. Exactly one hundred years after Muhammad's death, she fended off a great Muslim invasion in 732 at the Battle of Poitiers in France under the leadership of Charles Martel. (His grandson would be crowned *Holy Roman Emperor* in a conscious effort to maintain connection with the former Roman Empire now under Christian faith.) In 1571, Roman Catholic forces sank a vast Turkish fleet attacking off Lepanto in the Mediterranean. Nearly a thousand years after the victory at Poitiers, Europe resisted, yet again, another fierce attack, this by Ottoman Turks who reached the gates of Vienna in 1683. While earlier misguided Crusades had failed to permanently repossess Jerusalem and the Holy Land, they served a greater purpose *in further restraining* the advance of Islam into Europe for centuries. They also helped inspire Columbus to discover the Americas—as a boy in Genoa, he heard the refugees from Constantinople and later wrote of hoping to finance the recapture of Jerusalem with gold from the Indies. As it was, had the Reformation swept all Europe in the 1500s, a young and fractured Protestant front may not have withstood the great Islamic advances; but the Roman Catholic nations united in defense and kept Islam at bay with crucial victories at Lepanto and Vienna. To this end they had been made newly rich and powerful by their post-Columbus conquests in the Caribbean, Mexico, and Central and South America. In stark contrast, providence used the Protestants to plant Reformation theologies and biblical principles of family, freedom, rule of law, and representative government in the northern continent. Planting a line of colonies along the East Coast, they created the foundation for a future free and prosperous United States of America—and an untold expansion of the Gospel to the rest of the world at that very time in history when its population would soon explode (Acts 17:26).

Yet, even as Europe had exported a robust biblical worldview to the west and restrained Islam's encroachment from the east, her own long descent from Christian faith soon began. The seeds of her apostasy were being sown in the minds of intellectuals such as Descartes, Spinoza, Voltaire, Diderot, and Rousseau. Their degenerate ideas were passed on to the likes of Danton, Robespierre, and Marat; then to Marx, Engels, Darwin, Nietzsche, and Freud; and on to Lenin, Stalin, and Hitler, to name but a few of those who led and influenced others from the seventeenth to the twentieth centuries. Over a period of three long centuries, the effects of the Enlightenment slowly conquered a once-Christian Europe. It did so in the name of a skeptical, scientific, secular humanism. Questioning the need for God, it rejected the Church, the historicity of biblical faith, and divine revelation. In their place the Enlightenment deified atheistic Reason.

As a result, Christian Europe, historical home of a civilization deeply shaped by biblical faith, lost its way. Her leading lights became darkness, denying the existence of God, the reality of sin, and Christ's salvation. Instead they set out to create impossible utopias on Earth at terrible cost. The French Revolution was the bloody mother of them all, spreading terror, death, and destruction everywhere, and making way for the Napoleonic Wars, and a century later, two brutal world wars. In the process, Europe's vain ideas had spawned a brood of vipers that grew to be communism, socialism, and fascism, which murdered tens of millions. Now, Europe's new constitution even refused to acknowledge any previous Christian heritage.

THE APOSTASY

It was as I reflected on these things that it suddenly struck me like thunder that in this long collapse of Christian faith in our parent Europe—*former Christendom*—we were actually beholding the fulfillment of *the apostasy* Paul had prophesied nearly two thousand years earlier (2 Thess. 2:3). It wasn't something still to occur at some future point in time, as I had long believed—with a measure of hope for improvement. This great apostasy had been under way in the lands of the former Roman Empire—*Paul's restrainer*—for more than three hundred years. As a result of this apostasy, after centuries of Christianity's spiritual and intellectual dominance, Europe was now yielding itself to the vigorous influx of *Islamic immigration and to Islam itself.* In losing their historic faith, the Europeans had also lost their moral will and ability to respect and maintain their own rich heritage. They could no longer even reproduce themselves, having commenced an irreversible slide of depopulation by native races with their millennia of culture. Too spiritually weak and intellectually confused to resist, the Europeans simply allowed the prolific bearers of Islam to pour over their borders in every direction. Three times in history, Islam had tried and failed to conquer Christian Europe; but this time it seemed *a fait accompli.* With help from the liberal left, the followers of Allah would achieve their goal, perhaps without force of arms, simply by high birth rates and the fact that European Muslim men were importing poor wives from Muslims countries to intentionally breed and bear more Muslims. The price of its apostasy, secular Europe was in the process of falling to Islam, numerically and politically. Ironically, this was happening even as millions of Muslims in closed Islamic countries were having dreams and discovering salvation in Christ, and many living in the West were freely hearing the Gospel for the first time in centuries. Nonetheless, Paul had foretold the future fall of Christianity and the removal of the restrainer prior to the revealing of the lawless one. But while all the lands of the old Roman Empire, both East and West, would once again reunite, it would not be as the former ten provinces reborn under an authoritarian European rule, as many had thought. It would be their reunification under the imposition of Islamic faith and sharia law.

It was at that point I questioned what all this meant with regard to

Europe's historic role as the biblical restrainer of Antichrist. Clearly, that had been fading for three centuries and would soon end. But what did that then say about the United States? Weren't we the world's reigning superpower? Weren't we perceived by the leadership of Iran and al-Qaeda to be the principal barrier to the advance of Islam in the world? How did that fit with Scripture and the idea of a Christian Europe as the restrainer of the lawless one? Was I wrong about its biblical role? Or was the United States connected in some way to Paul's prophecy about the apostasy and the restrainer through our European heritage? Suddenly, the lights came on for me.

Created as we were from former colonies of England, the United States of America were clearly heir to Europe and its legacy. Centuries of mass emigration from that continent, before and after the founding of our country, brought with it European ideas, culture, languages, laws, learning, and most important, religion. Furthermore, going back to Julius Caesar conquering Gaul and Britain before the time of Christ, England and Europe would not be what they were without the Roman Empire and its heritage. As Chesterton wrote, "Britain was directly Roman for fully four hundred years."[4] It was a period equally as long in time as ours since Plymouth Rock. Without these things and Europe's long transformation by the Gospel, we would not have been who we were. In countless ways, the United States was the product of a Christian Europe transplanted.

Providentially isolated on a spacious continent between two great oceans and settled by Europeans within a century of the Reformation, our nation grew up from strong Christian roots, even as Europe fell from its faith. In the course of building our country, millions of Africans, Asians, and Native Americans played critical, essential roles; yet in God's plan and purpose, our country's most foundational influences came from Christian Europe. Our founding documents were products of worldviews brought to these shores by tens of thousands of largely Protestant European believers seeking religious and economic freedom, carrying their large Geneva Bibles with them; and later by ensuing generations of European immigrants. Profoundly Christian in nature and influenced by the first Great Awakening, our Declaration of Independence and our Constitution were imbued with the best of biblical thought and centuries of classical learning and practical European political experience that had produced the Dutch free republics and treasures like the Magna Carta and English common law. Indeed, as the Federalist Papers argued, we had been most influenced by England, the freest of Europe's nations by virtue of its own isolation on an island and its internal union. In God's wise providence, the English Isles had been thrust out on the western edge of the continent—to be the tip of Europe's spear to advance the Gospel and its culture across the seas and around the world. And despite what liberal critics claimed, our knowledgeable founders managed to keep much of the best while largely rejecting the worst of Europe's Enlightenment, Deist, and egalitarian ideas.

With such a rich heritage of faith and culture, America had been uniquely blessed by Providence, and despite its extensive failings, had been a blessing to the world. In thinking of these things, I wondered how we could be any more connected to Europe and its cultural, religious legacy without being there. It made absolute sense that we could be part of Paul's Thessalonians prophecy about the restrainer of the lawless one.

Furthermore, we were now the world's dominant power, just four centuries after the first European colonists had settled on our East Coast. In fact, from its humble beginnings as thirteen small colonies that formed a federal republic after the War for Independence, the United States had become *the first sole superpower since the Roman Empire*. Surely that was significant in God's plan. The symbol of our military might even traced back to the famous eagle of Rome's once-feared legions. Not only that, with our military might we had rescued mother Europe three times during the previous century from the ill effects of her Enlightenment experiments. We fought and helped win two world wars on her soil, wars that weakened Europe and made her vulnerable for the future. With the fall of the Berlin Wall and the collapse of the Soviet Union, we helped defeat communism in the Cold War. Unquestionably, in all these things, the United States had served in the role of "restrainer." In fact we had been the chief restrainer of evil power in the world for a century. In that capacity, however, it was also clear we were certainly the last in a line of powerful *restrainers* that could trace their lineage back to a former pagan Roman Empire that was converted to Christ. Yet, here we were, facing the advance of Islam into the former realms of Christendom, and our liberal elites were pressing us to follow in the path of Europe's spiritual decline. Having embraced the parent's apostasy themselves, they rejected and suppressed the truth about our own Christian heritage and purpose in the world.

At that thought, I grasped the further implication of Paul's prophetic words for America. First, wrote Paul, came *the apostasy*. After that, the restraining power *would be taken out of the way*. With Europe's apostasy, that left only the United States as the last Western power capable of restraining Islam's dominion, and with it, the coming of the lawless one. In a flash, I recalled how this role had been a part of our calling from the start. The founders of our first colonies had envisioned themselves planting a mighty bulwark to preserve and spread the Gospel. After the Revolution, when we lost the protection of Britain's powerful navy, the thirteen states sought a new federal government in part to provide for a national navy. For one, they wanted to defend against possible attack by the Barbary pirates of Islam, then blackmailing our sailing ships for tribute in the Mediterranean, and who they feared could potentially assault our long unprotected coastline. When our new navy and marines later defeated the Barbary pirates at Tripoli, a hundred years of peace and friendship ensued with the Middle East. In World War I, our involvement led to an allied victory that ended the Ottoman Empire, and with it, Islam's ruling caliphate *for the first time since its founding almost thirteen centuries earlier*. After World War II, the United States under Truman was instrumental *in establishing the new state of Israel*—costing us our long popularity and reputation in the Islamic world. In the last two decades, with our allies, we twice defeated the Arab world's strongest army in Iraq. Our soldiers also drove back and contained al-Qaeda and the Taliban in Afghanistan. In all these actions, with great sacrifices of blood and treasure, the United States had served as an instrument to delay the expansion of Islam's totalitarian darkness and the coming of Antichrist (Rom. 13:3–4).

While the Lord advanced His invisible kingdom, He had used our power to providentially serve His larger purpose. Generations of fallible American fighting men, like Washington, Grant, Lee, Pershing, Patton, Eisenhower, Halsey, MacArthur, to Westmoreland, Schwarzkopf, Franks, Petraeus, and millions of others, like my dad, my uncles, and my brother, had fought and purchased peace and time while the Lord built His Church during the period of history's most expansive growth of world missions since the apostles (Matt. 28:16–20; Mark 16:14–15; Luke 24:46–48; Acts 1:7–8; 1 Tim. 2:1–4).

How amazing it was to see God's work in such providence. An unsettled America could never have been a restrainer. An America settled without Christians could never have done it. A weak America that didn't become a union couldn't have done it. An America that remained divided after the Civil War could never have done it. An America that didn't spread across the continent couldn't have done it. The United States had to be a large, strong, moral, productive country to be a restrainer through World War I, World War II, the Cold War, Vietnam, the two Gulf Wars, and Afghanistan. Yet, ultimately, it wasn't about our so-called manifest destiny or exceptionalism. Any concept of America's economic success, military power, or moral character could never be rightly understood apart from God's larger purpose to complete the Great Commission in a fallen world. It was about His purpose as He built His kingdom. He had blessed America for a season to be a blessing to the world, not that she might boast and squander it on herself. Hers was to be a high calling, as the Pilgrims had first perceived.

As a melting pot of many nations and a land of freedom, America had even been a *type* of heaven and the Promised Land in a fallen world. Yet, her exceptionalism would last only as long as it served God's purpose in the world. But what about when America fell from power as a result of its own apostasy? What then? Wouldn't that complete Paul's prophecy about the restrainer being removed before Antichrist? Who could ever take our place with worldview *and* with power in the decades that were left?

THE FALL OF AMERICA

Before 9/11, I had thought it impossible that we could sink anytime soon to the same degree of apostasy and unbelief as in Europe. Christianity was so much a part of the fabric of American life and the foundations of our form of government. We had already resisted Europe's level of falling away for at least two centuries. Though many thought our country's culture war was a modern phenomenon, it traced back to the early 1800s, and influential Americans along the way, like Emerson, Thoreau, Mann, Dewey, Darrow, Sanger, Baldwin, Mencken, O'Hair, and hosts of others. But in spite of their influence, America had maintained a distinctly different attitude to faith than Europe. Even now, almost 90 percent of Americans believed in God.

But after 9/11, knowing of the Lord's purposeful judgment and our lack of repentance in response, I knew we were now a nation under judgment. Our sin had begun to bring the process of punishments that would inevitably break us. The situation seemed reminiscent of principles in Balaam's story in the Bible. He was hired to curse the Israelites in the wilderness after they had escaped slavery in Egypt. Finding it impossible to accomplish his purpose, Balaam counseled Israel's enemies to tempt them into rampant immorality and idolatry. That way, while he couldn't curse them, their sin would lead God to remove His hand of blessing and to punish the Israelites, which He did (Num. 22:5–6, 31:16; 1 Cor. 10:6–8; and Heb. 3:7–18).

Wasn't this just like where we were in America with our ever-increasing sin against God (Rev. 2:14–16)? Looking back in my lifetime, we had had great cause for thanksgiving for the blessings of peace and prosperity that were especially ours after victory in World War II. Yet, just nine years after such great victory, the United States Congress passed a law to muzzle pulpits in America for the first time in history, making it illegal for churches to preach about candidates for political office at the threat of losing their tax exemption. Nine years later, the Supreme Court outlawed both prayer and Bible reading in public schools. A decade later, the Court legalized abortion. With each progressive step, our nation fell further away from God and deeper into rebellion against His holy laws. We had grown so rich and powerful that we no longer saw need to humbly honor the God who had so abundantly blessed our nation. Instead, we chose to ignore the One who promised in His Word to bless those who honored and obeyed Him (1 Sam. 2:30; Prov. 14:34). As a result, the true and living God was now removing His blessing and favor from us. In their place, our country was beginning to experience the Lord's righteous wrath for its sins. As I knew for a fact, this had occurred with great severity on 9/11, and was then repeated not long after, when Hurricane Katrina nearly wiped out an entire American city.

But then I wondered, what about the millions of ordinary citizens who were simply living their lives in peace and quiet? They weren't practicing gross sins of greed, immorality, and violence. On summer Sunday mornings they could be seen out jogging or sitting peacefully on their porches, sipping coffee and reading a paper. But they saw the Lord's Day as just a day off, with no appreciation for its purpose or why they had its benefit. They just took it for granted. Yet, without loving or fearing the Lord who made them, they broke His greatest commandment, and did it in total ignorance of what was coming upon the nation and the world.

And what about the majority of Christians who were blessed to live in the freest and most prosperous nation in history? While lamenting the loss of godly standards, *three quarters* of all professing evangelicals—supposedly the most committed Christians—didn't give so much as a tithe of what they had for God's service. How, then, could a great spiritual war be fought and won when those who were called to supply provision for the battle kept it for themselves?

Even as I wrote these things, America's prosperity and the world's financial system were brought right to the brink of ruin in God's judgment upon us. And it *clearly* was His judgment, because the economic collapse was *directly* connected to 9/11. In attacking our financial center, bin Laden's goal had been to inflict severe damage on our economy. He had believed this would be the best way to undercut our power. However, the vibrancy and vitality of our large economy caused it to rebound quickly after the shock. Yet, responding to 9/11, Alan Greenspan made decisions in the Federal Reserve that economists later said were the critical factor in the subprime meltdown that nearly collapsed the world's financial system. As a result of the banking crisis, as much as 45 percent of the world's total wealth evaporated from the markets in 2008. But in reality, bin Laden had succeeded beyond his wildest imagination in his goal of injuring our economy. It took years, but the cracks in our economic system finally gave way. Yet, even enemies like Chávez and Ahmadinejad hadn't seen the connection with 9/11. They blamed our capitalist system and said it had proved inadequate; but they were wrong. The meddling of Greenspan by lowering interest rates to artificial levels too long; the foolish policies of liberal politicians that promoted home loans to those who couldn't afford them; and the greed of bankers and lenders to profit in this corrupt situation together crashed the system that bin Laden had attacked. But it was 9/11 that led Greenspan to keep the rates too low too long, which precipitated the financial crisis—*and 9/11 was God's judgment.* On that day just nineteen suicidal hijackers collapsed the World Trade Center, which in time helped crash our nation's banking system and others with it.

However, bin Laden and the hijackers were only instruments. The attack on Wall Street was the Lord's wrath at work, and therefore so were the economic crash and consequences that reverberated from it even to this day (see Prov. 1:20–27).

While there was no doubt we had not yet sunk to Europe's level of apostasy, without question I knew we had come under God's continued and increasing judgment for our sins since 9/11. Knowing this to be true and grasping the application of Paul's biblical teaching of our unique role in world history, I now could see with certainty that our condition was not just temporary, with hope for improvement. Our fall was inevitable *and* imminent. It must and would happen to fulfill Paul's critical prophecy connected to the revealing of Antichrist in our day. First came apostasy, and then the powerful restrainer would be removed. As *the last* restrainer in a long line of restrainers who had held the darkness back, the United States had played a great and vital role. But now, as a consequence of its declining faith and obedience, the shining city on a hill, the world's last best hope, the final bastion of Western civilization with sufficient power to hold back unrestrained evil in the world, was about to be "taken out of the way" (2 Thess. 2:7 NKJV). The process had already begun, and as I believed, would soon be accomplished by the consequences of a global war in the years ahead and related judgments to follow. These events would reduce the world's superpower to virtual powerlessness, thereby making way for Antichrist to be revealed.

Of course, with repentance, faith, and moral purpose, the United States could defeat any enemy, including long-term Islamic terrorism, but Scripture taught this would not be the case. America was under judgment, and this was only the beginning. We were destined to fall. Even now we were blind to the realities facing us. We lived in denial about a duplicitous enemy and refused to wake up. We deluded ourselves and underestimated our adversary with its aspirations for world domination. And while the caliphate had been dissolved after the Axis defeat in World War I, this bitter humiliation had never been forgotten. The Islamists would do all in their power to see the reestablishment of this institution, perhaps by the centenary of its loss. They would never rest until they had achieved the promise of a global caliphate. And who could stop them after we fell?

The apostle Paul had foretold these events nearly two thousand years ago when he wrote that *the restraining power* would one day be removed to allow for the revealing of *the lawless one*. As I now saw, this restraining power was first a converted Roman Empire that led to a Christianized Europe that developed into an expanded Western civilization and eventually to the birth of the United States of America, the country Madeline Albright called the "indispensable nation."[5] As the Islamists knew better than we, the United States was the final remaining bulwark of that religious, cultural, political, military identity standing in their way with power to prevent Islam's global agenda. It was so obvious to them. That's why bin Laden and al-Qaeda chose to attack us where and when they did. New York City and Washington were *the gates of the United States of America*, and September 11 was *a symbolic anniversary*. It was the date of *Islam's historic defeat* at the gates of Vienna in 1683, the decisive battle that stopped Islam's advance until our time. But with single-minded purpose, the Islamists did not forget their history. To them the point of this symbolism was that *this time Islam would be successful*. The jihadists believed the United States in its current form would fall following war, just as the once-mighty USSR had done. In their eyes we were a paper tiger with no stomach for a prolonged fight—and their last great obstacle. In time, they believed Islam would prove victorious in the enduring battle fought over fourteen centuries between civilizations. First, Islam had conquered all Roman lands in the Middle East and North Africa that had been Christian, then even Spain; later it conquered the great barrier city of Constantinople; in time all Europe would be taken; and lastly, the United States, that strong muscular child of Europe; and with us would fall the world. There would be nowhere else to go. At some point, America would yield up its precious Constitution, and with it, its form of government so shaped by Christian faith. With the rest of the world, we would also abandon Israel and ultimately succumb to Islam's ambition and sharia law (Rev. 13:7–8).

For me, the key to this picture was knowing the absolute certainty of God's judgment on our nation on 9/11 and its purposeful prophetic connection to Scripture through the book of *Revelation*. If not for this knowledge, I would be hoping against hope we could still turn back and recover our Christian heritage. But as I studied Jesus's Olivet teaching and John's vision of the Apocalypse with the knowledge of God's judgment on 9/11, the mechanisms for the end in this generation came into sharp focus: the War on Terror, the rise of Islam, the jihadist movement, a nuclear Iran, the danger to Israel, the instability of Pakistan, the rising power of Russia and China, and the specter of a World War III, with its dreadful consequences (Matt. 24:6–8; Rev. 6:1–8). Then I saw how the implications of a post-Christian Europe's irreversible depopulation, the rapid expansion of an Islamic population in its midst, and our own growing sin and declining faith all fit Paul's enigmatic prophecy about the coming of the lawless one: *the once-Christian West was being removed from its role as restrainer of the lawless one, and the United States as the last man standing must fall for him to come* (2 Thess. 2:6–8). Here lay the answer to the mystery restrainer of Paul's prophecy. This was the climax to the long, meandering course of world history. Through the lens of Scripture and providence, I could see a vision of the past and the future that was horrific and amazing. The whole scheme of providential history now made sense as never before. Western leadership, with its Christian heritage, will soon end with great and dreadful consequences for the world. The president of the United States will cease to be the most powerful leader on earth, thus leaving a vacuum to be filled. Ironically, it will be removing *the Great Satan*, as the Islamists label America, that will allow the real Satan to finally unleash *the lawless one*—who will be a Muslim, the Caliph or Mahdi of Islam.

21

THE ROLE OF ISLAM

And they worshiped the dragon who had given its authority to the beast.

—Revelation 13:4 CEV

S SCRIPTURE, HISTORY, AND CURRENT EVENTS all testify, Islam will be the enforced world religion of the Antichrist.

SATANIC ORIGIN

Islam has come too far and grown too large over a period of fourteen hundred years during the Christian era to be a mere product of human enterprise and wholly subject to human engineering. In opposition to the dictates of political correctness and multiculturalism, the Bible reveals to us that there is a driving force behind this religion beyond the purely human level. As Paul wrote, "Even if our gospel is veiled, it is veiled to those who are perishing, whose minds the god of this age has blinded" (2 Cor. 4:3–4 NKJV). Tragically, for hundreds of millions of Muslims caught up in its deception, there is a dark, spiritual power behind Islam. This power is what Paul called *the god of this age*, or in other translations, *the god of this world* (KJV). This powerful being has blinded Muslims to the truth. The Allah of Islam is not the triune Yahweh of the Bible known simply by another name. No real god at all, Islam's Allah is none other than the fallen angel, Satan—the devil, the ancient Serpent who deceives the world (Gal. 1:8–9; Rev. 12:9). Claiming to be the angel Gabriel, he appeared in a cave, offering a different gospel than the Gospel of Christ. But again Paul warned, "Satan himself masquerades as an angel of light" (2 Cor. 11:14 NIV), and elsewhere, "Even if we or an angel from heaven should preach a gospel other than the one we preached to you, let him be eternally condemned!" (Gal. 1:8 NIV). How much clearer could these warnings from the Bible be? They describe what happened at Islam's founding with its new revelation. Satan appeared with a powerful deception. But because Satan is the real Allah behind Islam, we can know that he will not yield in his battle against the Lord Jesus until forced to at the end. For this reason, Islam will never change its stripes in these last days. It will not evolve into a more peaceful religion as many wish and seek. The devil, who is both a murderer and a liar, won't permit it (John 8:44). Islam is his tool for ruling the world under the dictatorship of the Beast—the very lawless one of Paul's prophecy. Through the working of Satan in preparation for a worldwide caliphate, Islam will only increase its influence in the years ahead (2 Thess. 2:9). It has already begun this in the popular uprisings sweeping through Islamic nations demanding new governments and sharia law. The fact is, Satan offers Muslims the very same temptation he gave to Jesus in the wilderness: "I will give you all these things if you will bow down and worship me" (Matt. 4:9 ISV). In slavish response to the devil's lying promise of paradise and world conquest, Muslims literally bow to *the god of this world* five times a day in row upon row. His seductive promise to them will be fulfilled for a season in the coming of the Beast, who is Antichrist.

OPPRESSIVE GOVERNMENT

As Revelation 13:11–17 teaches, this Beast will lead *an enforced world religion* in the final generation. The reality is, there is no existing world religious system in our time that allows for such a leader but *Islam*. It is a religion *that demands a system of government* to carry out and enforce the imposition of sharia law. Not just the law of a few radical jihadists, sharia is the law of Saudi Arabia, *the birthplace of Islam and home of its "holy cities."* While jihadists fight for sharia's advancement, the Saudis seek to export this legal system to the world by underwriting mosques and madrassas. It is a system of religious law over all of life that requires active civil enforcement, even in a wealthy country like Saudi Arabia; how much more in a poor, primitive nation like Afghanistan under the Taliban? Furthermore, Islam calls for sharia to be *the law* of the land even in a nation like ours that recognizes freedom of religion to be a God-given right protected by our Constitution's First Amendment. Therefore, when proponents of Islam ask for tolerance in the name of freedom and diversity, it is not only about *religious* tolerance and diversity for them. Islamic *religion* demands Islamic *government* that must replace our Western freedoms and faith with its faith and law. To an honest observer, this situation is not about exercising Islamic religion in a free marketplace of ideas. Once in power, Islam removes all such freedom for others—by force of law—and requires submission to its requirements. By demanding that Islam alone be the dominant and exclusive religion and political system wherever it is practiced, it becomes entirely incompatible with our Constitution and form of government.

An example of Islamic duplicity to gain its way is seen in the mosque project by Ground Zero. When the promoter called for tolerance, claiming its purpose was to build bridges of understanding between communities and religions, he was being insincere to gain an edge. While he talked about getting along, this imam was actually a proponent *in writing* of sharia law being the rule in America, which would thereby end our freedoms of speech and religion. This man knew full well that his controversial mosque project sent a triple message to Islamists around the world: (1) *By planning to open this particular mosque on the anniversary of 9/11*, it recalls the anniversary of Islam's historic defeat on that date at the gates of Vienna—which halted Islamic advance for three centuries. At the same time, it celebrates the triumph of destruction in New York City on that date, thus announcing Islam's battle with the West is rejoined in earnest. (2) *By building this large mosque near Ground Zero, where the towers fell,* Islam demonstrates it is now inside our gates and this time it is only a matter of time before it will conquer. 3) *By calling this mosque Cordoba,* it is a reminder of Islam's former conquest of Spain—which it controlled seven hundred years—and is a symbol of its future victory in America. These messages are meant to encourage Muslim faithful worldwide that America will soon fall to Islamic advance.

The truth is, Islam was a militant religion for a thousand years, and *ceased its expansions by conquest only when defeated militarily by the West.* Now, enriched and empowered by oil wealth at the end of time, the followers of Allah are once again in position to spread their religion by overt and covert means. Despite its protestations otherwise, and the best intentions of moderates, Islam's single-minded intent since its seventh-century founding has been to see the whole world under Allah's religion and government. This is a fact of history. It will also be the agenda of Antichrist (Rev. 13:7). From the jihadists' point of view, all that is lacking for the masses to embrace Islam is for America's fall to be followed by the power and unity of a worldwide caliphate with a single leader to enforce it—as the Bible foretells. The so-called Arab Spring uprisings have helped prepare the way by bringing critical Arab nations into the Islamist camp. When one considers that *2032 will be the fourteenth-century anniversary of Muhammad's death and the founding of the original caliphate,* who can doubt that the followers of Islam will pull out every stop to celebrate this milestone in a worldwide, grand finale of fanatical adulation of Allah and his prophet? What a time for Antichrist! This fourteen-hundred-year anniversary will even echo the triple fourteen generations of Jesus's genealogy in Matthew's Gospel (1:17).

UNIQUE RELIGION

But for those who think the endtime religion of the Beast is not Islam, how likely is it at this late date that a leader can arise to found a new world religion that is like Islam, but is not Islam, and will be worse? It is implausible. It is also why the Beast's religion cannot be a peaceful amalgamation of Christians, Jews, Hindus, Buddhists, Sikhs, Shintoists, New Agers, and others, *along* with Islam in some *new generic religion*. Islamists will never allow such a thing without unending struggle. Not just one religion among many, Islam by its own doctrine must reign supreme over all. It is also the only religion ever to replace Christianity in any region where the faith was previously established, setting precedent for the future.

In addition, as the only major world religion founded *after* the New Testament revelation, Islam denies Christ's deity not merely out of prior ignorance, as others do, but with clear intent. Islam adamantly and specifically declares that *Allah has no son*. It's true the devil has no son, but the Bible reveals that *God the Father does—He is the eternally begotten Son, Jesus Christ our Savior*. Thus, Islam by its very doctrine is *antichrist in spirit* because it denies Jesus's divinity absolutely. Furthermore, John wrote, such a *one who denies the Son also denies the Father*, and "no one who denies the Son has the Father" (1 John 2:22–23 NIV). Jesus Himself said that "he who does not honor the Son does not honor the Father" (John 5:23 NKJV). He also said that *he who hates Him hates His Father as well* (John 15:23).

In light of such clear biblical teachings, how can anyone ever say the followers of Islam worship the true God of the Bible? How, indeed, can Muslims be saved by following Islam and worshipping Allah? They seek to earn their way to heaven by their works, while lacking an adequate conception of the infinitely just and righteous God who abhors even the smallest sin—but who sent His only Son to die on the cross for the salvation of sinners, whom He loves unconditionally. As difficult as it is to say these things, what good is it to hide the truth to spare the feelings of sincere Muslims when it will only lead to their eternal damnation and destruction? More than 1.5 billion adherents are now caught up in darkness, more than the population of China or India, and its numbers grow arithmetically as we approach the end and the time of the Beast. Real love would tell them the truth. May God help us to win them by His grace in every possible way while we yet have time. Sadly, many prominent Christian leaders at this key time in history have now been led to agree with Muslims that we both worship one God who is the same God. But the Allah that Muslims serve is an impostor whose antichrist teaching is at the heart of the religion that is destined to rule the world.

This turn of events is especially remarkable given that God promised Abraham that he and his offspring were *to be heirs of the world* (Rom. 4:13). While this singular promise was to be claimed by faith through Isaac's line, Ishmael's descendants apparently never forgot this promise of world dominion. Because they claim Ishmael was the chosen son of Abraham, they take it for their own, intending to accomplish the promise by deceit and force. And while God also promised that all the families of the world would be blessed through Isaac's future descendant, who is Jesus Christ, it can be said that the whole world will be cursed by Antichrist and Islam's counterfeit promise (Gen. 3:8–9, 12:1–3, 17:18–21, 21:17–18, 22:18). Though "salvation is of the Jews" (John 4:22 NKJV), Islam will be the final religion and government controlling the world. Therefore, what an amazing irony it is that human history should be coming down to the very conclusion that most highlights the ultimate importance of the salvation drama.

Yet, it seems so fitting in light of God's gracious promises to Abraham: all human history, with all its twists and turns, is coming down to *the age-old struggle between his two sons and their spiritual descendents*—with Ishmael's line and Islam winning the apparent victory before Christ returns (Gal. 4:22–29; Matt. 4:8–9). Islam's helper in this fight will be atheistic communism, duped into battle by its own dreams of world dominion. Yet, atheistic communism can never fulfill the endtime prophecy of an enforced world religion by its very nature: communism is anti-God. But Islam is anti-Christ. Islam will be the religion of the Beast.

THE REIGN OF ANTICHRIST

The beast was worshiped by everyone whose name wasn't written before the time of creation in the book of the Lamb who was killed.

—Revelation 13:8 CEV

B EFORE THE RETURN OF CHRIST, the whole world will be unified under a single authoritative religious leader—a powerful, charismatic Muslim who will be the Mahdi or Caliph of Islam (Rev. 13:7–8).

GROOMED IN PREPARATION

Within months of 9/11, I had come to the startling conclusion that the Antichrist could already be alive. It was in January 2002 when Betty and I were in New York City to meet with leaders at ABS to discuss our completed New Testament production. Arriving a day early on Sunday, we walked to Ground Zero in the afternoon and saw the massive empty space where the Trade Center towers once stood, what still remained of Dey Street, and the fenced-in grounds of St. Paul's Chapel guarded by police. After that we drove to see the old Dey Mansion in New Jersey, where an assassin's blood still stained the floor from a failed attempt on Washington's life and where Benedict Arnold had betrayed him. Later that night, as I prayed in our hotel room, the thought suddenly occurred to me that if we had entered into the time of the beginning of sorrows, and thus the final generation of forty years or less that Jesus foretold, then the Antichrist could soon be born or already living as a young boy to be of age at the proper time. It did not seem likely to me then that he would be an older man when revealed to the world. Such a leader could not long be anyone's understudy. When he made his appearance, he would have to be old enough to lead, and he would be on the world stage for a total of just seven years, ruling as the Beast for the last forty-two months (Rev. 13:5). This happened well before I had any understanding of the role of Islam, the caliphate, or the Mahdi; but that night I had wondered vaguely for the first time if the Antichrist could perhaps be Islamic and already alive somewhere in the Middle East or Europe.

That's why I wasn't surprised when I learned that many Shiites believe the Mahdi is already alive on Earth, and waiting to be revealed. Iran's President Ahmadinejad even claims to have communicated with him. He may have believed this Muslim messiah was Osama bin Laden before his death, or perhaps that Osama's youngest son, Hamza, is the one. Born in 1991, Hamza was nicknamed the "crown prince of terror" while in his teens.[1] Shortly before her assassination in Pakistan, Benazir Bhutto wrote that this Hamza was leading a hit team to kill her.[2] A potential heir to the leadership of al-Qaeda, Hamza is the only child of bin Laden's Saudi wife, herself descended directly from the prophet Muhammad. But it was in relation to the possible identity of the Antichrist that I thought this fact was important: the prophet was to have said the Mahdi would be a direct descendent of his line, which Hamza is through his mother. According to hadith, Muhammad also specified the Mahdi's army *would come riding out of central Asia into Khorasan*, an ancient region that incorporates northern

Iran and modern Afghanistan, and it borders on Pakistan in central Asia. In addition to all this, Pakistan's mountainous tribal region was one of the most *lawless provinces* on Earth, and would be an ideal incubator for the future *lawless one*. As it happened, when bin Laden was killed by U.S. Navy SEALs, he was found hiding in Pakistan. However, his son Hamza apparently still lives. Beyond this, Hamza himself had a little son of two or three who is also of Muhammad's line through him. In twenty years' time, this little one could be the age of Alexander the Great when he began his campaign to conquer Asia and the world. His name is also Osama bin Laden.

RULING FOR A SEASON

Whoever the *lawless one* proves to be, we can only speculate. But we can be certain that when he comes he will be well prepared for his role by religion, charisma, aptitude, commitment, reputation, and training. He may even have a unique genealogy that traces back to Ishmael and Abraham, perhaps fulfilling ancient promises to Hagar with their echoes of the real Messiah (Gen. 16:9–12). In his role as the Mahdi or Caliph, however, the Antichrist will be a true child of Satan, possessed and directed by the devil, and the whole world will come under his control (2 Thess. 2:9–10; Rev. 13:2–8). At that time, *the lawless one* will even change the dates and the keeping of time (Dan. 7:25). The Gregorian calendar of the West, descended from the Roman calendar of Julius Caesar, will be replaced with the Islamic calendar and dates; and the keeping of time will no longer be done at Greenwich, but in Mecca, where even now the construction of a great clock is under way. The lawless one will also remove the ancient landmarks of Western jurisprudence, but not replace them with a total lack of law, such as license or anarchy. He will substitute Islamic sharia, the law of evil codified, justified, and imposed, which approves and excuses murder, rape, abuse, torture, theft, idolatry, and covetousness by circumstance, and extends horrible punishments upon the guilty, as well as death to Christians, Jews, and the courageous Muslims who convert to Christ to save their souls.

As Scripture teaches, this Beast will win over the world by imitating the resurrection of Christ (Rev. 13:3–4, 12; 17:10–11). Supporting his claim to supernatural power and authority, he will miraculously recover from a mortal head wound, perhaps augmented by a chip implanted with artificial super-computer-level intelligence that futurists say will be capable of application in our lifetimes. After his recovery, no one will be able to withstand him. The Beast will quickly sweep aside opposition, controlling the world in Allah's name with brute sheer force (Rev. 13:7–8).

The Bible reveals that this Beast and his False Prophet will demand the world's allegiance and worship for three and a half years (Rev. 13:5, 19:20). The False Prophet, a leader in the Christian Church with *two horns like a lamb*, perhaps even claiming to be Jesus Christ, will work deceptive miracles and promote Islam as the true religion, and those who won't bow will be denied the right to buy and sell. Many will be killed (Rev. 13:11–17). Yet as quickly as the Beast's reign of terror begins, it will end. This Islamic ruler will meet his Almighty Maker in Israel, as Scripture has long foretold of his destruction (Zech. 14:3–5). At that time many Jews will recognize their Messiah, whom they pierced, and will be saved (Zech. 12:8–10). But the Beast, his False Prophet, and those with them will be defeated before the gates of Jerusalem by the true King of kings and Lord of lords—whose eyes burn like fire and whose tongue is a mighty sword—when He comes in glory with all His holy angels (Rev. 19:12–15; 2 Thess. 1:7).

On that great day, when the Lord Jesus returns on His strong white horse followed by the armies of heaven, He will capture the Beast and kill his followers with the sword of His mouth (2 Thess. 1:7–10; Rev. 19:19–21). Then the Lord will cast the Beast into the lake of fire, where he will suffer eternal judgment and destruction with all who had prefigured him in history: beasts like Nimrod, Pharaoh, Sennacherib, and Antiochus in the Bible; others like Attila, Genghis Khan, and Tamerlane who came later; and Lenin, Stalin, Hitler, Mao, and bin Laden in these last days, to name but a few. In that awful place of torment, Allah's Antichrist and his false prophet will suffer punishment forever with Satan, his angels, and all the lost (Ps. 52:5).

23

LIKE A JONAH

Yet forty days, and Nineveh shall be overthrown!　　　　　　　—Jonah 3:4 ESV

NOW I CRY LIKE A JONAH of the endtimes: "*Yet forty years, and the end will come!*"

Echoing Jonah's forty days of warning to Nineveh, this forty-year period is the length of a biblical generation that began with 9/11 (see Matt. 24:32–34). In our case, more than a decade has passed since it started, and the time may be shorter still, as these forty years are only meant to be symbolic. Nevertheless, as I've sought to prove, they represent a true reality—the season of the endtime judgments of our God and the return of Christ in this final generation.

WATCHMAN ON THE WALL

In July 2000, at the time of our mission to Madison Square Garden, I had believed the Lord's judgment on New York would be only an isolated sign of the fall of Babylon at the end of time. I didn't know this surprise attack would come in the first year of the New Millennium as a further sign. Nor did I foresee it as the Lord's great catalyst for *the beginning of sorrows* and the judgments of Revelation. I had thought nothing about the apocalyptic judgments happening in our time. I had never recognized America's role in prophetic Scripture. I had no knowledge of Islam's role in the endtimes. I didn't realize the Antichrist could be alive. But now I believe these things are true and that the final generation of the endtime judgments began with the attack on 9/11.

Nonetheless, to those who think or fear the end will come any day, I say it won't happen overnight. It won't happen next year, or the year after that, or the year after that either. The Great Commission must first be completed, and too many things must yet take place to fulfill Scripture (Matt. 24:6, 14; 2 Thess. 2:2). The next prophetic event must be the rider on the fiery red horse, who starts nuclear, biological, and chemical world war, with Iran the likely instigator and Russia its partner. While such a terrible war may seem unthinkable, the Bible teaches it will come before the end. Beyond this war and its attendant consequences, all the judgments and events described in the book of Revelation must also happen in the remaining years of this generation, even to the Battle of Armageddon and the return of our Lord Jesus in glory. In light of these things, may God give us grace to number our days to apply our hearts to wisdom (Ps. 90:3–12). The time is short, but there is much to do to reach the unreached peoples of the world.

To the skeptical, while I also stagger at the idea of such brevity, I say that so much can happen in forty years, as I know firsthand. Forty years ago was 1973, the year the Vietnam War ended, the year the Supreme Court legalized abortion, the year Nixon and Watergate dominated the news, the year Israel won the Yom Kippur War and the Arabs declared their oil embargo. Then consider all that has since transpired in the areas of science, technology, and historic world events in just these four decades—including the collapse of the Soviet Union, the advance of

China and India, the rise of Iran and radical Islam, the War on Terror, even to twice electing America's first African-American president, who ran two masterful campaigns. Ironically, the son of a British citizen, he was not legally eligible to be president under the "natural-born citizen" clause of the Constitution, which requires both parents to be US citizens. Nevertheless, this man served a fearful divine justice that never forgets: our nation, whose Constitution was a compromise that allowed *poor Africans to be stolen from their homeland at its start*, was justly weakened by God under the leadership of a president *of African descent, who stole its highest office near its end* (see Ex. 21:16; 2 Sam. 10:9–10; Rom. 12:19; Gal. 6:7–9; 1 Tim. 1:10). An Alinsky-style Chicago politician with a corrupt, radically progressive administration, President Barack Obama was God's chosen instrument to hasten the fall of the world's most powerful nation under divine judgment. His failed leadership was meant to pave the way for world war and the rider on the fiery red horse (Dan. 2:21, 4:17; Eph. 1:11). Even his Islamic name and heritage at such a time in history could be seen to foreshadow and presage our country's future under the coming Antichrist of Islam, for whom the president and his policies ultimately prepared a path (Dan. 4:22; Rev. 14:4–7).

As for me, I was converted in 1973, having laid my writing down to see if there was a God and if He would help me with my book. Instead, Christ saved me, gave me a true helpmate to love, and directed me in ways I never could have imagined. How could I have known that forty years later I would publish an account of His prophetic judgment on 9/11 and its purpose for the endtimes and the fall of America? This book is no novel. The United States is passing away, New York City is passing away, and the world as we know it is passing away—*in this very generation*—to make way for a better place than we could ever conceive (1 Cor. 7:29–31; 1 John 2:17).

Without question, I know what I have written about God's warning before 9/11, about the apocalyptic judgments, about America's place in Scripture, about her inevitable fall after world war, about Islam's certain victory, and about the reign of Antichrist in this generation will be dismissed, debunked, vilified, and ignored—just the ramblings of some "crazy Amos" the land can't bear (see Amos 7:10). One large Christian publisher wrote me that my topic was too narrow for its readers. I thought, if God spoke to our nation through a divine judgment like 9/11, as I know and prove He did, and American Christians aren't interested, what must He do to get our attention? But many professing Christians are like the rest of the country: they live chiefly for this life and don't want to see it disrupted; conservatives don't want their prosperity to be interfered with, and liberals deny these things as poppycock. In common, most leave God and His judgments pretty much out of their equations and want life to just continue on "as it always has" (see Matt. 24:37–39).

But I say, "What about our witness and warning in July 2000 of an attack on New York City that would point to the destruction of Mystery Babylon in the book of Revelation?" Wasn't the attack on 9/11 a reflection of the Scripture in chapter 18, in multiple ways, just as the Lord led me to believe it would be? This isn't theory and opinion. The attack was God's judgment, and we have not repented from what brought it upon us. This means more and worse are sure to come. And what of God's Word and what it *truly* teaches about the future for our country and the rest of the world (2 Pet. 3:2–13)? While many teach the United States of America has no place in the endtimes, we can be found in *at least* two major prophetic Scriptures: Revelation 6:1–2 and 2 Thessalonians 2:6–7. The first of these is the rider on the white horse. The second has yet to be fulfilled—namely, our loss of power and removal to make way for Antichrist—and it is heartbreaking to consider. I say this because I love our country. I am so thankful and blessed to have grown up in the United States of America. I thank God for the exceptional role He has given it in His plan to complete the Great Commission in world history. But we've lost sight of God, even as Scripture foretold, and terrible consequences lie ahead (Ps. 9:16–20).

In writing the sober things in this book, I've remembered the words in Ezekiel 40:4, which seem to speak in principle to it: "Son of man, look with your eyes and hear with your ears and pay attention to everything I am going to show you, for that is why you have been brought here. Tell the house of Israel everything you see" (NIV). I understand now that I was called to be a watchman to tell what I see by the light of Scripture and its application to the events of history and providence. When I came to Christ just weeks after the Vietnam War, I had concluded the world couldn't last another hundred years without destroying itself. I knew nothing then of the inspired prophets and almost nothing of the New

Testament writers. But since that night all those years ago, the Lord has trained me in His own school for His own unique purpose. For one thing, I wasn't constrained by denominational bias and presuppositions in our church with regard to endtimes eschatology; I was free to read the Scriptures for what they said. I also had opportunity to learn from some of the best Christian teachers of our day. I was exposed to a range of Christian churches—Evangelical, Reformed, Charismatic, Pentecostal, Catholic, Orthodox, and liberal too—and was not ignorant of their teachings. The Lord provided practical training in other areas, from writing stories and essays to learning about missions, Church history, fund-raising, production, marketing, and technology. Though I didn't have a conventional path to follow, and couldn't see what I would do or where my life was heading for years—like wandering through a maze—the Lord was at work in hidden ways the whole time. I was to be a *watchman on the wall*. I even had the idea for our video Bible while working at Cornerstone TeleVision that broadcast from a town called *Wall*. The 9/11 attack itself struck near *Wall Street*, where Betty's family had owned the property just outside where the old wall once stood. Even our project's name, chosen after our trip to New York in 1993, proved to be "prophetic." In Jeremiah 1:12, the Lord declared that He was "watching over [His] word to perform it" (ESV). In other words, His warning of imminent judgment was not an idle threat; He would act quickly to perform it. In our case, the project through which God spoke to New York before the attack was called the *WatchWORD Bible*. Its very name was a message and a testimony to the certainty that *the Lord was watching over His Word* to perform it, just as He warned, and then did on 9/11.

HISTORY'S DESTINATION

Now, the full outline of human history is becoming apparent, and that which has been hidden is being unsealed by Christ. Things happening at this time are not just more random points in the ebb and flow of world events. History has a destination. The 9/11 attack was God's providential sign that we are approaching that end point, and *that which restrains the coming of the lawless one* is about to be removed that he may be revealed—as Scripture teaches (2 Thess. 2:6 NKJV).

Without question, difficult days lie ahead of us. Nonetheless, multitudes of Christians believe they will entirely escape the coming darkness, while others with a different eschatology believe the world will be progressively transformed by the Church and presented to Christ. But overlooking much of Scripture and history, they will both be gravely disappointed. Many will have their faith shaken as a result. Unprepared to trust the Lord through such times, how will they weather the hard storms of persecution and suffering? They cannot conceive of enduring the coming global war, let alone worse to follow (Eccl. 3:8; Matt. 24:8).

Yet, in facing dark days, the Lord would teach us not to lose faith and wonder in despair, "Where is God?" (1 Pet. 4:12–13). We are to remember that He revealed these dark days in His Word beforehand, that we might trust Him in the trial. By foretelling the future, He demonstrates His absolute control and infinite knowledge (Ps. 147:5; Dan. 4:32). He is Almighty God! He laughs from heaven at the feeble machinations of the nations (Ps. 2:1–4)! Our Lord is building His holy Church, and nothing can stop Him, not even the devil (Matt. 16:18). In truth, all the coming sorrows are but brief pangs preceding the birth of new heavens and a new earth, where righteousness will dwell and sorrow will be banished forever. Our real home will be heaven!

In the meantime, the Lord reminds us that He will never leave us nor forsake us as we serve Him (Matt. 28:20). He has gone only to prepare a place for those who feed Him when He's hungry, give Him drink when He's thirsty, clothe Him when He's naked, visit Him when He's sick, and come to Him in prison (Matt. 25:31–46). His message is not one of selfish escapism, but of faith, love, and selfless service. He commands us to love our enemies. He wants us to share His Gospel even with our persecutors and to joyfully show God's love to a fallen world even in its darkest hours. Heeding His words, the early Christians stayed in Rome to care for the sick and dying after the pagans escaped in fear during the plagues that decimated the city. The selfless love and care of the Christians in the face of death won many to the Gospel. In coming days, some of us will be called to walk through the valley of the shadow of death for the sake of Christ (Matt. 24:9; Rev. 6:9–11, 13:10). But He promised that death can't separate us from Him. He tells us to look up: He is coming again to raise us up to meet Him in the air and be with Him forever (1 Thess.

4:15–18; 2 Thess. 2:8). In the twinkling of an eye, we will be changed, and the sufferings of this life won't be worthy to compare to the glory we will know (1 John 3:2; 1 Cor. 15:51–52; Rom. 8:18).

But, the Lord warns, there will be only wrath to come for the unrepentant (Ps. 9:17).

On God's great day, the living and the dead will be judged according to the absolute standard of His perfect law (Rev. 20:1–12). Believers who have been redeemed from sin by faith in Christ's death on the cross will be delivered from everlasting damnation. But there will be no excuses, no second chances, and no escape for those who reject His salvation; only *sudden destruction*, as Scripture warns (Heb. 2:2–3; 1 Thess. 5:3). No one who has ever lied, lusted, hated, stolen, coveted, dishonored parents, worshipped false gods, or the like, will be able to stand on his merits before the infinite wrath of the Holy Judge (James 2:10). Without Jesus as Savior, they will be found guilty and be utterly lost for eternity—no matter who they are, or how sincere or zealous their religious practice (Gal. 3:24). For all have sinned, and there is no salvation apart from faith in Christ, who alone died to pay for sin (Rom. 3:24–25). Without their justification by faith in Him, they will be condemned to suffer God's eternal wrath in the fire of hell (Rev. 20:15). The Lord will once and for all put an end to the great rebellion of unrepentant people who will be cast into destruction forever (Matt. 25:46; Rom. 2:5–10).

How inconceivable these things are to the fallen human mind. People in our culture today assume everyone goes to heaven when they die if they are not serial-killer-monsters. It is almost impolite to think otherwise. But they are deceived. It is not true. Jesus taught the way is broad that leads to destruction, and many are on it; the way that leads to salvation is narrow, and few find it (Matt. 7:13–14). That is why the apostle Paul wrote, "Knowing therefore the terror of the Lord, we persuade men" (2 Cor. 5:11 KJV). It will be sheer terror for the unredeemed to fall into the hands of the living God (Jude 15–16).

But to all who trust in our righteous Savior, the Lord declares, "Behold, I create new heavens and a new earth" (Isa. 65:17 ESV). On that great day, just as Peter and the prophets foretold, this entire universe groaning under God's curse will melt in a vast cataclysm of fire to make way for new heavens and a new earth—the home of righteousness (Isa.

34:4; Rom. 8:18–23; 2 Pet. 3:10–13). Here the Lord's redeemed sons and daughters will experience unending joy in the glorious presence of the Father and the Lamb and the Holy Spirit with all the saints forever. They will come from every place and continent: Africans, Asians, Australians, Europeans, North and South Americans, and the islanders of the world (Dan. 7:13–14).

This happy goal has been God's gracious purpose from the beginning. In the presence of Adam and Eve, He made His great promise at the Fall that He would one day send a deliverer born of a woman into the human race (Gen. 3:15). The rest of the Bible is the story of God's work to fulfill this one great cryptic promise in the process of human history. In the flood, the Lord preserved only Noah and his family, keeping the race alive to keep His promise. Nine generations later, He called Abraham and assured him that He would bless all the peoples of Earth through this patriarch's descendent (Gen. 12:1–3). In the fullness of time, Jesus Christ, the sinless Son of God, born of a Jewish mother into the human race, came as promised with power to defeat Satan, sin, and death. Who else but the perfect God-man could do it—pay the debt for human sin, yet survive the wrath of God? After His death and resurrection, the Lord Jesus commanded His followers to go and make disciples of all nations, Jew *and* Gentile, for all the families of the earth will be blessed and united in Him (Gal. 3:26–29; Eph. 2:14–17). Indeed, Scripture says, "For God so loved the world that he gave his one and only Son, that whoever believes in him shall not perish but have eternal life" (John 3:16 NIV). In His holy kingdom, He will have some from every tongue, tribe, people, and nation, for He has promised (Rev. 14:6–7). Their names were written in the Lamb's Book of Life from the foundation of the world.

Now the fulfillment of these things is finally at hand. Even as God planned before the beginning, the good news of salvation and the lordship of Jesus Christ are being preached to the ends of the earth. The Great Commission is poised to be accomplished in *the generation that began with 9/11*—a time that radically demonstrates God's amazing wisdom and fairness in all salvation history. From the *calling of Abraham* in 1921 BC *to the outpouring of the Holy Spirit on Cornelius* in about AD 40, the Jews were the almost exclusive beneficiaries and stewards of salvation for *some 1,961 years*—at a time when Earth's population was smallest (Gen.

12:1–3; Acts 10). Depending on exact dates, from the *outpouring of the Holy Spirit upon Cornelius*, that first Gentile convert, *until the 9/11 attack in 2001*, the Gentiles have been principal beneficiaries and stewards of the Gospel for the very same period of *1,961 years*—but during the time when Earth's population was its largest and the greatest numbers of Gentiles were living. In fact, it can be seen that the modern missionary movement began about the time Earth reached its first billion people and has been most active while that population exploded seven times. Oh, the wisdom and goodness of our God! What a remarkable sign these things are of where we are in history. Arriving at an equal number of years for Jews and Gentiles *in 2001* is no incidental fact in the hands of the sovereign God who orders the affairs of the universe. Now, despite the opposition of the evil one and his followers, may He raise up laborers *in this final generation* to complete the Gospel task across every culture and boundary—to Jew and Gentile alike—so that *the full number of Gentiles come in* and the Jews be grafted back into the olive tree, *that all Israel may be saved* (Rom. 11:23–26).

"Even so, come, Lord Jesus!" (Rev. 22:20 NKJV).

EPILOGUE

The grass withers, the flower fades, but the word of our God stands forever.

—Isaiah 40:8 NASB

THE 9/11 PROPHECY wouldn't exist without the *WatchWORD Bible*. In His sovereign providence, the Lord used the production of *The Book of Revelation* to get my attention before the film festival in 2000. Then He spoke through it in a still, small voice to warn New York City of His coming judgment on 9/11. These experiences became the basis of *The 9/11 Prophecy*, without which this witness would not have been written.

Long before I knew about 9/11 and its prophetic purpose, however, our vision for the *WatchWORD Bible* had been to create a whole new way to increase Bible reading as a catalyst for revival and spiritual awakening in America. If at all possible, the key would be helping millions more people to read God's Word on a regular, daily basis so their minds could be renewed and transformed in the process. That's what our little team set out to accomplish. Upon seeing the first finished chapters in 1994, I then had two immediate ideas that we openly discussed. One, I believed the ultimate best use of our production would someday be on handheld players, if we could finish it. Without question, we were making the Bible effortless and compelling to read on video. And by producing it in chapters, unlike a movie meant to be watched all at once, we had designed it for regular daily use. It just wasn't convenient yet with existing technologies. But someday being handheld would make it convenient too.

The other idea had to do with promotion. By way of strategy, I thought the ultimate best way to promote this new *videobook* and achieve the goal of making an impact on the entire country with God's Word would be by means of a Super Bowl commercial. I thought this would be the single most effective way to introduce our new Bible on video to the largest possible audience in a media world growing more fragmented by the day. If one truly wanted to help increase biblical literacy at a level that would spark a spiritual awakening, something of the magnitude of a Super Bowl commercial would be required, where almost everyone in America would be on the same page at the same time. There were more than 350,000 different congregations in the country and countless denominations that didn't often communicate with each other.

There were also tens of thousands of ministries and millions and millions of individual believers of all sorts. How could one ever reach such a wide and diverse group in a unified way using conventional means that would make any really significant difference? If we were only interested in selling some products, we could simply pursue normal marketing efforts. Then our product would just be one more product among many. But what if we sought to make an impact on the entire nation? Hollywood, which surely knew its business, spent as much as $35–45 million to create brand awareness for a single film that came and went in a matter of months. How could we hope to match a marketing budget like that, even though our production was evergreen and meant to have years of use? But a commercial in the Super Bowl would reach as many as 40 percent of all thinking Americans at one time, and at a tenth of the cost of a conventional Hollywood marketing budget. I also knew people had no idea what our video Bible was until they actually saw it and how it worked. There was nothing quite like it for reference. It wasn't a dramatic reenactment or an animation, as nearly everyone imagined it must be. There had also never been a Christian product ad in the entire history of the Super Bowl. An engaging, unforgettable commercial for a video Bible would stand out from all the rest by its very uniqueness. It wouldn't be just another ad. And being a Super Bowl ad, people would actually sit up and take notice. After the game, tens of thousands of believers would continue promoting it by word of mouth. These were my thoughts when we first began, and I never gave them up.

As it has turned out, the idea for the *WatchWORD Bible* on handheld players finally came to fruition sixteen years later. In January 2010, a friend walked into my office to say we needed to make *WatchWORD* available as a new smartphone app. He then showed me how the app store worked, which was crucial for distribution. He said no one could easily replicate what we had accomplished over the years, giving us a huge head start and advantage. He also said he would love to watch a chapter every day after work to unwind with God's Word. Shortly after, another friend came to show how great one of our Gospels looked that she had loaded to her iPhone from the computer. Focusing our limited resources after that on developing an iPhone app, our prototype *WatchWORD* Video Bible App was released in the App store in December 2010.

Some who might have helped us over the years had declined because they didn't see how we would ever get major distribution for our production as an independent producer. I had thought if God truly called us to produce it, surely He had a plan for its distribution, even if it wasn't fully clear when we started (Gen. 12:1). Now, here was a vast means of distribution. Through the app stores, the *WatchWORD* Video Bible would eventually become accessible to literally hundreds of millions of people around the world. Already, there were more than five billion cell phones in operation on the planet. In the future, most mobile phones would become smartphones of some type—portable minicomputers that could play the *WatchWORD* Video Bible anywhere in the world.

As it happened, within days of the app's release, a great idea for a Super Bowl commercial popped into my mind. I had thought about ideas for an ad for years and had never come to a viable solution. And here was this idea just when we finished the app. I couldn't help but wonder at the timing. But how could we hope to raise sufficient money to buy a Super Bowl commercial? Airtime alone would cost at least $3.5 million. Yet within weeks, I thought through a possible solution for the funding too. Then, reading the Sermon on the Mount one morning and urgently asking the Lord to help me know whether I should pursue the idea or not, I came to the verse Matthew 5:15. Jesus said, "No one would light a lamp and put it under a clay pot. A lamp is placed on a lampstand where it can give light to everyone in the house" (CEV). The Lord's words seemed so directly applicable to our situation. Twenty years before, we had set out to light a lamp with God's Word on video to make an impact on the country. Yet, our lamp was still hidden away (Ps. 119:105). And here, the Super Bowl offered the largest commercial lampstand in the nation. An ad there would bring our unique video Bible to the attention of "everyone in the house." Encouraged by these words, I decided the time had come to pursue the idea, in spite of how impossible it looked. The plan was to enlist a Gideon's army of three hundred smaller sponsors, who in turn could each receive promotion on our website for the commercial. In the meantime, the Super Bowls in 2011 and 2012 had the largest TV audiences in history. If we could present our video Bible product in that venue, we would be sharing a passage of Scripture with the largest audience ever at one time. And while the networks rejected ads for proselytizing, we had a unique product, twenty years in development and certainly worthy of attention. And the promotion wouldn't stop with the game! A Super Bowl commercial would be a powerful springboard for the project to build on. Lord willing, such an ad would put our lamp on a lampstand to give its light to the whole country. May He *open a door to us for the Word,* and may *the word of the Lord run swiftly and be glorified in the lives of many* (Col. 4:3; 2 Thess. 3:1).

Without question, the day is coming when there will be *an enforced* famine of God's Word on the land, and how will people learn it then, when it's too late (Amos 8:11–12)? How will they be ready to stand if they don't know what it teaches? How will they be transformed without regular engagement with God's Word? While many believe the Bible to be trustworthy and true, most people don't read it and are for the most part ignorant of its truths, not knowing God's Word enough to be changed or guided by it (Rom.15:4). As George Gallup Jr. and Jim Castelli said, "Americans revere the Bible but, by and large, they don't read it."[1] They say they are too busy or find it too difficult when they try.

To help solve these problems, we devoted years to produce a video Bible that would be compelling to use and as easy to read as possible. The video pulled you along. The audiovisual elements focused attention and increased comprehension. The text was divided into individual thoughts that were delivered by their natural phrases—difficult work the reader didn't have to do. Viewers heard the words and read them at the same time. Because they watched, read, and heard it all at once, they could recall multiple times more than if reading print. At the end of each screen, seconds of "wait time" were added, allowing readers to grasp what was being said without noticing because of images, text, and music. At the end of each chapter, additional "think time" was added, allowing opportunity to absorb what had passed. All these elements were built into *WatchWORD* to make it possible to focus on the message rather than on the work and difficulty of reading. The technology and presentation made the work as easy as possible, more so than any other Bible that existed. Viewers could even multitask, reading while using their hands or exercising. The books were also produced by chapters, so they could be watched in short increments on a regular basis, like reading a book, rather than watching a movie.

As it turns out, this last element has proved to be vital. Research by the American Bible Society discovered *almost no measurable difference* in *the moral lives of believers in our culture except for a single factor*—whether a person engaged with the Bible *at least four or more times a week*.[2] Those who engaged God's Word in this way lived differently than other Christians. Activities such as church attendance, giving, or even reading the Bible three times a week showed little difference in how believers lived in the culture. It was the practice of engaging with God's Word *at least four or more times a week* that transformed a person's life under the work of the Holy Spirit. In fact the research paper concluded that "disengagement from the Bible is the most critical challenge facing the Christian community today." This finding so excited me because it went right to the heart of what we had set out to accomplish a decade before 9/11, and now more than a decade since. We sought to produce a video Bible that would help people easily read God's Word *on a Monday–Friday basis to change their lives.* With a mobile app, it was now convenient and practically effortless. People could just tap a button *to watch* a chapter daily and make it part of their lives, like eating or exercise (Matt. 4:4). Then the Holy Spirit will work through God's Word to transform them by the renewing of their minds (Phil. 2:12–13; 1 Thess. 1:5; Rom. 12:2). As a result, they will go on to impact others and the culture disproportionately.

In addition, we have also produced the *WatchWORD Bible* as an online streaming video service that is managed for us in the UK by In2itive. It has an automated reading plan designed to take users through the New Testament in a year—with 260 video chapters matching the 260 weekdays a year. A new chapter is scheduled every weekday, five days a week, fifty-two weeks a year. The average chapter is only six minutes in length. Churches can even use the service as a program to help members develop and maintain a Bible-reading discipline as a group. It offers random viewing by book or chapter, a viewing log, and a search engine. In the process of working on the project, In2itive's owner, Jeff Lenton, also came to faith in Christ. A former agnostic, he says managing our service at TheBibleChannel.com has made him an *e-missionary*—spreading God's Word in electronic video form to change lives.

And once again, we're distributing our *WatchWORD Bible* New Testament DVDs. People regularly tell us how much they love *WatchWORD*, what it means to them, and how much it has helped them better understand God's Word. In one case, a maximum-security prison in California has broadcast the entire New Testament on its in-house channel a total of *forty-two times* to seven thousand inmates over a four-month period. Men that no one expected to do so had watched it in the privacy of their cells. Spontaneous Bible studies sprang up as a result. The chaplain was amazed that it crossed racial and religious barriers. Reaching that many inmates by conventional means would have required thousands of Bibles, many of which would have remained unopened. Furthermore, two-thirds of inmates have poor reading skills, for which *WatchWORD* provided an effective solution.

Beyond these things, we hope to continue with other productions in the future. Lord willing, our plan has always been to produce the New Testament in at least the ten largest world languages. In addition to our original

English version, two others have been produced, and one other started.

In 2006, the Japanese New Testament was finished with CHEA in a coproduction in the Land of the Rising Sun, where only 1 percent of the Japanese people had put their faith in Christ after 150 years of outreach. With a population of 120 million, this hi-tech nation has been considered the world's second-largest unreached people group. Yet, the Lord has promised His name will be praised even from *the rising of the sun* (Ps. 113:3 NKJV), and there is now a growing openness among the young. As it happened, this version was produced in Sendai, where the tsunami struck in 2011.

To date, twenty-four books of the Arabic New Testament have been produced and broadcast throughout the Middle East, North Africa, and Europe by SAT-7. Nine of the world's largest unreached people groups speak Arabic, totaling 120 million people who live in Islamic nations difficult to reach by conventional means. Tens of millions of Muslims live in additional Arabic-speaking nations with a small Christian presence.

ERF, Germany's largest TV ministry, has produced *The Gospel of Mark*. Lord willing, this project can complete the German New Testament in the future.

Beyond these, three other productions could serve two billion more people. The Chinese New Testament in Mandarin would serve the world's largest population. The Spanish New Testament could serve the world's third-largest group, and the 10 percent of US homes in which Spanish is the principal language spoken. The Hindi New Testament would serve those who speak the chief language in India, which has the world's second-largest population. Because of Hindi's strategic importance, we struggled for five years at great expense to launch this production, to no avail. About 20 percent of the earth's population lives in this rapidly developing nation, yet less than 1 percent of Hindus have come to Christ after almost two centuries of Christian outreach. Yet, with God's Word on video in Hindi, it could be broadcast to literally hundreds of millions on TV, and used on inexpensive DVD players to plant house churches in any village with electricity. Watching just thirty minutes a week, villagers could read the New Testament yearly and know more Scripture than many in the West learn in a lifetime. Nonreaders could learn to read their own language in the process. Beyond these, versions have been requested in Farsi, Urdu,

Turkish, Armenian, Russian, Korean, Portuguese, French, Italian, and Romanian, just to name a few.

Lastly, we've also produced twelve books of the NIV New Testament, recording perhaps the best NIV New Testament narration available. Its narrator is the Reverend Dr. John Guest, possessor of a superb voice with impeccable diction and the most appealing British accent. He had had a popular radio program that broadcast his preaching and, in his early years in America, he also recorded the first contemporary Christian music album ever in the United States. Now John has narrated God's Word to help reach a culture where two out of three Christians have never read the entire New Testament even once. To have his involvement in our project was like coming full circle. He was the one who gave me a ride many years ago and asked people in church to pray for a young writer living in a tree house, and I later married his secretary. As it happened, running out of money once again after completing the NIV narration, we lost our medical insurance. Within weeks, Betty became seriously ill, but refused to see the doctor, not wanting to add to our financial difficulty. A month later, her stomach perforated from a hiatal hernia. She had bled internally all night before I found her downstairs, and emergency room staff didn't think she would live to reach surgery. The doctor told me he couldn't believe the pain she must have endured. But the Lord mercifully spared her life in a miracle of grace (Ps. 68:20). Countless people prayed for her, and I had asked the Lord to save her life, even as He had spared Epaphroditus, who nearly died in his service for the Lord (Phil. 2:25–30). Betty came home after forty-six days in the hospital. I don't know what I would have done without her.

Lord willing that we complete the NIV New Testament production in the future, we hope to follow with the Old Testament in phases. As long as thirty-five feature films and three times the length of the New Testament in phases, this seventy-five-hour-plus production would be one of truly "biblical proportions." Should we finish reproducing "the whole counsel of God" (Acts 20:27 NKJV), the *WatchWORD Bible* will be more than one hundred hours of digital video, all readily available in the palm of your hand (Acts 20:27). Hundreds of millions of people around the world could watch it, a river of God's Word flowing out to the world, as we prayed so many years ago.

Should we be unable to complete the whole Bible, however, the various New Testaments will continue to deliver God's Word in this new way on video. And the *WatchWORD Bible* will also serve another purpose. It is not just another video. The Lord chose this production of His holy Word to warn New York City of the judgment He would use to usher in the endtimes. Now, this story has been told.

How amazing all this is to me. Forty years ago, the World Trade Center opened in the same Lent that I gave up my writing for what I thought would be forty days to see if there was a God. Now, forty years later, *The 9/11 Prophecy* is being published as a witness and a warning of the endtimes. May its message be shouted from the rooftops and its witness help spark an awakening in these last days—even to the ends of the earth, for the time is near (Acts 1:8; Rev. 1:3). To God be the glory!

I will stand my watch and set myself on the rampart, and watch to see what He will say to me, and what I will answer when I am corrected. Then the Lord answered me and said: "Write the vision and make it plain on tablets, that he may run who reads it. For the vision is yet for an appointed time; but at the end it will speak, and it will not lie. Though it tarries, wait for it; because it will surely come, it will not tarry.

—Habakkuk 2:1–3 NKJV

APPENDIX

Over 30 Amazing Providences in Support: (each one remarkable in itself!)

- Converted when I gave up writing during the *same forty-day Lent* in which the World Trade Center opened in 1973.
- Vowing not to marry until midlife, I would marry a wife who had a *direct connection* to the World Trade Center.
- Betty's birthday is December 7, *the same date* as the surprise attack on America before WWII.
- I had the original vision to produce a video Bible in 1991—the year bin Laden became America's enemy.
- I met with ABS to license the translation in New York City—one week before the first WTC attack—1993.
- Eight years later, we finished the final scene of the first full NT production—one week before the 9/11 attack.
- We completed the first-ever full production of *The Book of Revelation* during the Millennium Year.
- The video was accepted by the 2000 New York International Independent Film and Video Festival.
- Scripture and providence led me to foresee an imminent judgment on New York City before we went.
- I told the staff we were being sent to warn of a surprise attack in a single hour—a sign of Revelation 18.
- I told our composer at the foot of the Empire State Building on July 9, 2000, that *tall buildings would fall*.
- My name and the production title appeared on the Madison Square Garden marquee, July 9, 2000.
- When we returned home, an offer to purchase Betty's *Family History* was waiting for us in the mail.
- *Family History* shows that Betty's first Dutch ancestors had possessed the World Trade Center property.
- Trinity Church later proved its ownership of their major landholdings with the former Dey lease.

- Like the sign of Ezekiel lying on his sides, we had two bad accidents after the festival falling *on our sides.*
- Reflecting Ezekiel's 430-day sign, 9/11 hit exactly 430 days after our NYC premiere.
- Three clear confirmations made a pattern of where, how, and when the attack would strike.
- As forewarned, the attack was an amazing reflection of Revelation 18.
- Providentially, I began writing this 9/11 book in California in 2006 *in room 911 of an oceanfront tower.*
- This 9/11 book is being published *forty years* after I quit writing for *forty days* to seek God's help.
- Also, evidence for 9/11 and future judgments is published forty years after *Roe v. Wade.*
- My nickname had been the same as the name of the prophet of sycamore trees who wrote Amos 3:6–7.
- After I was converted, I earnestly prayed Isaiah 6:8—"Send me"—from my home on *Sycamore Road.*
- In time God sent me to warn of a judgment, the sign of which would be *the sycamore trees cut down.*
- *The Harbinger* states that the sycamores cut down were a sign of God's judgment in Isaiah 9:10.
- A sycamore tree was cut down on Chapel land that my wife's Dey ancestors possessed at the city founding.
- *The Harbinger* also linked Washington's dedication service to this very same ground.
- In the American Revolution's last year, General Washington had headquartered at Dey Mansion in New Jersey.
- The New York City mayor attending Washington's presidential inauguration was this Dey's *grandson.*
- Dey's grandson helped found ABS—which licensed the translation used in our warning.
- The Isaiah 9:10 pattern was preceded by a warning, *like the advance warning God sent New York City.*
- Isaiah 9:10 is linked to the Messiah prophecy, and 9/11 began pre–Second Coming endtimes.

NOTES

PROLOGUE

1. See Ezek. 3:17; Isa. 21:6–9; Dan. 2:28; Amos 3:6–7; Rev. 18:4–18.
2. Rev. 18:18.
3. See Rev. 17:16–18; 18:9–20.
4. Rev. 19:11–16.
5. See Jon. 3:1–4; Acts 26:26.
6. See Jon. 3:10, 4:1–3; Matt. 12:41; Ps. 28:5.
7. See Matt. 24:32–33.
8. Matt. 24:6–8; Rev. 6:1–8.
9. Matt. 24:34.
10. 2 Cor. 5:11; Matt. 10:28, 24:34; Isa. 46:9–10; Lam. 3:37–39; Dan. 4:34–35; Amos 3:6.
11. See Rev. 1:19; John 21:24.
12. Jer. 4:19; Matt. 24:14; Ps. 98:9; Matt. 24:29–31; Acts 17:30–31; Rev. 20:11–15.
13. See Amos 3:7–8; 1 Thess. 5:20; Rom. 12:6.
14. Rev. 6:1–2; Matt. 24:6; Luke 21:9.
15. Rev. 6:3–4; Matt. 24:7; Luke 21:10.
16. Jon. 3:4.
17. See Rev. 6:3–8, 13:4, 7, 11–12; Matt. 24:7–8; 2 Thess. 2:1–12; Dan. 11:36–39.
18. Rev. 6:1–8, 9:13–16; Matt. 24:7–8, 21–22.
19. Rev. 6:9–11, 13:7, 9–10, 20:4; Matt. 24:9–10; Luke 21:16; Dan. 7:25.
20. Rev. 17:15–18; Dan. 11:38–39.
21. 2 Thess. 2:8; Rev. 19:20.
22. See Matt. 24:33–34; Luke 21:29–32; Ezek. 12:21–28.
23. See Rev. 18:4–19; Mark 13:4, 28–30.
24. See Acts 17:11.
25. 2 Thess. 2:1–4 NKJV.
26. 2 Thess. 2:6–8.

27. See Ps. 25:14; Jer. 33:3; Dan. 2:22; Matt. 24:6–8; John 17:7; Rev. 6:1–8.
28. See Ps. 2:1–5, 19:7–11, 33:4, 34:8–11, 115:3, 119:160; 1 Chron. 29:12; Dan. 4:35; 1 Tim. 6:15.
29. Matt. 24:30–31, 28:18–20; Rom. 15:4; 1 Thess. 4:13–18; Rev. 5:9, 14:6–7.

CHAPTER 1: DIVINE REVELATION

1. David Wilkerson, *Set the Trumpet to Thy Mouth* (New York: World Challenge, 1985; New Kensington, PA: Whitaker, 2001).
2. Alan M. Stibbs, *The First Epistle General of Peter*, Tyndale New Testament Commentaries (Grand Rapids: Eerdmans, 1981), 176.

CHAPTER 2: DIVINE PROVIDENCE

1. Ralph D. Winter, "The Task Remaining: All Humanity in Mission Perspective" in *Perspectives on the World Christian Movement: A Reader,* eds. Ralph D. Winter and Steven C. Hawthorne (Pasadena, CA; William Carey Library, 1981).

CHAPTER 10: GOD'S PLAN

1. "Religion: God & Steel in Pittsburgh," *Time*, March 21, 1955.

CHAPTER 12: VIDEO BIBLE

1. Wikipedia, s.v., "The War to End War," http://en.wikipedia.org/wiki/The_war_to_end_war#cite_note-1.

CHAPTER 13: WATCHWORD BIBLE

1. The Pittsburgh Experiment, "History," http://www.pittsburghexperiment.org/history. Accessed June 5, 2013.
2. Martin Luther, *The Bondage of the Will* (Grand Rapids: Fleming H. Revell, 1992), 319.

CHAPTER 14: THREE CONFIRMATIONS

1. Rebecca Stetoff, *The Patriot Act* (Tarrytown, NY: Marshall Cavendish Benchmark, 2011), 10.

CHAPTER 16: FIRST HORSEMAN

1. See Ronald Jose Morelos, *Performing Victory: The Different Kind of War of Bush 43*, http://www.academia.edu/215738/Performing_Victory_The_Different_Kind_of_War_of_Bush_43. Accessed June 5, 2013.

2.   George Bush, speech transcript provided by the *Guardian* (UK), May 1, 2003, http://www-guardian.co.uk/world/2003/may/01/usa.iraq. Accessed June 5, 2013.

3.   *Wikipedia*, s.v., "Axis of evil," http://en.wikipedia.org/wiki/Axis_of_evil.

4.   Jonathan Edwards, "God's Awful Judgment in the Breaking and Withering of the Strong Rods of a Community" (sermon, 1748), available at http://www.biblebb.com/files/edwards/rods.htm. Accessed June 5, 2013.

CHAPTER 17: SECOND HORSEMAN

1.   Fouad Ajami, "Osama bin Laden, Weak Horse," *Wall Street Journal*, May 3, 2011, http://online.wsj.com/article/SB10001424052748704436004576299110143040714.html. Accessed June 5, 2013.

2.   Dr. Hugh Cort, AFCPR.org, "Can We Stop Osama bin Laden's 'American Hiroshima' Plan?," 2007, http://www.afcpr.org/articles/6-7-08_stop_american_hiroshima.html. Accessed June 5, 2013.

3.   Amir Taheri, "The frightening truth of why Iran wants a bomb," *Sunday Telegraph*, April 16, 2006.

4.   Address by H. E. Dr. Mahmood Ahmadinejad, President of the Islamic Republic of Iran, before the Sixtieth Session of the United Nations Assembly, New York, September 17, 2005.

5.   Patrick Poole, "Ahmadinejad's Apocalyptic Faith" FrontPageMag.com, Thursday, August 17, 2006, http://archive.frontpagemag.com/readArticle.aspx?ARTID=3029. Accessed June 5, 2013.

CHAPTER 20: AMERICA'S HIDDEN ROLE IN PROPHECY

1.   Governor Edward Winslow, *Hypocrisie Unmasked*, 1646.

2.   G. K. Chesterton , *A Short History of England* (1917), 15.

3.   Edward Gibbon, *Decline and Fall of the Roman Empire,* 1845 revised, Chapter 15, "Progress of the Christian Religion" Part I.

4.   Chesterton, *A Short History of England*, 10.

5.   *Today Show*, NBC, February 19, 1998.

CHAPTER 22: THE REIGN OF ANTICHRIST

1.   *Wikipedia*, s.v., "Hamza bin Laden," http://en.wikipedia.org/wiki/Hamza_bin_Laden.

2.   "The Bin Laden who got away: Was 'Crown Prince of Terror' the son who escaped U.S. special forces raid?," *Daily Mail Reporter*, May 10, 2011, http://www.dailymail.co.uk/news/article-1385588/Osama-Bin-Laden-Did-Crown-Prince-Terror-escape-special-forces-raid.html. Accessed June 5, 2013.

EPILOGUE

1.   Collin Hansen, "Why Johnny Can't Read the Bible," Christianity Today, May 24, 2010, http://www.christianitytoday.com/ct/2010/may/25.38.html.

2.   Arnold Cole, EdD and Pamela Caudill Ovwigho, PhD, Center for Bible Engagement, "Understanding the Bible Engagement Challenge: Scientific Evidence for the Power of 4," December 2009, 7 and 14.

INDEX

War on Terror, 148, 151–55, 160, 161, 169, 173, 189, 202
Warren, Richard, 122
Washington, DC, 4, 40, 46, 106, 188
Washington, George, 84, 111, 120, 122, 150, 183, 197, 219
WatchWORD Bible, The (videobook) 109–16, 211
  Gospels, 113–14
  New Testament production, 109–16
  NIV New Testament, 216
  upcoming versions in German, Hindi, et al., 215
  Revelation, 114–16
WatchWORD Productions, 107
WatchWORD Video Bible App, 211
WatchWORD Worldwide, 126
Watergate, 201
weapons of mass destruction, 160, 162, 170, 173
Wen Jiabao, 164
Wesley, John, 81
Westinghouse studio (Pittsburgh), 108
White, David N., 63–64
White, Stanford, 63, 64, 90
White House (U.S.), 150–51
Wilkerson, David, 3
Williams, Arlene, 97
Winter, Ralph, 93
WMDs. *See* weapons of mass destruction
world religion, enforced, 190, 192, 195
World Trade Center, ii, 39, 42, 43, 45, 54, 76, 107, 119–20, 125, 186, 197, 217, 218. *See also* Ground Zero; Twin Towers
World Trade Center bombing of 1993, 41, 107
World War I, 31, 118, 123, 158, 168, 169, 183, 184, 187
World War II, 62, 101, 118, 140, 151, 158, 172, 183, 184, 185
World War III, 157, 159–60, 163–66, 169, 189. *See also* global war
WPCB-TV, 95, 99
Wycliffe, John, 96, 104
Wycliffe Bible Translators, 9, 142

Y

year 2000, vi, 7, 8, 10, 12, 14, 18, 20, 26, 27, 115, 116, 128, 138, 146, 151, 201, 218
Yom Kippur War, 201

Z

Zechariah, 139, 140, 199

PRESENTS

GOD'S WORD COMES TO LIFE ON DVD

WND films PRESENTS

THE EASIEST WAY TO READ AND UNDERSTAND THE BIBLE

THE WATCHWORD BIBLE

THE NEW TESTAMENT

Over ten years in the making, The WatchWORD Bible New Testament (26 hrs) presents all twenty-seven books of the New Testament on video. It makes reading God's word easier and more compelling than ever—with thousands of scenes shot on location from Jerusalem to Rome, word-for-word text on screen, a world class narration, plus 130 original music compositions written scene by scene for the underscore and countless sound-effects. Over 260 chapters of video!

TEN DVD SET

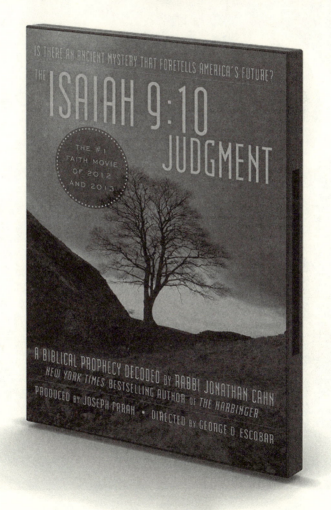

PRESENTS

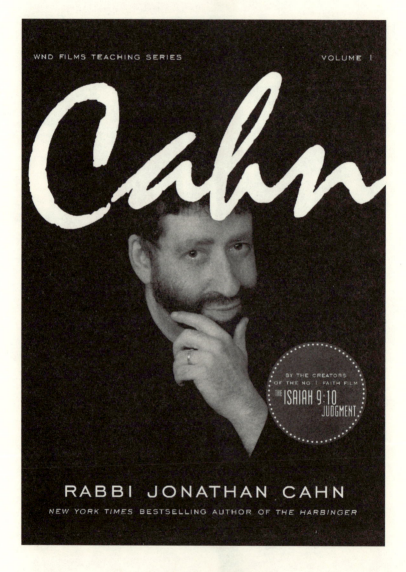

IN PARTNERSHIP WITH WND FILMS, MESSIANIC RABBI JONATHAN
CAHN IS RELEASING SOME OF HIS FINEST TEACHINGS,
DELIVERED AT CONFERENCES AND AT HIS OWN NEW JERSEY
CONGREGATION, THE BETH ISRAEL WORSHIP CENTER.

THREE DVD SET

PRESENTS

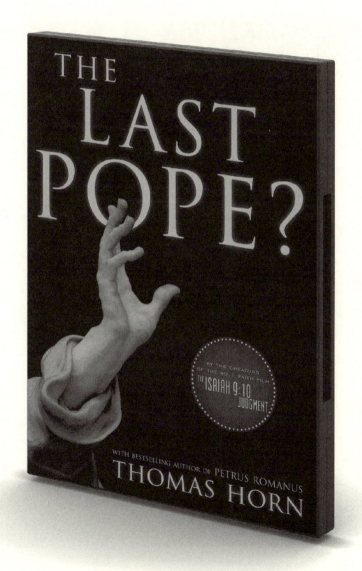

A JUST-ELECTED POPE.
AN ANCIENT PROPHECY PREDICTING THE
END OF ROME AS IT EXISTS TODAY.

THIS FILM EXPLORES THE UNWITTING CLASH BETWEEN THEM.